Children's
Experience
With Death

Children's Experience With Death

By

ROSE ZELIGS, Ed.D.

Clinical Child Psychologist
in Private Practice

CHARLES C THOMAS • **PUBLISHER**
Springfield • Illinois • U.S.A.

Published and Distributed Throughout the World by
CHARLES C THOMAS • PUBLISHER
Bannerstone House
301-327 East Lawrence Avenue, Springfield, Illinois, U.S.A.

© *1974, by* CHARLES C THOMAS • PUBLISHER
ISBN 0-398-02984-9

Library of Congress Catalog Card Number: 73-12698

*With THOMAS BOOKS careful attention is given to all details of
manufacturing and design. It is the Publisher's desire to present books that are
satisfactory as to their physical qualities and artistic possibilities and
appropriate for their particular use. THOMAS BOOKS will be true to those
laws of quality that assure a good name and good will.*

Printed in the United States of America
R-1

Library of Congress Cataloging in Publication Data

Zeligs, Rose.
Children's experience with death.
1. Children and death. I. Title.
[DNLM: 1. Adolescent psychology. 2. Child
psychology. 3. Death. WS105 Z51c 1974]
BF723.D3Z44   155.9'37   73-12698
ISBN 0-398-02984-9

To my brother
Mendel Zeligs, M.D.
Who helped me with this book

PREFACE

WHAT is this book about and why is it needed? The meaning of the mystery of life and death is the eternal quest of man. To understand death is to understand life, for death is part of life. The child, like primitive man, is deeply involved with the mystery of birth and death. He has deep anxiety about death and needs clear and honest answers to his questions about death. To be able to answer those questions to the best of our ability, we need to understand the child's developmental attitudes toward death, his fears, his knowledge, and his experiences with death in general and especially in the way it touches his life.

Death has been a taboo subject in our present death-denying society, where most people die in hospitals rather than at home. Children lack personal experiences with death, and when a member of their family dies they are often overprotected and misinformed. This confuses the child and may be traumatic to him, especially when he is not permitted to participate in the mourning ceremonies, to talk about the meaning of death, and about what happens to the body when a person dies.

Therapists are beginning to realize that the subject of death should be faced and discussed in order to deal with death as a part of life. Some books have recently been published on the subject relating to adolescents and adults, but very little attention has been focused on death as children experience it, how they understand it, and how they are emotionally affected by the way parents and other authoritative figures deal with death.

As a psychologist, I have worked with children who have been disturbed by experiences with death. Their trauma was increased because their parents did not know how to handle the problem, so that the children became confused, frightened, and emotionally upset.

This book is written for all people who work with children and are interested in children. This includes professional people, parents, students, and clergymen, as well as laymen.

Every intelligent person would be interested in such a book, since death touches all our lives, for the bell tolls for everyone and we cannot avoid death. Therefore we must all try to understand the mystery of life and death and learn to deal with it with understanding, wisdom, and fortitude. It is important that such understanding and attitudes begin early in the life of the child, in order to help him face the eventualities of life and death with courage and maturity.

The style of this book is simple and concrete but the material is based on authoritative sources. It can be easily understood by high school students as well as professional people. The material is derived from research of recent books, medical and psychological reports, attendance at symposiums, seminars, and workshops, and a number of personal case studies of children in therapy. The children had been disturbed by some experience with death and the author worked with them and with their parents to help them gain a better understanding of the meaning of death and what their experiences really meant. The case studies report the conferences of the psychologist with the child and with the parent. There are topical center headings, a summary, and list of references at the end of each chapter.

The focus of this book is always on how the child and adolescent is affected by death. It therefore deals with the developmental concepts of death, the dying child himself, his experience in hospitals and with medical personnel, his reactions to the loss of a parent, and to being handicapped, and the influence of religion on his attitudes toward the meaning and experience with death.

What experiences and circumstances enabled me to write this book? As a psychologist and teacher in the public elementary and high schools of Cincinnati, I have had the privilege and opportunity of working directly with a large number of children. Much of my research and writing is based on my daily experience with these normal, everyday children.

Later as a child psychologist in private practice in California, I again became occupied with children of all ages — normal everyday children, children with emotional problems, and parents who have problems with each other and with their children.

In this work I have been associated with my brother, a pediatrician, Mendel Zeligs, M.D.

Today, in the nuclear family, young parents do not have, nor want, the guidance of their elders in child rearing. They look to professionals for advice in every detail of child care. It has now become the responsibility of the pediatrician and the psychologist to advise and direct parents in both the physical and psychological upbringing of their children.

Because the present focus in pediatrics is on understanding and helping the whole child, the pediatrician is concerned with preventing as well as curing disease; preventing emotional and personality maladjustment; and advising parents when problems occur.

To achieve these objectives it is helpful for a pediatrician and a psychologist to work together. Through such cooperation they can better help each other and their patients.

This book grew out of my experiences and association with my brother. He brought to my attention and discussed with me all the references and other material presented in the medical literature concerning children's experiences with sickness and death. Without his help this book could not have been written.

ROSE ZELIGS

14256 Ventura Boulevard
Sherman Oaks, California

ACKNOWLEDGMENTS

The author thanks THE NATIONAL ASSOCIATION FOR MENTAL HEALTH, publishers of *Mental Hygiene,* for their kind permission to reprint her article, "Death Casts Its Shadow on A Child," as the first chapter of this book.

She also wishes to express appreciation to Mr. Payne E. L. Thomas, for his wisdom, guidance, and encouragement that made the development and preparation of this book an enriching experience.

CONTENTS

Children's
Experience
With Death

Chapter I

DEATH CASTS ITS SHADOW ON A CHILD

A simple child,
That lightly draws its breath,
And feels its life in every limb,
What should it know of death?

William Wordsworth
"WE ARE SEVEN"

WHAT does death mean to a little child? What should we tell a child about death? Every child, at some time in his life, has an experience with death that may be deeply disturbing to him. Parents, teachers, and sometimes professional therapists must help children meet such a crisis with the least amount of trauma. Mrs. Brown came to me because death had cast its shadow on her child and she felt unable to deal with it adequately.

August 26th: First Conference with Mrs. Brown

Mrs. Brown: Fear gripped my heart as I rounded the corner leading to my home. Two hours ago I had left my one-year-old son in care of my cleaning woman while I went to see my doctor, then stopped for a short time at the supermarket. Now I saw crowds of people standing in front of my house, almost surrounding the two police cars on the driveway.

I forced my way into the living room. Policemen were questioning the cleaning woman. I rushed into the baby's room. My husband tried to put his arm around me, but I pushed him away and ran to the baby's crib. The pediatrician was covering the baby's face with his little blue blanket. My baby was dead! My beautiful, adorable baby would smile at me no more. His sparkling

3

blue eyes were closed forever. What had happened? Who killed my baby?

Paul, my husband, put his arms around me and lead me to a chair. Suddenly I screamed, "Where's Robert? Where's Louise?" Fear for my son, who was five years and nine months old, and for my three-year-old daughter clutched at my aching heart. Perhaps something had happened to them, too.

"The children are all right," Paul said. "Our neighbor, Sandra, took them to her house." His voice was filled with tears.

Then Dr. Good said, "No one harmed the baby. It was no one's fault or negligence. It would have happened just the same if you had been home. David died of natural causes. He had an acute respiratory infection which developed rapidly."

Later, the coroner's report confirmed my doctor's diagnosis. Our pediatrician explained to us that infection of the respiratory tract can cause sudden and unexpected death in infancy. Nevertheless, the shock and the pain seemed greater because I had not been with my baby when he needed me most. That thought keeps nagging at my heart all the time.

After the crowds left, my empty arms ached for my children. My good friends Ethel and her husband, Dr. John Green, said they would bring the children in from the neighbor's house and would later take them to their own home until after the funeral.

When they brought the children in, Robert ran up to me and said immediately, "Is David all right? I want to see David."

I tried to hide my grief and said, "You can't see him now. He is asleep. But remember, we promised that you could visit overnight with Uncle John and Aunt Ethel, and now we are going to let you do it." Louise was willing to go, but Robert still looked worried and kept asking about the baby. Finally Uncle John promised them a treat, and the children went with them.

The next morning John phoned us. "Robert has been worrying about the baby all night. I had to give him a sedative so he could sleep. He wants to come home. I think you had better come over and talk to him."

Paul and I decided that the children would have to be told the truth. But we would not take them home until after the funeral. As soon as we entered the Green's home we saw that Robert was disturbed. "Is David all right? Is he all right? I want to go home. I want to see David," he cried.

How can you explain sudden death to a little child? It was heartbreaking. We didn't know what to say or how to say it. But still we had to tell them. Robert had seen the hand of death on the face of his little brother. He could never forget that. Paul took Robert on his lap, and I held Louise on mine. We could not fool these children if we had wanted to. Our voices reflected the sorrow in our hearts. "We didn't want to tell you yesterday, but now we know that we must tell you the truth. David is not all right. He got sick suddenly, yesterday. He died and fell asleep, never to awaken. He is with God in heaven, now. His memory will always be in our hearts, but he will not be with us any more. God took him." Paul spoke quietly and sadly.

"He's not dead! He's not dead! I want my baby! I want David! Tell God I want David back!" Robert jumped up and down and screamed hysterically, "I want my baby! I want my baby! I want to go home. " His grief was uncontrollable; and he wept bitterly.

Louise repeated the words, "David died, David died." But she did not really understand what was going on.

Robert had always felt great responsibility for the care of the younger children. Every time David cried he would run up and talk to him. The first thing he did when he came home from school was to look for the baby. They would have so much fun together. David loved him and would gurgle in delight when Robert played with him.

"We want him, too, but we can't have him. God took him," I said.

"Why did God take our baby? Will God know how to change the baby's diaper? Are the angels watching him? Will they give him his bottle?"

We did not know what else to say. But we were determined to protect our children from the tragic experience of the funeral, from the crowds of people, and especially from the fact that our hearts were filled with grief. So we said, "We are very busy now and have to attend to a lot of things. If you stay here two more days we will give you any present you want."

"I want a slinky toy," Robert said.

"All right, Uncle John will go out and buy you a slinky toy. Now we have to go. Be good children."

We did not see the children again until after the funeral. Robert was very sad. He cried a lot, especially when it was time to go to bed. He seemed afraid to close his eyes.

Paul and I tried to hide our grief in the presence of the children. But visitors were still coming, and the children seemed to sense our sorrow. When Paul had to go back to the office, I felt very frightened and insecure. "If I'm not here and your mother cries, you must help her," Paul said to Robert. When my husband left, a great loneliness swept over me, and I could not control my grief. Robert clung to me, and we cried toegther. The child was very frightened to see me cry. "If I draw horses for you, will it help?" he asked. When I said it would help, his face brightened, and he drew horses for me all morning. He felt a great responsibility for taking care of me.

I'm afraid we have always burdened this willing child with too many responsibilities. Once, when Louise was a baby, we left her in the car alone with Robert while we went into a store to shop. "Watch the baby, Robert," Paul told him. When we came back, Robert was hysterical. He was afraid something would happen to the baby. After that he refused to be left alone with her. He was afraid something would happen to her and he would be blamed.

My pediatrician said that Robert may be jealous of Louise, but I don't see how that could be. He has always been overly concerned about her, and he acted the same way about David, too, after he was born. But Paul always warned Robert to look after the younger children.

Paul is a strict father, especially with Robert. He was an only child, and his mother was very strict. She made him practice his music until he hated it. She spanked him hard. Sometimes I think that Paul is using the same strict methods with Robert, although he spoils Louise. Because Robert is tall for his age and is the oldest, I think that we expect too much of this six-and-a-half-year old boy.

At bedtime I used to sing lullabies to the children and we would all have fun together. But after David died I could not bear to sing those lullabies. When I put the children to bed, I try to tell them stories to make them laugh. But Robert keeps on talking about David. He lies there with his eyes wide open and seems to be afraid to close them. He just can't fall asleep.

Robert has had some serious illnesses. At nineteen months he had to be in the hospital for a week, and it frightened him very much. When he was five years old he had his tonsils out; but I was allowed to stay in the hospital with him the entire time.

Three months after we lost our baby, Robert became ill with nephritis and had to stay in bed for two months. One day, while he was in bed watching television, he saw a program about Abraham Lincoln. It showed the grave of Ann Todd. Suddenly Robert burst into tears. "What is this — a cemetery? Is David buried in a cemetery like this?" he asked in amazement. Then we had to tell him that the baby is buried.

"I want to go see him. I want to see David in the cemetery," he demanded.

"We can't take you now. You are sick, and the doctor says you must stay in bed till you get well." The last thing we wanted to do was to take this little boy to the cemetery. Robert wept bitterly and we really did not know how to comfort him.

After we lost David we decided to have another baby. We are trying to feel that it is not a replacement, but I can hardly wait two months until I have a baby in my arms again.

Robert seems very concerned about my pregnancy. "Would you have another baby if David hadn't died?" he asks. "Is this baby going to be healthy?" I think he secretly harbors the idea that David will come back in the form of this new baby. He wants to name it David. We don't want him to think of the new baby in that way. He seems so confused about birth and death. He wants to know if I will become thin again. He doesn't like fat people.

Robert was put into the first grade when he went back to school after his illness, because it was the beginning of a new semester. He got nervous over the reading. One day he came home and his eyes were wet. When I questioned him he burst into uncontrollable sobbing. When his group was reading, the teacher said, "Robert, you're not paying attention." He started to cry and she sent him out of the room. He cried all afternoon.

I went to see the teacher and she told me that Robert is always on edge and cries at the slightest thing. He is a bright boy, but he is not doing well in reading because he just doesn't have his mind on his work. She believes that something is troubling him — some deep emotional problem outside of school.

This summer Robert has been going to day camp twice a week. Monday he came home from camp and climbed into my lap. "Mommy, I have a problem — I don't know why I cry so much. Do you know why I cry, Mommy?"

A few days later he got an infected ear and had to be put to bed for a week. Most of the time he kept on crying, yet he says he doesn't know why he cries. Just a little frown from me or Paul will upset him. A scolding will make him hysterical. If Louise cries, it upsets him too. He was the same way with David. He took care of him like an adult. He would talk and play with him and watch him.

Robert has always been a good boy and wants to be good. His greatest joy is to have us talk to him. But Paul is so busy with his work, and I have a tendency to push him off when I'm busy. I know we should include him in our conversations more often. I guess the main thing is that my hurt has not been healed, and I am always running to the cemetery to my baby's grave.

School starts again in two weeks. Robert will start in a new school with a different teacher and children he doesn't know. He keeps saying that he is afraid to go to this new school because he cries so much and the children will call him a cry-baby.

He is so fearful and insecure that he cannot make the slightest decision. He can't even decide the kind of ice cream he wants. It is now nine months since we lost our baby, but Robert still has not been able to get over it. Paul and I finally decided to consult a child psychologist. That is why I have come to you.

Psychologist: From your description and background it seems to me that a number of factors may well be responsible for your child's emotional disturbance. Robert sounds to me like a highly sensitive child. He has had many illnesses, and there are other factors in the family constellation that may have contributed to his sense of insecurity. Such a child is more vulnerable when he has a severe traumatic experience. But before we discuss this further, I would like to make an appointment to see the child.

August 28th: First Conference with Robert

Robert came in with his mother. She had told him they were going to see a child psychologist, a doctor who helps children with their problems. He could tell this doctor anything and it would be kept a secret.

Psychologist: Your mother will wait for you in the waiting room while you are in my private office. Sit down at this little table. You may use these crayons and this drawing paper if you feel like drawing anything while you talk to me.

Robert: My problem is that I cry too much and I'm afraid to go to school because the children will call me a cry-baby. I don't know why I start to cry.

Robert took the yellow crayon and drew a closed half-moon outline and filled it in. Around this he continued to make similar drawings in different colors until the paper was covered. On another paper he drew a house, outlined in black, with a black roof and a solid, tightly covered window, and a tightly closed black door. With the orange crayon he drew two windows and a crooked chimney, and filled in the rest of the house. Outside the house he made a little crooked man, a cat, and a mouse. He explained that his drawing represented the crooked house from the nursery rhyme.

Psychologist: If a fairy came and gave you three wishes, what would you wish for?

Robert: First I would like to have a big farm — 30 acres big, with a big barn where I could keep many horses. For the second wish I would like a private office of my own. For the third wish I would like a great big airplane so I could fly way up and far away. I could fly to Chicago by myself.

Psychologist: Who would live on the farm with you?

Robert: Well, I would have my dog to help take care of the horses. I would have my granpa, my mother, and my daddy. But I and the dog and the horses would be most important, because it would really be my farm.

Psychologist: Who is your family?

Robert: My granpa, my mother, daddy, Louise (in a small voice), the dog, and the bird.

Psychologist: Why do you think you cry?

Robert: Sometimes my mommy yells at me and is mean to me. Sometimes I fight with Louise and then she lets me have it. In school I had a mean teacher. She said I didn't pay attention to the reading. She sent me out in the hall.

Psychologist: Parents and teachers sometimes scold children. That doesn't mean that they don't love them. Even if a teacher scolds you sometimes, she only does it because she wants to help you learn. You should not take it so hard. Besides, you are going to have a new teacher this year. I am sure you will like her and she will like you.

Robert: Could I come back to see you again? Will you give me your phone number? I have another problem. I don't like to go to sleep. I am afraid to close my eyes.

Psychologist: We will ask your mother if she can bring you again.

Robert: Do I take these drawings home or leave them here?

Psychologist: You may do it any way you like.

Robert: I think I would like to leave them here.

Psychologist: I will put them away in a drawer.

August 28th: Psychologist's Interpretation of Interview with Robert

Although Robert refrained from mentioning his sister, the loss of his little brother, and his mother's pregnancy, his drawings revealed his concern in this area. His first drawing is a classic example of symbols and colors children use to express concern over the birth of a new baby in the family, as described by Alschuler and Hattwick (1947) in their study of nursery school children's paintings.

The second drawing indicates that Robert felt that he lived in a crooked house with a heavy black door that kept him out, because he was a little crooked man. In other words he had been sent away because he was somehow responsible for David's death. This made him feel alone, insecure, shut out, because he had been sent to another person's house when his little brother died.

Robert's three wishes are efforts to deal with his problems. He would have his own big house where he would be the master. His dog would help and protect him. He would sometimes invite his grandpa, daddy, and mother. He doesn't mention his sister, indicating that she is a competitor for love and he would feel safer without her.

His wish for a private office again suggests the desire for independence, power, and privacy.

The third wish, for a plane in which he could fly far away, shows his desire to escape from his problems. He would fly to Chicago, where his grandparents live.

August 30th: Second Conference with Mrs. Brown

Psychologist: I think Robert is an interesting child, with a strong conscience and a deep sense of responsibility. He has been emotionally disturbed by unusual experiences of personal illness and the sudden loss of a little brother. Certain other facts in the family constellation have made him feel insecure and uncertain of himself, lessening his ability to meet a crisis when it occurred.

Robert may have felt less loved than his sister or brother. We often do expect more from the eldest child in a family, give him less attention and more responsibilities. Sometimes a father who has been an only child and always received all the attention unconsciously resents the attention given his first-born son. He may express this jealously by being very strict with the child, having too high standards for him, and giving him many responsibilities beyond his age.

Paul's strict discipline and severe criticism may make Robert feel inadequate and inferior, unworthy and unloved. He may be fearful of failure in school because he lacks self-confidence. He needs to have a better picture of himself.

The child takes on the responsibilities given him, such as the care of his mother or the younger children. Consciously or unconsciously, he may become jealous of the attention bestowed upon them and resentful or being burdened with their care. At the same time, he may assume a parental attitude of concern and responsibility. He develops a bivalent attitude toward them — that is, he both loves and hates them.

Jealously is a sign of insecurity — of feeling dethroned by

another person who is believed to be stealing the love of parent or loved one. When an older child finds himself with a rival, a new baby who gets all the attention, he feels left out in the cold. This does not mean that we deal with jealously by *neglecting* the younger child. It is much better to *include* the older child in the picture of family togetherness. He can learn to associate the baby's nursing period with a pleasant time for him, too. Give him a cookie, tell stories, or just make it *listening time* when he can talk to you and you really hear him out.

Recognize his feelings of jealousy, accept them, and deal with them in a constructive way. You might say, "I know you are mad that I can't help you with that puzzle now, because I have to bathe the baby. But when he goes to sleep we will have our special time together *to do anything you like*."

The natural wish of the older child who is jealous is to eliminate the usurper of parental love. "Give him back to the doctor. We don't need him. You've got me." He may have conscious or unconscious death wishes against the new baby. When left alone with the younger child and told to watch him, he may actually hurt the baby. Or, if he has a strong conscience, the fear that he might harm the child may make him panicky.

When Robert was left alone with the baby Louise, he became hysterical because he was afraid something might happen to her and it would be his fault.

You said that Robert is very good and has always done everything to help the younger children. His father's emphasis on his responsibility for them lay heavily on him. He may have overcompensated for feelings of jealousy by loving the children *too much* and doing too much for them. The result could be conscious or unconscious resentment and rejection.

What do we do when someone stands in our way? We want him to leave — to get out of our sight — out of our life. In other words, we tell him to "drop dead" — to disappear. Every language has different expressions for such death wishes. A child will wish someone dead if that person interferes with his emotional or other needs.

Children are very confused about the meaning of death. It is just a word to a three — or four-year-old like Louise. The five-year-old may associate life and death so closely that it may be a reversible process to him. Of course, this idea of life after death is found in many religions. The six-year-old is more aware of the meaning of death and the sorrow it may bring.

The child's learning about the meaning of death should be gradual and a part of everyday experiences. He learns that the flowers have dried up and are dead. When he sees a dead insect or goldfish or bird, let him satisfy his curiosity by inspecting them, if he wants to. He can have a funeral and bury his little pet.

To a young child, death may just mean someone getting out of his sight — being gone — vanishing into thin air. The child feels he has magic power. When someone near him actually dies he may feel that his wishes caused the death. Robert felt that it was his responsibility to take care of the younger children. He may feel that he did not carry out his responsibilities and that his death wishes caused the baby to die. A sensitive, insecure child like Robert is more vulnerable when tradgedy strikes.

Now, let us look at this from the parents' point of view. The shock and sorrow of the sudden death of a child are bewildering and heart rending. You and Paul did the natural thing. Your first thought was to protect your children from the tragic experiences associated with death and funerals. You sent them away. You planned to hide your grief from them.

But sorrow as well as happiness must be shared. Children can take a great deal if they have their parents to lean on. Especially in time of trouble, they need the security and strength of family togetherness. But, if they are out of the picture, they feel rejected, alone, unwanted, and somehow responsible for what happened.

Robert's feelings of rejection and guilt for the baby's death were reinforced when he was sent away, when he was not told the truth about what actually happened to the baby, not allowed to come home to participate in the mourning, and not given a true picture of what death and a funeral are. Because he felt pushed aside, out of the family, *to his way of thinking,* he must have caused all the trouble.

Louise, being only three years old, did not understand what had happened. When she said, "David is dead," in unemotional tones, she was just repeating what she had heard. To her it just meant that he went away some place. Besides, she had no feelings of personal responsibility toward the baby.

Robert, on the other hand, felt your grief. When Paul told him to cheer you up, he was again burdened with responsibility, and he spent the entire morning trying to cheer you up by drawing horses.

All these months you have been grieving and running to the cemetery. You made your secret sorrow a wall separating you from Robert. But your child sensed your grief. When you are ready to accept God's will and turn from negative to positive thinking, you will be able to concentrate more of your love and attention on your living children and less on the one you lost. That is not easy to do. It takes time to heal the wound, and the scar will always remain. But Robert will know when you have accepted what happened, and he will also be able to accept it. Children sense these things, and we cannot fool them.

You also have to help Robert understand the facts of David's death. It was no one's fault. The baby became ill suddenly. This does not happen very often, but unfortunately it did happen in this case. Then explain about the funeral. Tell him that the body is buried and the soul is with God. If he wants to visit the cemetery, take him there. If he wants to bring flowers or anything else, let him do it. Let him discuss it freely and answer any questions he asks, honestly and clearly. He must have a concrete picture of the facts. Otherwise, he may have a feeling that death means sudden disappearance, vanishing into nowhere, something that can happen to anyone at any time. Such thoughts add to a child's disturbance and insecurity.

Don't try to hide your grief. A child may feel that parents who do not mourn for their lost baby are really not loving parents. This may make him feel insecure and unloved. Sharing sorrow will unite you, and parents and child will gain strength in togetherness.

Do not try *not* to talk about David. Remember the shared joys. Sine the lullabies and tell the stories you did before. It will help unify the family and make Robert feel that he is an important part of it.

When the child understands what death is, he will not confuse it with sleep. It is not good to tell a child that death means going to sleep and never waking up. He must know that sleep and death are *two separate things.* Otherwise he may be afraid to go to sleep. Prayers should not suggest the possibility of not awakening. "If I should die before I wake, I pray the Lord my soul to take," is not a comforting bedtime prayer. The child may feel that he has to keep his eyes open to watch his soul so it won't be taken away from him.

Lullabies and prayers should reassure the child that God will watch over him and protect him, that his parents are near to take care of him. Children need that assurance to let go of wakefulness and to give in to sleep. Let the child make up his own prayers. It will make him feel closer to God and will give you an idea of what he is thinking about.

After you talk things over with Paul and both of you explain some of these things to Robert, I think it would help if I saw the child again.

Mrs. Brown: Robert will jump at the chance to see you again.

September 3: Second Conference with Robert

Robert was eager to come in. He looked relaxed and at ease.

Robert: My problem is getting better. My mommy and daddy talked to me and it helped. I didn't think it would help, but it did help me.

Psychologist: Are you less worried about going back to school now?

Robert: This thing happened a long time ago!

I think I will draw a battleship, now. I think I'll use this brown crayon. There are three decks. Brown smoke is coming out of the smokestack. Now I'll have to cover up the whole picture with the blue crayon. I have to cover it up to match the smoke. Can I have more wishes, today?

Psychologist: Sure, what would you wish for?

Robert: I would like to have three great big bars of gold and silver.

Psychologist: What would you do with them?

Robert: It would cost too much to have people make things, so I guess I would make things myself. Statues. The Statue of Liberty. I would make another wish that I could have magic power. I could say abracadabra, and it would happen in a second. I would wish my room would be cleaned up and in a second it would happen. My mother would be surprised. I could make myself so big I could reach the sky, or so tiny that I could float on a leaf. Then I could hide in tiny places. Maybe I would like that better than being real big.

Another wish is for a golden building with sixty-one rooms. It would be filled with beautiful things made of gold and diamonds.

Psychologist: Who would live in the house with you?

Robert: I would live there all by myself. I wouldn't have any doors in it — except a door for me to get into my house. I wouldn't want strangers to come in. They might steal something.

Psychologist: Would you ever invite anyone to visit you?

Robert: I would invite my mom and dad, sometimes. But I would have to watch them, too, a little. Mostly I would live there by myself. Another wish is for a magic plane so I could fly through space in a short time. I could fly to Chicago in a second. I would wish for a diamond tower through which I could talk without dialing a number. I don't know many numbers, and I can't look them up.

Psychologist: Do you feel better about school?

Robert: Yes, I think talking to Mom and Daddy helped me. You helped me, too. I am not so worried about school and crying now. But this is a new school. All the children will be strangers.

Psychologists: When you start school the first day, every child is a little afraid. Maybe the boy next to you feels lonely. You could just go up to him and make friends with him. You would both feel better. In a short time you will know everyone in the room, and you will all be friends.

Robert: I am still worried because I don't like to go to sleep. That is something everyone has to do, so I want to be able to sleep without worrying about it.

Psychologist: It is all right to have a light in your room, if you want one.

Robert: I know, but when I close my eyes it gets dark and I can't see what is happening.

Psychologist: You're afraid something will happen while you're asleep. But nothing will really happen. You can hear things and

feel things in your sleep. You are breathing. Your body and your heart are working. What happens when an alarm clock rings?
Robert: It wakes people up.
Psychologist: Yes, and they hear it in their sleep, so they wake up. If someone would throw some cold water on your face, you would wake up. It would make you mad, too. Sleep is good because it helps your body rest from the work of the day. If you don't feel well in your sleep, it wakes you up. Your mommy and daddy have especially good ears when it comes to hearing if their children are all right while they are asleep. They watch over you. And God watches over you. Being asleep is resting. It is not like being dead.
Robert: Yes, I know. Being asleep is not like being dead. When a person is dead, he does not wake up. I know it is different.
Psychologist: Yes, it is very different. Don't be afraid to close your eyes and go to sleep. You will be all right and you will get a good rest. It is time to go now.
Robert: Could I see the drawings the other children make?
Psychologist: I'm sorry I can't show them to you. They are secrets like all the things the children tell me. But I have a little present for you. Here are some little picture cards of animals with funny little poems on them. Would you like one or two sets?
Robert: If the sets are all the same, I only need one.
Psychologist: I am going to give you this baby book. You can give it to your mother for a present.

In the waiting room Robert quietly handed the book to his mother as they were leaving.

September 3rd: Psychologist's Interpretation
of Interview with Robert

Enabling parents to deal with a problem themselves gives them greater self-confidence and brings about a closer relationship between them and their child. After Mrs. Brown's second interview, she and her husband explained to Robert that David had died suddenly of an illness, which does not happen often. Unfortunately, it did happen to their baby; but it was no one's fault.

Robert said he wanted David back, but they told him they

could not have the baby back. It was God's plan, and they just had to accept it. Then Robert said he wanted to name the new baby David. They explained that it would be a *different* baby and would have to have a *different* name. They answered all his questions honestly. He wanted to go to the cemetery, and they promised to take him.

In the second interview, Robert told the psychologist that his parents talked to him and it helped him. When asked if he was less worried about school, he said, *"This thing happened a long time ago,"* indicating that the worry about the death of the baby made him cry and made him afraid to go school. Sometimes children who are emotionally insecure are afraid to go to school for fear something will happen at home while they are away.

Robert's drawing of a battleship suggested that he was gaining enough courage to battle with his problems and fight it out, instead of giving way to crying and despair. But his covering the brown ship with blue showed that he was still fearful of expressing aggression.

His wishes reinforced those expressed in the first interview. He wanted power, privacy, and security. He wanted to feel free. He wished for gold and silver from which he would make the Statue of Liberty, symbolic of his own desire for freedom and independence. His wish for a beautiful building with sixty-one rooms but without any doors, except one for him to enter, indicated his desire for security and independence. There he would live by himself and feel safe. He would not let anyone in because strangers might steal something. Although he might invite his mom and dad sometimes, he would have to watch them a little, too, so he would rather live there by himself most of the time. Again, the sister was not mentioned. And again he wished for a plane in which he could go through space in a short time to get to Chicago, where his grandparents live.

Robert's wish to be big enough to reach the sky was another attempt to gain strength and power. But his desire to be tiny and float on a leaf and be able to hide indicated his feelings of insecurity and the wish to hide or regress to a more infantile stage in which he would be safer and would be given less responsibility. Robert's wishes indicated feelings of insecurity and inadequacy, unsureness of his parents' love. He was still too fearful to mention the loss of his little brother.

His fear of falling asleep was probably due to the idea that a person who falls asleep may die, and he must keep his eyes open to protect himself. When it was made clear to him that a person who is asleep can still hear and feel, that there is a big difference between sleep and death, he felt reassured.

Robert's jealousy of Louise was shown when he did not mention her as someone to visit him in his big house. When offered another set of pictures, he did not accept it to give to his sister, but said he needed only one set. He was given the baby book for his mother to help strengthen the realization that she is going to have a baby and that fact must be accepted.

September 10th: Mrs. Brown Phones the Psychologist

Mrs. Brown: What did you say to Robert last week? We are amazed. He is such a different child. We never saw him so relaxed. We took a vacation trip to Santa Barbara for a few days, and it was one of the best times we ever had. Robert was marvelous. He showed self-confidence, poise, courage. He ordered what he wanted from the menu. He didn't cling to Paul and me, but went out on his own. He asked the hotel clerks for what he needed. When we left, he thanked them for their kindness and told them he had a good time.

We visited the museum of natural history and the mission. Before we realized it, the guide had led us into the cemetery. "Is David buried in a cemetery like this?" he asked. When I said he was, Robert asked us to take him to see David's grave. We promised him we would do it as soon as we had a chance.

School started yesterday, and Robert did not object to going. When he came home, he was happy and said he had a nice teacher. I feel that Paul has had his eyes opened to many things and that he is doing much to improve the situation. He is giving Robert more love and attention. He takes time to talk to him and explain things rather than spanking him. With Robert, you can do so much with love and patience that I don't see why Paul ever thought of spanking, except that his own mother treated him that way.

But now Louise is getting to be a problem, because she senses that Robert is getting more attention. So we are trying to give her more attention when he is in school and give him individual attention when she is playing. We will also try to plan activities in which both children can have fun together. We will try to stress *family* togetherness for some activities.

November 10th: Mrs. Brown Phones the Psychologist

Mrs. Brown: My baby was born three weeks ago. At first Robert was hysterical when he heard that it was a girl. I guess in his mind he still hoped that David would come back. Finally we convinced him that it is better to have a healthy girl than a sick boy, and he was satisfied. I think this helped him feel assured that nothing would probably happen to this baby.

Last week, on a quiet, peaceful, sunny day, we all went to the cemetery, as I had promised Robert. He brought his favorite stone from his stone collection, for David, and placed it on the grave. We all said a little prayer. Louise was getting restless, so Paul took her back to the car while Robert and I stayed on. Then tears came to my eyes and I started to cry.

Robert put his hand in mine. "You are sad, Mommy?"

"Yes, I am sad. I miss David, but we have to accept God's will. Our David's spirit is with God."

Robert began to cry softly as he held my hand. "I miss him, too, Mommy. But that is the way God wants it. He wants our David, too, I quess. Let's go now, Mommy."

"Yes, let's go. Our little baby girl will be waiting for us at home."

Three years later: Mrs. Brown Meets Psychologist

Mrs. Brown: It is now three years since my little girl was born. Last week we went to the Cemetery. Robert came along. He became very upset when we got home. I said, "Look here, young man, you have had a loss, but I have, too, and so has your dad. It is enough — stop it. You are thinking of yourself." That ended that.

Psychologist: When you said that, it made him realize that it was not his fault. So he did not feel guilty. He just felt the sadness as part of the family sadness. He could finally accept the reality that death is a separation that must be accepted by everyone who experiences the loss of a loved one.

REFERENCES

Adelson, L. and Kinney, E. R.: Sudden and unexpected death in infancy and childhood. Pediatrics, 17(5):663, 1956.

Alschuler, R. H. and Hattwick, L.: Painting and Personality. Chicago, University of Chicago Press, 1947.

Zeligs, R.: Death casts its shadow on a child. Ment Hyg 51(1):9-20, 1967.

Chapter II

CHILDREN'S DEVELOPMENTAL CONCEPTS OF DEATH

THE meaning of birth, life, and death has preoccupied the thoughts, emotions, beliefs, and cultures of all men throughout the ages. The child, like primitive man, is deeply involved with the mystery of birth and death.

Steiner (1965) finds that the child's ideas follow the sequence of cognitive development as described by Jean Piaget. Bender (1963) quotes Piaget as saying that death represents the greatest mystery to the child and that the finality of death is beyond his conception. The questions children ask about death grow out of their experience in daily living. Where did I come from? What is death? What happens when you die? Will my parents die? Will I die? Does everyone die? What do you do when you die? Where do dead people go? Why do they put dead people in the ground? These questions occupy the growing child's thoughts and feelings. If he is not given honest answers, in accordance with his age and understanding, he may develop all kinds of weird and distorted ideas. If he is afraid to talk about his thoughts and fears about death he may become confused and disturbed.

DEATH: A TABOO SUBJECT

In earlier times, more people died and children had more experiences with death. Our medical knowledge and preventive medicine were limited; many mothers died during childbirth; infant mortality was high; and plagues of all kinds spread among the population. People lived, became ill, and died in the home. The funeral took place in the home. The death of a relative or neighbor was a common occurrence, so that death was no mystery to the growing child.

Today, fewer people die at an early age. The child has less experience with the death of a relative, because it usually occurs in a hospital. The child does not have a chance to see the person get sick, gradually grow worse, and then die; so that when death does occur it becomes more of a shock to the child. In his mind, the person seems to disappear into nowhere. In speaking of those who have died, people usually try to avoid the word "death" and say the person has departed or passed away.

Psychologists at St. Louis University drew up a list of twenty words and phrases that they found aroused anxiety and the fear of death: "birds, journey, candle burning out, to burn, across a bridge, a trip, old man, statue, thunder, to drive away, black water, the silent one, river, to depart, stranger, terminal, the end, four, the thirteenth."

Adults' attitudes toward death are absorbed by their children. Many adults have an unrealistic attitude toward the fact that man is mortal and will eventually die. They refuse to talk about death or to face the fact that *death is part of life.* Feifel (1959) states that "concern about death has been relegated to the taboo area." He says that "we have been compelled, in unhealthy measure, to internalize our thoughts and feelings, fears, and even hopes concerning death."

CHILDREN'S EARLIEST CONCEPTS

Children's ideas about death grow and change with their development. A child of two and three has little comprehension of the meaning of death (Jackson, 1965). He lives in the present and has little understanding of time. But he is interested in the origin of life and wants to know where babies come from. To a three-year-old, the concept of not being born is the same as being dead. He wants to know *where he was* when he sees a wedding picture of his parents and that it does not include him. When told that he wasn't born yet he feels sad and left out. He can be comforted by telling him he was in his mother's tummy.

The morbid fear of death (Wahl, 1959) starts as early as three years of age, though Nagy (1959) believes that children below ages eight or nine cannot comprehend the process of dying. The three-year-old begins to distinguish between animate and inanimate objects. He is beginning to notice that living things move and can make sounds. When a bug does not move, he may inspect it and ask why it is lying still. This is the time to say casually that the bug is dead, and let him satisfy his curiosity by examining it. To the four-year-old, death has a limited meaning. Jimmy doesn't want mother to sew on the dolly's hand that was torn off, because it will hurt dolly, but four-year-old Debby says, "It's not real, Jimmy. It won't hurt dolly."

Three-to five-year-old children have no concept of the finality of death. To them everything has the quality of permanence. They talk about death freely as they play with their guns and pretend to shoot each other. The pre-school child, according to Piaget, is so egocentric and so related to the cosmos, that he attributes purpose and feeling to the events of nature. His notions are colored by animism and sometimes by magic, and often bear striking resemblance to primitive mythology.

The child who is less than five years of age usually does not recognize death as final — in death he sees life. To him, death is a departure, a sleep. This denies death entirely. The child recognizes the fact of physical death but cannot separate it from life — he considers death as gradual or temporary (Nagy).

To most children between the ages of three and five death is regarded as another form of existence (Chesser, 1967). The five-year-old associates life and death so closely that it is a reversible process to him. The young child seems to believe that death is accidental rather than inevitable. At first the child refuses to accept the idea of death. Then he tries to substitute severe and curable illness for death. Being in a hospital equals death (Nagy quoting Cousinet, 1959). At a later age death simply disappears as a troublesome concept. At this stage the child realizes the truth about the meaning of death and represses it as a fearful thought.

Nagy, studying Budapest children ages three to ten, used their drawings, compositions, and discussions, to learn their concepts of death. She says that at first the child up to age five does not accept the reality of death and thinks of it only as a temporary separation. Going away, being absent, is the same as being dead. The young child attributes life and consciousness to the dead but on a more limited plane. The dead person thinks and feels and is aware of what is going on in the world, but under changed circumstances. The child thinks about how things become different *for him,* not for the person who has died. The dead person is separated from him, lives on in the cemetery, but under more restricted conditions that limit movement and activity, because the coffin and grave hold him in. His life consists mostly of sleep.

This concept is similar to that of many primitive peoples who identify death with sleep. They may provide food, clothing, and arms for their dead. The dead communicate with them through their dreams. Also, in psychoanalytic thinking sleep and death are considered synonymous in the unconscious.

The six-year-old is becoming more aware of the meaning of death as final and the sorrow it may bring. He may worry about his own death and that his parents may die, but unless he has had other experiences, he usually connects death with old age, especially if he has had a grandparent who died.

The seven-year-old knows that he will die sometime. He is interested in the ceremonies with which death is connected, the coffin, funeral ceremonies, burial, and the cemetery. The eight-year-old has learned that people, animals, and plants die. Children from eight through ten are interested in the cause of death and in what happens after death.

Many children between the ages of five and nine develop an increased sense of the reality of death, fear it, and keep it at a distance. They personify death, think of it as the most powerful ruler in the world, except God. Death is like a skeleton, king, or ghost, and the companion of the devil. He is invisible, white as snow, and very dangerous (Nagy). He goes around secretly and carries people off. At night, he goes about and carries children off, especially if they have been bad or have done wrong things. To many children death is related to darkness and they may want to have a light in their room when they go to sleep.

Beginning at age nine, the child recognizes that *death is part of life;* that it is inevitable and universal. No one escapes bodily death, although the soul is believed to live on.

Adolescents think of death as fearsome yet fascinating. The transition from adolescence to maturity is a time of maximum emotional insecurity. Chesser (1967) says they do not want to die without having had the opportunities of life's fulfillments. So they rebel against war and the insecurity due to the atomic bomb. Some turn to religion as an insurance against the risk of death. The majority repress and deny their anxiety. The psycho-analytical literature treats the fear of death as an infantile castration anxiety or the dread of losing the love object.

Schilder and Wechsler (1934) report that to the tiny child, killing means personal retaliation, the complete removal of the unwanted person. Death is a kind of deprivation which is not definite or final. It is not the natural end of life but the result of violence. Aggression and deprivation are unconsciously connected with it. In their destructiveness and aggressiveness, the children expect the destroyed object to be restored. An unbearable degree of deprivation of love may cause children to have aggressive and death wishes against other people. The child feels that he has the power to invoke death on others through the magic of wishful thinking. When a death does occur, he may feel that he has caused it in some way. This may create deep fears and feelings of guilt in the child and result in unconscious anxieties and trauma.

We see that children's ideas about death grow with their age and development. As experience with death grows, from the death of flowers, insects, birds, to that of pets and people, the child's concepts widen. They not only vary with age, but also with the experiences, personality, and intelligence of the special child. Sylvia Anthony (1967) says that "to one child death may be signified by immobility, to another sleep; to another being put into the ground; to another, going up in the sky; to another, going to the hospital, or going on a journey, or disappearance." She says that when we try to explain the meaning of death to children we must know that in ages seven through twelve they do not realize the generality and impersonality of death.

Marjorie Mitchell (1967) says that all children have deep anxieties about death. Her book is concerned with the depth of children's fears about death, the resulting harm to their personalities, and ways to help them find positive answers to their problems.

When a child realizes that death is final, it may arouse separation anxiety in him. Since every child lives in a world where he has some experience with death, we cannot and must not try to conceal the existence of death from him. It should be a gradual learning experience for him as part of his general picture of the world.

RURAL AND URBAN CHILDREN'S EXPERIENCES

How do rural and urban children differ in their experiences with death? Rural children have more opportunities than urban children to witness the birth and death of living beings, so the meaning of death becomes more of a reality to them. The walls of houses and the cement of cities separate the city child from nature. Although schools sometimes have animals in the classrooms, where children learn about them as part of their science lessons, it is not enough. Also, the animals are not in their natural habitat. Urban children should be given more opportunity to visit farms and to have pets and animals around them. Beginning at a very young age, they should spend at least a few weeks on a farm.

A country child, living on a farm, is close to nature and to God. He is close to Mother Earth, the giver of life and nourishment. He feels that he, too, is part of Mother Earth and he does not fear her. To her he entrusts his seeds and she brings forth food and flowers. He senses the serenity of stars; the peace and quiet of the star-lit skies. He senses the cycles of the seasons — of spring and summer, fall and winter, with all the changes they bring forth. All around him he sees living and growing things. He sees the birth of calves and lambs, kittens and puppies. He watches the sprouting seeds; the growth of flowers and fruit, of wheat and corn. He may have his own little garden and his own pets to nurture and care for.

Being closer to earth and sky, he learns to accept life and death as part of life's rhythms. Just as he experiences life through close and intimate contacts, so he also comes close to death. He thereby learns to accept the ever-changing world of living things — of plants and animals, insects, birds, and bees, of pets and puppies; yes, and sometimes even of people, for he learns that man, too, is mortal.

This awareness does not mean that he is not saddened by the loss of pets or people; but he learns to accept such loss as reality. He learns that death is part of life, without the great surprise and shock that comes to the city child, who is far from nature and her constant cycle of life and death. The country child absorbs the facts of life and death gradually, intuitively, naturally, as an ever-present experience.

When flowers fade and die, he finds the seeds to plant and thus he resurrects life; for to him, the secret of life is in the seed that will sprout again into living flowers. The country child can be more tender to every living thing. He identifies himself with it. But he is also more aware of the possibility of death. Death is more of a reality to him; a part of his experiences.

His parents discuss the meaning of death with him. "Mother," John asks, "Why did the ewe die?"

"The mother just happened to die because she got sick. When something happens to a mother we take care of the little ones; then they grow up and have their own little ones; so life goes on."

John was able to learn that death is part of life, and gradually to meet the crisis with fortitude and understanding.

THE DEATH OF DANNY'S PET

Danny came into the psychologist's office in a very sad mood. Although Danny was a bright seven-year-old boy, he was still confused about death and reluctant to accept its finality.

Danny: My lizard died this morning and I can't make him wake up.

Psychologist: What would you wish for if a fairy godmother gave you three wishes?

Danny: I would wish that I could own the whole world.

Psychologist: What would you do with the world?

Danny: I would make people happy and make lizards live forever, and nothing would die; even if they got sick, they would live forever. A lizard would live 95 years and would die 7 days later.

Psychologist: How would you make people happy?

Danny: By making people live a long time. When they got sick they would never die, and everybody would live forever and stay alive forever. The world would never stop.

Psychologist: Did you ever have anything else that died?

Danny: My turtle died once and my fish died a couple of times. The lizard was my favorite pet. I found it in my yard. I had it for a week. I liked him as much as my iguana. I liked my lizard better than my toad — better than my turtles — the new ones — and better than my fish. I like them both the same — the lizard and the iguana.

Psychologist: How did you feel when your other turtle died?

Danny: I do miss him a little, but I really didn't feel very bad because I knew I could get a new one. It didn't cost as much — a couple of quarters. My dad is not going to spend all that money for another lizard. The iguana cost $2.50 and the cage cost $3.00 — altogether $5.50. The lizard would cost that much.

Psychologist: How much money have you got saved up?

Danny: I have $1.12 at home. I found a dollar on the street and I got my allowance — 10 cents.

Psychologists: What did you do with the dead lizard?

Danny: My father put it in a little box. It is in the garbage can.

Psychologist: Why don't you and your father bury the box with the lizard in it in the ground. That is the way dead creatures are treated.

Danny: O.K., we will go home and bury the lizard.

A week later Danny came into the office.

Danny: I buried my lizard — about three days later I unburied him. He still looked the same. After I came to see you I unburied him four days after I unburied him before. He was gushy and he stinked, and all kinds of flies, slugs, beetles, worms, potato bugs, weevils were all over him. He stinked like anything. I put him back and I'm not going to unbury him again. It stinks so much! The worms had half eaten him up. They were almost finished with him, he was so little. That's all I have to say about him.

Psychologist: Why did you unbury him?

Danny: I wanted to see if he was eaten up by the worms. My dad showed me where he buried him. I took some rocks and made a circle around his grave, so I know where his grave is. I just thought it up myself so I could find the grave.

Psychologist: Have you got over your sad feelings? How?

Danny: Yes, by not thinking about him — thinking of happy things. But I'm still a little sad about it.

The death of Danny's pet lizard illustrates a seven-year-old boy's inability to conceive of the finality of death. He learns about the differences between death and sleep when he finds that he cannot wake up his pet.

After burying and exhuming his lizard several times he is finally convinced that living things die, and disintegrate in their grave. So, when given three wishes, one of them was that people and pets should be happy and live forever.

THE SUDDEN DEATH OF A PUPPY

Nine-year-old Peter and his seven-year-old sister, Mary, were walking with their seven-month-old puppies, Dale and Simona. Mary was holding Simona on a lease when suddenly the puppy got loose, dashed into the street, and was instantly struck by a car. This is the way Peter told it to the therapist a week later.

Peter: Dale was chasing Simona into the street about twenty feet. A car dashed by and hit Simona head first. She stuck onto the wheel of the car. Then she flew away from the car twenty feet. Then I ran out to get her. I hugged her and I got blood all over me. Her neck and her back were broken. Then Mary ran out in the street to get me. But a lady stopped her and put her arms around her. Mary was crying. Another lady came out and tried to take me away from the dog, and she did. She said, come off, get off. Then me and Mary ran home to tell our dad.

I felt TERRIBLE. Me and Mary were crying. Dale was right by Simona. I put his leash on and he ran faster than anyone. When we got home our dad came out and got Simona. He put her in a bag in a trash can for some guys to pick it up.

We couldn't stop crying. Dad took us both on his lap. He said it was nobody's fault. He said a dog runs out in the street before you know it. Simona died instantly, without suffering too much, so we can be thankful for that. But we still miss her. Dad said the important thing is that while Simona lived you were good to her. You took good care of her and gave her love and fun. Now we must try to comfort Dale because he will miss her. We don't always understand why such things happen, but we must have faith in God and help the living while we can.

Psychologist: How do you feel about it now?

Peter: It was out of my mind until you asked me about it.

Psychologist: Does it bother you that I asked?

Peter: Not that much.

Psychologists: It's better to talk about it. How has this accident affected your life?

Peter: Me and Mary thought that Simona and Dale were the only dogs in the world and we loved them very much. Because we loved them so much we wished that it was a dream and didn't really happen.

Psychologist: But when you found out it wasn't a dream — so what now?

Peter: It's over, so I don't have to worry about it. Simona is gone. My dad promised me another dog. He said he might get me another dog.

Psychologist: Do you want another dog right away?

Peter: No, because it wouldn't be so nice for Dale. As soon as Dale forgets it, we can get another dog.

Psychologists: How is Dale acting?

Peter: It's like yes and no put together. He doesn't tear up the house like he used to tear up people's slippers and pieces of paper. He doesn't chew up so many things anymore.

Psychologist: How did your parents help you deal with this problem?

Peter: They didn't help me. We had to do this by ourselves. We had to learn that we had to deal with it. That is the thing. Simona just cannot pop out from under our bed again and say, "I'm here." She is gone. We will never see her again.

Psychologist: Have your parents been acting any different to you?

Peter: Mom's been nicer. She got me and Mary some new roller skates. She's not yelling so much. Dad is different, too. He gets up early to be with us. He takes time to be with us and takes us places. He's not mad at me — is talking things over with me instead of yelling.

Psychologist: How does that make you feel?

Peter: Good. I'm behaving better, too.

To see their puppy suddenly dash into the street and instantly be killed by a car is a very traumatic experience, especially for children. Peter and Mary were helped to accept the death of their puppy, when they were told it was not their fault. They felt comforted when their parents held them on their laps and talked to them. Peter expressed deep empathy for their living puppy, when he said that he didn't want to get another dog until Dale had time to forget the loss of his sister puppy. The children learned the meaning and finality of death and the sadness that it brings.

SUMMARY

The child, like primitive man, is deeply involved with the mystery of birth and death. Steiner believes that the child's developmental ideas of death follow Piaget's ideas of cognitive development. Children have deep anxiety about death. They need clear and honest answers to their questions about death, according to their age and understanding. The meaning of death should be a gradual learning experience for the child as he becomes aware of it through the death of insects, birds, animals, pets, and people. The country child is closer to life and death than the city child. In his daily experiences he learns that death is a part of nature, so he learns to accept it as a reality. The city child should spend some time on a farm and get close to nature in order to learn through personal experience about the rhythms of life and death, and to accept the fact that death is part of life.

REFERENCES

Anthony, S.: The child's idea of death. In Talbot, T. (Ed.): The World of the Child. Garden City, N. Y., Doubleday, 1967.

Bender, L.: Aggression, Hostility, and Anxiety in Children. Springfield, Ill., Charles C Thomas, 1963.

Chesser, E.: Living With Suicide. London, Hutchinson & Co., 1967.

Feifel, H. (Ed.): The Meaning of Death. New York, McGraw-Hill, 1959.

Grollman, E. A. (Ed.): Explaining Death to Children. Boston, Beacon Press, 1967.

Jackson, E. N.: Telling a Child About Death. New York, Channel Press, 1965.

Mitchell, M. E.: The Child's Attitude to Death. New York, Shockcn Books, 1967.

Nagy, M. H.: The child's view of death. In Feifel, H. (Ed.): The Meaning of Death. New York, McGraw-Hill, 1959.

Schilder, P. and Wechsler, D.: The attitude of children toward death. J Abnorm Soc Psychol, 45:406-451, 1934.

Steiner, G. L.: Children's concepts of life and death: A developmental study. Doctoral dissertation, Columbia University, 1965.

Talbot, T. (Ed.): The World of the Child. Garden City, N.Y. Doubleday, 1967.

Wahl, C. W.: The fear of death. In Feifel, H. (Ed.): The Meaning of Death. New York, McGraw-Hill, 1959.

Chapter III

CHILDREN'S FEAR OF DEATH

Do children fear death? Freud said that death means little more than a departure or journey to the child, and that there was no unconscious correlate to be found for the conscious of death; that the fear was symbolic of the fear of castration, caused by improper resolution of the Oedipus complex. But Wahl (1959) disagrees with Freud and states that thanatophobia, the morbid fear of death, is frequently found in some children as early as three years of age, at a time when the child is able to develop concept formation and feelings of guilt. Family stress, that may bring about intense frustration, rage, or anxiety, or threaten parental loss, may contribute to the fear of death in children, especially if they have failed to receive parental love and care.

The privileged, nondeprived child retains in his unconscious the infantile omnipotence whereby he controls his outside environment by his powerful wishes, and by identification with his parents who are all-powerful. This gives him a persistent feeling of personal invulnerability to death, so that he thinks it cannot happen to him, although it does happen to others. Thus, the child's earliest experiences affect his fears and attitudes toward death.

When the child later learns that death is final, instead of being reversible, he becomes frightened about his death wishes toward ambivalently loved significant persons whom, at moments of frustration, he wished to banish. *To think of a thing is the same as doing that thing,* according to the law of Talion, therefore the child thinks that his death wishes towards others will ensure an equal punishment for himself. He now tries to revoke those wishes through magic maneuvers. He applies this magic before he goes to

34

bed, by going through a form of prayer in which he blesses all his loved ones. This is similar to primitive man's rites and spells to achieve God's blessings for himself and death for his enemies.

An unloved or underprivileged child is especially vulnerable to greater trauma if his parent or sibling happens to die. It proves to his way of thinking, that the magic power of his thoughts caused the death of his loved ones. He may develop strong feelings of guilt and fear that his own death is imminent.

The death of a parent may bring to consciousness the child's earlier fears of separation. David Moriarty (1967) says that the trauma of the death of a parent or sibling is always followed by profound and complex psychological reactions which may permanently distort further maturation of personality. Levinson (1967) states that "bereavement presents a seriously traumatic event in a child's life, frequently resulting in insecurity, anxiety, fear, distrust of the world, and physical discomfort."

When the child conceives the parental death as being a hostile act of abandonment, for which he is responsible and for which he will have to pay, his feelings of anxiety, insecurity, and aloneness may become so traumatic as to affect his daily activities, schoolwork, eating, sleeping, and self confidence. Professional help may be needed to reassure the child that he was innocent, did not cause the death, and that it was no one's fault. He must also be told that the person did not want to die and leave him, but that he had no choice in the matter. The real cause of death should then be clearly explained to him. We must remember that the child's thinking is neither logical nor reasonable. He is filled with confusion, with feelings of guilt and anger, of deprivation and abandonment. He dares not admit these thoughts and feelings to himself.

In order to repress the fear of his own death, the child builds up defenses in his own mind against such possibilities. A great deal of his fears and fantasies could be allayed if we did not make death a taboo subject but spoke of it freely and factually, so that the child could satisfy his insatiable curiosity about what death is, the cause of the death of someone, and where people go when they die. But he senses the evasion and subterfuge of the taboos against talking freely with his parents, about the meaning of death, and learning that death is part of life.

Wahl suggests that the deeply repressed fear of death becomes heavily symbolized into other fears and anxieties. But if a child's parents, from whom he gets his self-image as a worthy person, can accept the reality of death and deal with it, he too can be less fearful. He can then have the expectations that his own death and that of his parents are probably a long way off. Freud (1957) said, "To deal frankly with the psychology of death has the merit of taking more into account the true state of affairs and in making life more endurable for us."

Various explanations of death fears in children have been reported by Alexander and Adlerstein (1958). They found that death words were responded to with increased affect especially in the early school years and adolescent years.

Chadwick (1929) relates children's fear of death to the fear of excessive physical restraint, masturbation guilt, fear of darkness, and especially to infantile separation anxiety. It is also associated with guilt, pain, and fear of the unknown. Actual experiences with death and funerals bring the child closer to the reality of death and the fear that it may happen to him and to his loved ones.

We see that children's reactions to an experience with death are greatly influenced by the way their parents and other authoritative figures conduct themselves during such an event.

The adults' attitudes toward death are absorbed by their children. Many adults have an unrealistic attitude toward the fact that man is mortal and will eventually die. They refuse to talk about death or to face the fact that sooner or later they will die. Feifel (1959) says that concern about death has been relegated to the taboo area and that "we have been compelled, in unhealthy measure, to internalize our thoughts and feelings, fears, and even hopes concerning death."

Because death has been a taboo subject, many of these childhood fears and thoughts linger on in the unconscious and appear in adult life when death strikes a significant person in our life and makes the loss more difficult to cope with. When a parent is overwhelmed by the death of a child and is unable to come to grips with his own feelings, his living children absorb his anxiety. If the parent is afraid to talk about the death, the child is influenced by this taboo and represses his fears, guilt, and confusion.

The following cases deal with children who became emotionally disturbed by experiences with death. Their disturbance was increased by the unwise handling by authoritative figures, who did not understand the children's feelings. They tried to protect them by not explaining the meaning of death and the real cause of the death of their loved one. Some parents did not let the children participate in the funeral and mourning ceremonies, but sent them away during those times. In many cases the adults were so engrossed in their own grief that they were unable to understand the children's feelings and reactions.

Dicky: Fear Father Will Die

Eight-and-a-half-year-old Dicky was brought to me because he was restless, fearful, and disturbed. In school his attention span was short, he could not concentrate on his lessons, and he was having trouble with his peers. I found Dicky to be a very frightened little boy. When he played checkers he was afraid to move his men. Each time he asked, "Am I safe? Am I safe?" He decided that he did not want to finish the game, so we put away the checkers. He told me that he saw an alley cat dying. In his Rorschach cards he saw a "skeleton in a haunted house."

Dicky was seven-and-a-half years old when his father died suddenly in his office, of a heart attack. Dicky was not taken to the funeral. When his mother later told Dicky that his father had died, the child ran outside and played with all the children, acting as if nothing had happened. When a child exhibits such behavior adults may think that he does not care and is indifferent to the death of the loved one. Actually, the shock is too great for the child to bear, so he denies to himself that the death has occurred. To prove to himself that everything is the same as before, he continues with his normal activities of play. But sooner or later the child will have to face the truth and learn to deal with it.

Dicky's mother could not give the boy the special attention he needed at this time, because she was not only involved with her own grief, but also had the care of her little daughter who was born two weeks before her husband died.

When Dicky's mother remarried and became pregnant again, Dicky showed great anxiety about the health of his stepfather. He was afraid that after this new baby would be born, something would happen to this father, too. Young children sometimes confuse birth and death. They may think that when someone dies he may be reborn again and come back to life as a baby; or when a baby is born he may take the place of someone who is going to die. This is similar to the idea of reincarnation.

Dicky's parents and I tried to make clear to him that his first father did not die because of the mother's pregnancy and the birth of his little sister. We tried to explain to him that his father just happened to get sick and die at that time, but it had nothing to do with the new baby. But Dicky was still anxious and restless. He would not go to sleep until his father came home from work and he knew that this new Daddy was safe. When his father got sick with a cold, Dicky had to come along with him to be reassured by the doctor that his father would get well after taking the medicine. But this little boy still continued to be fearful and anxious during the mother's entire pregnancy. He felt great relief when his mother gave birth to a little boy and his father still remained in good health.

Fear of the Dead and Viewing the Body

Fear of the dead may cause serious disturbance in children. Sherry, now twenty-five years old and the mother of three children, is still afraid of dead people. She said to me, "When I was seven years old we lived near a cemetery. My fifteen-year-old cousin took me there. She said to me, 'If you don't do what I tell you I will press a button and the dead person will come out of the grave and get you!' When I was fifteen years old my grandfather died. Until the viewing I was scared to walk to the casket. When they lowered him into the grave I was so relieved. I was so afraid that I slept with all the lights on in my room."

The custom among some religious groups of "viewing the body" can be very frightening to children. At age fifteen Sherry was still very disturbed by being required to view the dead body of her grandfather. She was still afraid that the dead body of her grandfather would jump out of the coffin and get her.

How can we really know what a child feels and thinks about the death of a relative? The events that stand out and are remembered from childhood may continue to affect him, consciously or unconsciously.

Dr. Charles D. Aring (1968) writes of his own childhood involvement with death. His mother, who was forty-three years old when he was born, and an invalid ever since that time, died in their home six years later. He was her only surviving child. He writes, "I have no clear memory of her suffering or death. As far as I know, I was as composed as a youngster might be during the obsequies that took place in the parlor of our home — that is, until some oaf coming up behind me picked me up and held me over the coffin for a good look... If this memory is a screen, it tells something about my unconscious; death had no untoward conscious connotation to a young lad, perhaps because I had no firm ties with a sickly mother. But this is mainly speculation; it is not among my earliest memories."

A Jewish Child at his Grandmother's Funeral

Vivid descriptions of children's experiences with death can sometimes be found in autobiographical accounts. Maurice Samuel (1963) in his book, *Little Did I Know,* describes the death of his grandmother in 1904, in Manchester, England, when he was nine years old. He tells how he wept for this old lady who was a loving soul in a small shrunken body. Experiences with death was more common to children in those days. Maurice was one of the younger children in a family of nine, three of whom had died.

While describing his thoughts and feelings about his grandmother's death and the rituals associated with it, he recalls the death of his little sister when he was about five or six years old. Orthodox Jewish customs require a simple wooden coffin. Viewing the body is not permitted and the coffin is closed. His reactions to Jewish rituals and ceremonies are vividly described in the following quotation from his book:

Grandmother's was the second family death I witnessed, the first having been that of my shadowy little sister, Bessie, in Rumania. At the age of five or six I had gone through the common childhood preoccupation with death, my own and that of others, and was reminded poignantly of it when my first granddaughter, at the same age, snuggled close to me and whispered: "You're not so old, Grandpa Moish; you won't die yet for a long time." But at nine I had forgotten my early terrors, and the transformation of my grandmother into an image which was held in a box and carried out of the house amid hand-wringing and loud sobbing was a totally new, totally unexpected and ghastly event, bewildering and shattering in its effect.

How could such a frightful thing happen? What was the matter with the grown-ups, the bosses of the world, that they should let themselves be pushed around in this incomprehensible fashion, not lifting a finger, but rather joining with abandon in the monstrous procedure? There was so much frightening play acting, too: the bucket of water at the outside door into which you had to dip your fingers entering and leaving, the mirrors and pictures turned to the wall, the entering and leaving without salutation, the sitting in stockinged feet on low stools, the tearing of lapel of your coat. I wept for my grandmother and felt I was a part of a conspiracy; I wished I could thrust into her hand all the ha'pennies she had ever given me. She might need them where she was taken."

Fear that Mother Will Die

Fear that a parent will die and disappear in the middle of the night, can unconsciously continue to disturb a child for many years, until the cause, buried in a past experience, is brought to consciousness and the facts explained.

Dolly, a gifted child, now ten years old, who was coming for therapy, had a hard time falling asleep. Almost every night, since the age of three, she would come to her parents' bedroom in the middle of the night, wake up her mother, and insist that she take her to the bathroom. This disturbed the mother's sleep every night. At a session with Dolly and her mother I asked her to explain what happens.

Psychologist: Why do you think you wake your mother up every night?

Dolly: It's a little impulse that makes me do it; an urge to do something — made by something you don't know.

Psychologist: Maybe it is made by some past experience buried in your unconscious.

Dolly: There are two halves of your mind. In the conscious there is a lot of thoughts you know while in the unconscious the thoughts are buried under dirt, with a tooth pick trying to pry it up. It turns your mind from bolts to screws, to realization, so that thought comes into view. It shapes into a tumble jumble ready to be unjumbled — into a jumbled thought in your conscious mind. Then you think more about it and it comes into a dim view of a thought facing the conscious mind.

When I was little (age three), I had a real bad dream. I dreamed about the witch in *Hansel and Gretel.* I saw shadows on the wall. It scared me. There was a canopy over my bed. I used to see horrid faces on the border of the canopy. Sometimes, when I woke up I was startled and afraid. I looked up and saw faces. It was almost like they were coming to kill me. Hardly any of the faces will have body forms. The forms of the different faces keep changing. They are staring at me and staring and being witches. Then I hide my face — then look at them quickly — and when it was morning I jumped out of bed. There were really flower baskets with handles on the canopy. You could easily take notice of dim shadows in the dark. I would get a shudder — a tightness feeling.

Psychologist: Can you try to remember something way back that frightened you about your mother's health?

Dolly: I've got a memory for distant things. Just ask me any questions and I will be free and ready to answer. Ask anything about the past and I can remember.

During the day I loved the canopy. My mind sees the flowers. Then I'm thinking. I stare with my eye — my mind transforms it into faces — then I get scared. I was thinking of nice things — then I would look up — and boo — a reflector mirror between my mind, my eyes, and the canopy. The canopy relates to the shadows of the dream.

That night, about seven years ago, I went to sleep. It was early in the morning. I had a dream like *Hansel and Gretel,* that I had wandered away and fell down. The witch threw me about. I woke up and looked at the canopy and saw the faces of the witches. I had wandered away from the house. I came to a wooded clearing.

I came upon a mean-looking house. The witch tugged me into the house. She threw me again and again and again. Then I woke up. Then I saw the faces. I was scared. I was afraid to move. It was almost like a reality dream, but the clearest part I remember. I looked up and saw the witch in the shadows blended within the walls — in the old house. That was before we came to California.
Psychologist: Did anyone ever shake you hard when you were little.
Dolly: The maid — she was real mean. I hated her! Mother, you fired her suddenly. She spanked me and yelled at me. She hit me. She was sort of fat. There was green furniture in the room we were in — a sofa — a TV. I did something you wouldn't even bother me about. She took hold of me and shook me a little and hit me. I didn't like her in the first place. She was wicked and pretty ugly and I hated her.
Mother: Dolly was less than three years old then.
Dolly: It just made me mad at her. I kind of felt something would happen. I got so frightened about it. I remember all those incidents before.
Mother: Dolly, do you remember what Lena said to you that terrified you when we both had the mumps?
Dolly: She said, "If you don't let your mother have her rest she is going to go back to the hospital and never come back again!"
Mother: Daddy and I jumped up and said, "That's a lie!" I told you that was not true. You said, "Mommy, I didn't mean to make you sick."
Dolly: Sometimes when Lena talked to me it got me frightened.
Mother: When Lena talked sharp to you it frightened you. What happened when your teacher shook you last year and you got very upset? I guess that in your unconscious mind you were seeing the maid again and were frightened.
Dolly: She held me tight and tried to shake me.
Mother: That's why when Daddy holds you tight you panic.
Psychologist: You are remembering things from way back that are very important and very helpful. Do you remember anything else from that time that may bother you?
Dolly: When I happen to wake up in the night I get fear-strucken and run out. I think there are other thoughts I can bring out.

When I wake up I seem to get visions in my mind. I get frightened and I run to my mother. Visions are bad things in general. Sometimes when things happen to be my fault, I cry also. Talking is just an advance form of thinking. You got to think before you talk and talk before you do something. *"You'll wake up your mother! She will get sick and die,"* the maid said. I remember another time when I woke up in the morning and my mother was gone from her bed. My daddy told me that Mommy got sick in the middle of the night and had to go to the hospital. *I thought going to the hospital meant being dead.* Following incidents related to this just panicked me. Here is a picture I am making of the maid. She is an ugly woman − uneven eyes   a square corky nose − a horrid mouth and eyebrows, with a ridiculous icky hair-do.

Psychologist: You see, Dolly, not finding your mother in bed brought back the unconscious fear that she had gone to the hospital and was dead, and that you caused the death by being bad, because that was what your maid told you in order to frighten you. So unconsciously you wake up in the middle of the night and run to your mother to see whether she is still there, safe in bed. What will you do now when you wake up in the middle of the night?

Dolly: Now, if I wake up, I will just think about it. I will understand it and go back to sleep. I know how to deal with urge now. Last night I would have been frightened. Now, I would wake up − think about it, realize there is nothing to worry about, be comforted, and go back to sleep. Sometimes, if I do get visions, I won't just cover it with a blanket and push it deeper down in the dirt, but I could deal with it.

This analysis ended the compulsion of a ten-year-old gifted girl, who woke up every night, compelled to check if her mother was in bed, so that she might be reassured that her mother did not die and disappear in the middle of the night.

Death and Fear of Abandonment

When a parent threatens to leave a child as punishment for bad behavior, the fear of abandonment may be aggravated if the child suddenly loses a relative through death. Such a child may already have been frightened and confused by the death of the relative, who went to the hospital and did not come back. This is especially true if the child was not permitted to attend the funeral, the parents avoided talking about the dead person, and the child had no clear, concrete picture of what actually happened. He may feel that if a person suddenly dies and disappears into nowhere, this can happen to anyone, especially to him or his parents. His fantasy may create all sorts of fears and anxieties: fear of being abandoned by parents for misbehavior, fear that the death of the relative was his fault, fear that his parents will suddenly die and disappear, fear that accidents and sickness will strike him and his parents.

Such anxieties can grow into wide-spread phobias of all kinds and cause the child to withdraw from many normal activities. He may become emotionally disturbed, be unable to concentrate on his schoolwork, and may even be afraid to go to school, and insist upon staying home to see that nothing happens to him or to his parents.

CHILDREN'S REACTION TO THE DEATH
OF PUBLIC FIGURES

Children's reactions to the sudden death of public figures by assassination have been studied. Murphy (1964) reported a wide range of reactions in children age 12 to 15 to the assassination of President Kennedy. She said that some children were overwhelmed, whereas others did not seem disturbed . . . in some children the death "loosened defenses and evoked residues of emotional expression found in past experiences." Wolfenstein (1964) studying adolescents said, "After the death of a parent the predominant tendency was inhibition of emotional response, often to a level below the surface of reality, with denial of the loss. In contrast, the President's death evoked intense emotions and grief."

This suggests to me that children who lose a parent may feel singled out for suffering such a loss, and they cannot share their sorrow with others who are more fortunate. But when there is a universal loss and everyone suffers, they can understand and share their feelings with others.

Kliman, working with Wolfenstein, pointed out that the

younger emotionally disturbed children showed increased anxiety and bizarre behavior at the news of the assassination of President Kennedy. It invoked the "perception of death in some children as a threat to defenses against their own death wishes against their parents."

Seven months after the death of President Kennedy I asked an eight-year-old girl what she would wish for if a fairy godmother gave her three wishes. Her third wish was that President Kennedy would not be dead. The tragedy was still in her mind.

Levinson (1967) says, "Bereavment presents a seriously traumatic event in a child's life, frequently resulting in insecurity, anxiety, fear, distrust of the world, and physical discomfort."

Harrison (1967) reports a study of President Kennedy's assassination as it affected children hospitalized at Children's Psychiatric Hospital, University of Michigan Medical Center. He states that there was adult confusion and misperceptions among the staff in their interpretation of how the children reacted to the news of the death of President Kennedy. The staff also disagreed over what the children's appropriate response should be. "There appeared to be numerous distortions in the staff's perceptions of children's reactions, apparently as consequences of the participant's own grief."

I think that their experiences should alert us to the way adults may react to their own grief during the death of a member of their family, and how their neglect or misunderstanding of the way such a death is affecting their children, and that it may result in the emotional disturbance of youngsters. Anthony (1967) says, "The adult is often ready to suppose that his own distress at thoughts of death will be shared by the child . . . this is seldom the case."

The assassination of Robert Kennedy was another unfortunate occasion to study the reaction of children to this tragedy. Helen, a 16 year-old high school girl, was very disturbed by this event. She said, "I was very upset by Bobby Kennedy's getting shot. Thursday morning, when my mother told me that Bobby Kennedy was dead I just couldn't believe it. I lay in bed for ten minutes without moving, although I had to get up to go to school. When I passed the American flag on the way to school I kept thinking about Bobby Kennedy. The Battle Hymn of the Republic kept going through my head. We had been singing it in Glee Club.

"When I was in my house I had the feeling that someone was going to shoot me through the window. I ran into my bedroom. I was scared to go any place in my house, but I had to go, of course. I ran into the bathroom. I felt secure only in my bed. This happened all day Thursday. My girlfriend, Jane, had the same fears and feelings. She didn't want to talk about it. I talked about it a lot with my mother. It helps to talk about it.

"When we had a test in math I just couldn't concentrate. I just couldn't get it through my head that he was dead. What Kennedy said kept going over and over in my mind. I just kept saying, 'You're not dead! You can't be dead.' My mom said it was just like a member of the family had died. I think Sirhan should be killed — a life for a life. During school I just started staring at the American flag. The Battle Hymn of the Republic pops in my head all the time. It's not till a person dies that you realize how good he was. Last night I was reading in the encyclopedia about John Kennedy and Robert Kennedy. They were both great Americans."

How were other children affected by this tragedy? Three months after the assassination I talked to 11-year-old Catherine about it. She said, "I was in the fifth grade. We had elections in our current events class and Bobby Kennedy won. Later, at 1:30 A.M. Bobby Kennedy was shot. He was in very serious condition. If he would have lived there would have been something wrong with him. It was very sad. Out teacher didn't want to talk about it. Neither did the rest of the class. Then, after his death, they had three days of the funeral. The family was there and all the relatives, and other people. There were so many people there — it was twenty blocks long. It was the worst tragedy since his brother died. That's why elections were postponed to September.

"The class had been watching what was happening on TV. The man who shot him was part Mexican and part Spanish. He was in the hall where Bobby was talking. He entered the kitchen and he saw the guard and Kennedy walk out. He shot four of the guards and he shot Kennedy; two bullets in the back of the head — two bullets on the side of his neck — one bullet on his left arm. Some man saw him shoot and the police immediately rushed in, captured the man, and Kennedy's wife was immediately called.

Then the ambulance came and they took Kennedy to the nearest hospital. Four guards took care of the man who shot him — Sirhan Sirhan. The crowd tried to rip Sirhan apart — tore his coat off. They forced him into the police car and drove away."

I asked her, "Do you think teachers should talk about it?"

She answered, "They could talk about it but should not rub it in. It's sad. Don't rub it in. Don't talk about it. About two weeks ago Sirhan's brother was in court and a girl shot him. He was wounded."

Catherine's seven-year-old sister said, "Bobby Kennedy — he was president. Someone shot him — a man with black curly hair."

These conversations reveal the way children of different ages interpret in their own way, according to their age and knowledge, what they see on TV, and how they absorb the concern and disquietude of the adults around them. It also shows the influence of the teacher who didn't want to talk about the death. Neither did the class want to discuss it, although talking about it would have helped the children learn to face the fact of death in a situation that was tragic, yet not as close to them as a member of their family would be. The younger child was much more confused than her sister. She had vague distorted ideas about what happened. But she did absorb a vivid picture of killing and violence by watching TV.

Robert Hertz, (1960) an anthropologist, says that Wertham has labeled the murder of famous people "magnicide." Hertz says, "In tribal societies unexpected death of young and important citizens seems to shake the community's faith in its own power of survival. Intensified mourning rituals result."

I suppose that the leader represents the protective father figure and the tribe suddenly feels unprotected and vulnerable. This is also the way a child feels who suddenly loses a father and has no one to turn to for guidance, support, and protection. He feels alone and helpless, as if the bottom has been pulled out from under him. Jackson (1965) says, "Children think their parents are all-powerful and are confused when their parents cannot meet a crisis with complete mastery." At such a time it is no wonder that a child feels deserted and unprotected in a frightening world.

SUMMARY

As soon as children become aware of the fact that man is mortal, the fear of death is upon them. Their reactions to an experience with the death of a significant person in their life are influenced by the way their parents deal with it. Deprived children are more vulnerable than those who feel secure and loved. Some children have fears that they have caused the death by disobedience or death wishes at a time of anger.

Childhood fears linger in the mind, may be repressed in the unconscious, appear in unexplained disturbing behavior, and make an experience with death more difficult to cope with in adult life. Most adults can remember the childhood fears and feelings they had when a member of their family died. Religious mourning and funeral rites affect children's attitudes and fears about death.

The sudden death of a close relative can have a traumatic effect on a child who is already vulnerable to emotional breakdown because of other disturbing experiences. Conscious effort must be made to learn how to diminish the trauma caused by the fear of death in children.

Studies indicate that children were seriously disturbed by the assassination of President John F. Kennedy and later his brother, Robert Kennedy. Our children today feel closer to leaders and identify with them, because they see and hear them on television and actually feel that they know the leaders of their country.

Children who lost a parent through death had repressed their personal grief, because they felt singled out by sorrow. The universal sorrow brought on by the death of public figures enabled them to express and share their sadness with others. The assassinations as reported on television affected children of all ages.

Parents can help children face the problem of death by freely discussing it with them; and in the case of assassination, by explaining the facts clearly, so that the distorted and confused ideas children may get will be corrected.

REFERENCES

Alexander, I. E. and Adlerstein, A. M.: Affective responses to the concept of death in a population of children and early adolescents. J Genet Psychol, 93:167-177, 1958.

Anthony, S.: The child's ideas of death. In Talbot, T. (Ed.): The World of the Child; Essays on Childhood. New York, Doubleday, 1967.

Aring, C. D.: Intimations of mortality: an appreciation of death and dying. Ann Intern Med, 69:137-152, 1968.

Chadwick, M.: Notes upon the fear of death. Int. J Psychoanal, 10:321-334, 1929.

Freud, S.: Thoughts for the times of war and death. In The Complete Psychological Workks of Sigmund Freud. London, Hogarth Press, 1957, Vol. XIV.

Harrison, S. I., Davenport, C. W. and McDermott, J. F., Jr.: Children's reaction to bereavement. Arch Gen Psychiat, 17:593-597, 1967.

Hertz, R.: Right Hand. New York, Free Press, 1960.

Jackson, E. N.: Telling a Child About Death. New York, Channel Press, 1965.

Levinson, B. M.: The pet and the child's bereavement. Ment Hyg, 51(2):197-200, 1967.

Moriarty, D. M. (Ed.): The Loss of Loved Ones. Springfield, Ill., Charles C Thomas, 1967.

Murphy, L.: Bereavement is studied in children. Medical Tribune, July 11-12, 1964, p. 19.

Samuel, M.: Little Did I Know. New York, Alfred A. Knopf, 1963.

Wahl, C. W.: The fear of death. In Feifel, H. (Ed.): The Meaning of Death. New York, McGraw-Hill, 1959.

Wolfenstein, M.: Death of Kennedy stirs nation's youngsters. Medical World News, May 8, 1964, p. 11.

Wolfenstein, M. and Kliman, G.: Children's Reactions to the Death of the President. New York, Doubleday, 1965.

Chapter IV

THE HOSPITAL SETTING FOR THE SICK CHILD

DEATH was no stranger to children in the nineteenth century when medical knowledge was limited and epidemics ravaged the population. Children's diseases were common and infant mortality took its toll. Death occurred in the home and children witnessed its arrival. Children's literature in the nineteenth century reflects their awareness, acceptance, and sadness of death as a reality.

But with the growth of medical science and the greater use of hospitals to care for the sick, our children have been spared many experiences with death. People have denied death and avoided discussing its existence, especially in the presence of children.

Physicians and psychologists are now trying to overcome the taboo against talking about death and dying. They are stressing the need to face the reality of death and to deal with it with understanding and wisdom, for we are learning that a child who is suddenly confronted with the death of a close relative may undergo the shock of a permanent traumatic experience, unless the event is handled with professional guidance.

A child who is himself confronted with his own death, throws everyone into a state of anxiety or even panic, for the fatal illness of a child is unexpected and shocking to all concerned. Yet such illness is not rare, since malignancy in children between the ages of one and fifteen is the single greatest cause of death in children in the United States. Pediatricians who have to deal with dying children need to learn and teach their younger colleagues how best to deal with their own emotional involvement, so that they can help the child, the medical staff and the parents as well as the child's grandparents and other relatives.

Dr. Robert H. Moser writes (1969) "The leukemic children I have known, loved, labored with, wept over, and watched die in helpless anguish, will never cease to haunt me. The unfilled promise of youth, the mysterious vitality of children, the taunting thought that someone, somewhere, may unlock the secret within the next weeks or months, drives one to exhaust every rational therapeutic possibility to preserve the small life. However, in the presence of fatal disease, in the agonal hours, . . . I feel it is cruel . . . to prolong life . . . of a brief survival."

A study of the *Year Book of Pediatrics* from 1950 through 1970 contained only two references, (Friedman et al, 1963; Weston et al, 1963) to the way a child and its parents were treated in cases of a child suffering from a fatal disease, in spite of the tremendous need to deal adequately with this problem. (Gellis, 1964-65).

WHEN A CHILD IS DYING

How can we meet the crisis of a child who is dying of a lingering, fatal illness? How do we relate to him and help him meet the problems he must face in the most constructive way?

Who are the significant people concerned with the case and how can they be organized to function in a cooperative, constructive manner? How can we help parents and relatives meet the situation with strength and acceptance? How de we encourage parents to participate cooperatively in the care and treatment of their child?

Who are the professional people involved, and what are their responsibilities and attitudes toward the child and the family? What are some health authorities and hospitals doing today in facing this problem? What procedures do they follow that will make the experiences of the child who is dying most meaningful and least emotionally traumatic for all the people concerned?

The Child

How do we face the child who is dying? What do we tell him? How do we treat him? How de we answer his questions about death, about himself, about what is going to happen to him? Do we dare to face him with the truth? Can we look him in the eyes?

The most important ingredient in the relationship between doctor and patient is *trust*. Without trust in one's doctor great fear is aroused in the patient, for his health and life are in the hands and heart of his doctor. He is dependent and fearful, insecure and inferior in his position of dependency.

You cannot ever fool a child. Intuitively he senses another person's thoughts and feelings. He is closer to the deep inborn collective unconscious and senses any default in defensive, destroying, dallying with the truth. No matter what the seriousness and shock the truth may invoke, the child *must not lose trust* in those who attempt to serve him, be they parents or professional personnel. With trust, the patient will put himself into the hands of those who care for him and thereby feel safe and secure no matter how serious his illness may be.

Should we then speak outright to the child and say, "I am sorry, but you are about to die." Of course, that is not the way to deal with death at any age. First, we treat the child, as we should treat any human being, with respect as a person, with warmth and attention, with professional care and assurance that we are using all our knowledge and competence to help him; that we are not running out on him but will stand by at all times as long as he needs us. We emphasize the present and deal with every need, big or small, that we can assuage. We do not pretend that he is not a sick child, nor do we frighten him with hopelessness.

The Doctor

The doctor sets the pattern of care and concern as he creates the atmosphere that surrounds the child. All the activities of the hospital and the outpatient clinic reflect his attitudes and actions. His professional and personal manners are emulated by the staff, as he trains them in the method of treating patients with kindness and consideration. He provides plans for the constructive participation of parents in the care of their child.

The doctor must be able to face and care for a dying child with strength and fortitude. It is especially hard for the pediatrician to accept the fact that a child is dying. He has selected his specialty because it is more concerned with the prevention of what used to be called "childhood diseases" and now concentrates on the care and supervision of the healthy and growing child.

But death may be a part of life even in children, and a doctor who cannot face the fact of death should not try to care for a dying child until he has learned to understand his own fears and deal with them in a realistic way. If he denies death he will avoid seeing the dying child who is a constant reminder of its reality. To avoid seeing and facing such a child is to make him feel unloved, rejected, abandoned. Only a doctor who has learned to accept the reality of death can help a child learn to face it with courage and acceptance. Instead of passing the room of a sick child, the doctor must make every effort to see the patient, even if it is just for a moment to say hello or bring him a small gift. If a doctor feels the need to turn away from a dying child or his family, he has not received the proper guidance in his medical school training. It should be a "part of the curriculum at every medical school" (Robinson, 1970).

The doctor who has to care for a dying child must be able to accept the probable outcome with courage and control. However, he must never really lose all hope in both the outcome of his immediate case and the continuing research of science.

Physicians respond to the fact that a child has a fatal illness according to their own age. The resident responds with *rage;* the middle-aged physician responds with *denial;* while the older physician often *accepts death* as a normal process, without too much emotional involvement and last minute heroic efforts to prolong life. The physician who regularly treats children with life-threatening disease must know how to manage his own emotional attitudes toward death in order to be most effective in the way he handles the child and his family (Lascari et al., 1970).

"The physician should not give the impression of being rushed. Appearance, manners, tone of voice, gestures − the entire gamut of nonverbal communications exert subtle but very definite effects on the patient's mood" (Verwoerdt, 1965). "As long as the patient remains alive there should be nothing which happens to him that his doctor cannot help relieve," Dr. Verwoerdt explains. Patients' complaints and physical symptoms offer a wide range of opportunities to provide relief. Whenever fresh complaints arise, the patient should be re-examined, especially to avoid any appearance of futility. Palliative therapy should be continued to the very end.

The doctor must be professionally competent and emotionally mature so that he may contribute to the support and confidence of the child and his family. They must feel that he has special expert knowledge and understands what there is to know and do about the medical management, that he will call a consultant any time he is unsure about the situation or anytime they ask for one. A good doctor should always be willing to consult another doctor whom he respects. If the consultant has new suggestions it will help the patient and the doctor will feel that he has tried every possibility for the treatment of the child. However, if the consultant agrees with the doctor's treatment, it will serve to contribute to his own self-confidence and to that of the child's parents. This will provide the security of knowing that everything possible is being done, Dr. Morris Green explains (1967).

Although other doctors will participate in the care of the child, it is very important that the family and child know who is their main doctor. The family should be able to reach this doctor *at all times.* He should also provide the name and phone number of a substitute in the event that he cannot be reached in an emergency. The doctor's relationship with the child and his family must be that of a warm and strong friend, who will instill in them the confidence and comfort so necessary for facing the long ordeal. Frequent visits will reassure them of his interest and concern and give them the opportunities to express their fears and anxieties. It will permit him to attend to present needs and discomforts, no matter how slight they may seem, for to accentuate the present is of the greatest importance.

It is important that parents should not be afraid of the doctor but should feel at ease in talking to him and expressing their thoughts and feelings. They should feel free to ask questions and bring up problems with the assurance that he will respond with honesty, patience, and friendliness. He should explain in clear and simple terms what is being done during the treatment in the hospital or clinic, and what the parents should do when they care for the child at home.

The Doctor and the Patient

The child should be able to look forward to the doctor's visits with confidence and anticipation as the relationship grows more friendly and informal. The child's faith in the strength, knowledge, and friendship of his physician, whom he can trust, who is consistent and reliable, will have tremendous therapeutic significance in easing the child's fears and pains. If the doctor is able to gain the child's confidence and bring out his repressed fears the continuous moral support and interest in the child will be mutually meaningful and rewarding.

"Many children interpret illness as punishment and respond by regression, persistent dependency, rebellion and/or chronic invalidism . . . The physician, to allay a major fear of the child, must reassure him that his illness is not his fault and is not punishment for anything he did" (Lourie, 1962).

By the doctor's frequent visits he is able to keep informed about the child's progress with his disease. He can show a personal interest in the child by talking to him about his daily activities at home and in school. Interest in the child's school work may stimulate him to pay more attention to his studies. The doctor may bring him a book, a map, or pictures related to some school subject, ask to see his report card, and compliment him on his progress. Talk about his experiences with peers and parents, sisters and brothers, may lead the child into reflecting his own self image — his fears and hopes about his place in the world.

Thus the relationship grows closer and stronger, as the doctor remembers birthdays and holidays, hobbies and interests, until the child finds comfort, confidence, and trust in the doctor who is now the most important person in his life, next to his parents. So the patient looks forward to his physician's visits with hope and anticipation, although it may bring painful treatment as well as strength and friendship.

Open communication between the child and the doctor will contribute to the understanding and cooperation so important for all necessary treatment. The basic principle to remember is that the child should be prepared in advance before treatment is administered. He should not suddenly be taken by surprise and wheeled away in mystery, for a major medical procedure, without some honest and factual explanation by the doctor. Such procedure should be explained in enough detail to satisfy his curiosity. He should be permitted to ask as many questions as he wants, to express his concerns, anger, and fears. This does not mean that every detail of the treatment must be explained, but the child must be given some general idea of what to expect. He should be told what will be done, whether the treatment will be painful, if an anesthetic will be required, and what happens when it is used. This will eliminate unnecessary fears and trauma, and contribute to the child's trust and confidence in his doctor, so essential to his comfort and peace of mind. Of course, such explanations should depend upon the child's age and understanding. Tell the child as much detail as will give him reassurance, but do not give him misinformation that will later make him feel that he has been let down by those whom he trusted the most.

The doctor should encourage the child's interest in his illness and allow him to take an active part in its management (Morris Green, 1967). This will help him gain self esteem as he tries to cooperate with the doctor and willingly follows instructions regarding his own care and welfare. The child will take pride and pleasure in his attempts to cooperate when the doctor praises him for his efforts, so that they both work together as partners in the project of contributing to the child's health and happiness.

PREPARING THE CHILD FOR HOSPITALIZATION

The child will absorb the parents' attitudes toward his hospitalization. They must therefore try to understand their own feelings about his need to be hospitalized and accept it as necessary for his health and welfare. Such acceptance will help them focus on the child's anxieties to allay any fears he may have.

The parents should prepare their child for hospitalization a day or two in advance, so that he can get used to the idea. They should encourage him to ask any questions that trouble him and try to answer them honestly and simply, according to his age and understanding. They should tell him why he is going, what will happen there, how long he will probably have to stay, and when they can be with him in the hospital. They should explain to him that it is no one's fault that he happened to get sick. When he is brought to the hospital his parents should be allowed to be with him during the admittance procedure and stay with him until he gets settled and used to his surroundings. If he cries a little, they should accept it quietly and put their arms around him, as he resigns himself to the inevitable.

The younger child might be allowed to bring a favorite toy and even something belonging to his parents, or a photograph of them so that he may feel they are with him. The older child might want some favorite book or familiar object that he usually keeps in his room. Words used by the younger child to express his toilet functions, his nickname, the foods he loves as well as those he is allergic to, and eating, sleeping, elimination and play habits should be written down for the nurse. This will help her make the child feel more at home and safe.

When the parents leave the child in the hospital they should not sneak out but should tell him they are going and when they will return. They should also tell the nurse they are leaving so she can comfort him if necessary. If possible, they should phone him when they get home so that he may feel he has a line of communication open and is not completely separated. This will not be necessary if the mother is allowed to stay in the hospital.

Parents should try to visit their child frequently, especially if he is a pre-school child. More and more hospitals are permitting parents to help in the child's daily routine of eating, washing, and dressing. It is good for both parents and patient to participate in such care. If the child has to go through surgery or some painful procedure it is very reassuring to him to have his parents with him, or have them waiting in his room after such treatment.

However, if the child is adjusted and learning to get along with nurses, doctors, and peers in the hospital, his parents need not stay with him so much. They need time to take care of the rest of the family and carry on with home responsibilities as well as to get a little rest and relaxation. This will help siblings and spouse from feeling neglected and contribute to a more normal home life.

When the child returns home from the hospital he may regress to more dependent and immature habits. He should gradually be helped to grow into his former, more mature and independent ways and assume his own responsibilities and self-confidence. His hospitalization may then have contributed to a growing, maturing experience as he realizes that it must sometimes be accepted as a part of life. Ten-year-old Danny who underwent surgery in the hospital said, "I'll never again be afraid of an operation. They are all so nice here, I think we should write them a letter telling them how nice they are."

THE CHILD IN THE HOSPITAL

Children must be prepared in advance for a basic hospital experience. The child must be told that hospitalization is not punishment or abandonment; but that it is an opportunity to get the best and most modern care known by doctors, who are always learning through research to find better methods and medicines to heal the sick.

A change away from the security of the home and parents is in itself disturbing to any child. When this occurs to a sick child, brought to a hospital and cared for by strange hospital personnel, he may be upset and frightened. In the hospital the child is restricted in his mental and physical activities. Prolonged bed rest interferes with freedom of activity and produces negative physiologic reactions. There is a great need for a climate of warmth and friendly concern in the hospital to counteract the general procedures that sometimes make the patient feel that the hospital staff is against him. The less unnecessary change that occurs the easier will be the child's adjustment to the impersonal climate of the modern hospital.

Especially under prolonged hospitalization, children develop friendships and form a group. Therefore, the child should not be moved around from room to room as if he is a piece of equipment. The daily routine of meals, medical treatment, visits by doctors and parents, educational and recreational activities should be as regular as possible so that the child knows what to expect. "Sameness is reassuring in the face of death" (Verwoerdt, 1965). Children in general find security in a structured daily program.

A spirit of solidarity and cooperation of hospital staff is

required for good teamwork among various specialties, departments, nurses, and other hospital personnel. Doctors, nurses, and dieticians should try to anticipate and fulfill the patients' wishes about meals and other details. Good food contributes much in bringing comfort and satisfaction during the daily routines of hospital living.

Every personnel member should be constantly alert to the comfort and needs of the child, so that he may feel that there are always friends around to whom he can turn. They should comfort him when he is in pain and give him some attention and reassurance, rather than ignore him with indifference and hopelessness. "Children frequently complain about being alone, cold, in the dark, or behind a closed door" (Smith and Schneider, 1969).

Dr. William B. Rothney, (1970) a pediatrician, reported a study of the emotional problems of hospitalized children at Tufts-New England Medical Center in Boston, and declared that the study supported the need to treat the whole child, rather than to focus only on the physical illness. The center's parent unit at Boston Floating Hospital has nine parent-child cubicles with two registered nurses wearing brightly colored dresses, always on duty. They are a part of a team that includes a pediatrician, a social worker, and a child psychiatrist, who work with the parents and the children. They often maintain a continuing relationship, particularly with children who may be hospitalized more than once.

"This approach reflects the changes in pediatric care which have led to long periods of hospitalization for prolonged, chronic care, and often fatal illnesses, such as leukemia or kidney diseases . . . The health care team helps parents and children learn how to handle grief, the anxiety of hospitalization and often, impending death. The focus is on sustaining ego strength and coping ability," Dr. Rothney explained. "The presence of the parent is a major help to the child, but the parent does not do the nursing."

Children with chronic illnesses have special emotional problems and fears. Adolescents with chronic diseases, such as diabetes and asthma, *live with a constant fear of death,* yet this fear is mixed with the hope that they can live with their illness, according to Dr. Stanley G. Werner, Children's Hospital, District of Columbia. He asked 32 children who had been treated in the hospital's adolescent and specialities clinics to write essays on "What I know about asthma (diabetes etc.) and how it affects me" (Werner, 1970).

Dr. Werner found that diabetic children knew a great deal about their disease process, its complications of hypo-hyper-glycemia, acidosis, and most precipitating factors, and that they would need insulin injections all their lives. *The great fear in both groups was death,* either from acidosis or from an acute asthmatic attack. To offset that fear the essays included a detailed account of the conduct required of a patient with the chronic disease they had.

All the diabetic youngsters said they felt different from their friends because they were deprived of certain foods, but some of them were able to accept it because they realized that there were other people who were also suffering from diabetes. The diabetic children were hospitalized for training in the basic physiology of glucose metabolism, the need for insulin, possible reactions, self-injection, and proper diet. They learned to develop self-reliance, but continued to maintain a relationship with the clinic and with one special physician.

Asthmatic children did not know as much about their condition as the diabetic children. They were only aware of wheezing and tightening of the chest. They gave heredity and allergies as the cause for their illness, but would not accept the emotional factor as part of it. The asthmatic children were given hyposensitizing injections weekly for the first three to six months, and monthly thereafter. They were treated by the same doctor and same nurse, thereafter. The adolescents all came in regularly at the same time, so they got to know each other and felt more at ease with their peers and the medical personnel.

Every child who enters a hospital for medical treatment, whether it is for minor or major care must be prepared in advance for such an experience. An unexpected procedure that is frightening, may not only be traumatic to the child during his stay at the hospital, but his fearful experiences may later be transferred to other medical treatments that are really not as serious or painful as the child anticipates because of his past disturbing experience.

Nine-year-old Johnny had to go to the pediatrician's office to get an injection for an infected ear. He was frantic with fear and resisted for half an hour, although his pediatrician told him that it would not hurt much. after the injection Johnny acknowledged that he hardly felt it. The next day, before the second treatment, he talked with the psychologist in the pediatrician's office.

Psychologist: You see the shot yesterday was not so terrible. You must have trust in your doctor. You know that Dr. M. has never told you a lie; you can trust him. He told you it would hurt a little. Trust between people is the greatest thing in the world.

Johnny: I am not really afraid of Dr. M. because he always explains everything and he always tells me the truth. But I was still scared about what happened last year, when I went to the hospital and Dr. B. had to operate on me. I had three moles — one on my back, one behind my ear, and one on my side. I stayed in the hospital 14 hours — from 6:00 A.M. to 8:00 P.M. I was put into a bed, wheeled in by the nurse. I felt kind of chicken. My mother and father were with me in the room. When I went to the operating room they wouldn't let Dad and Mom go in with me.

They put a weird mask over my face. The doctor did. We had a big fight — the doctor and me. I started to squirm and wiggle. I wouldn't let them put the mask on — like on an airplane — the pilot and copilot. It was for oxygen — not hydrogen. I thought I was going up — they were going to wheel me into a plane. I thought a plane was in the back of the hospital. So they gave me a teaspoon of gooooy medicine — barrrch! to take. They were the boss. The doctor and nurse were the boss. My parents were not around. I fell asleep. So they had the easiest time of putting the mask on. I hardly remember the mask.

When I went into the operating room I felt scared. When I first came into the hospital I felt like I had to barfff. I was asleep till I went to my room again. When it was all over and they wheeled me into my room again my Dad gave me a walkie-talkie. I had to eat awful food — potatoes, string beans, sloppy joes. My parents were in my room all of the time. After I came out of the operating room my parents were with me till 8:00 P.M. and we went home.

Psychologist: What about the nurse who gave you the shot in the operating room? You see, you forgot to tell me about the nurse who gave you a shot, because you tried to forget it. The mind sometimes blocks out − pushes out of memory − fearful things, but it stays hidden in the mind and comes out at another time.

Johnny: Oh, I remember, I was wheeled in. The medicine didn't work. Then she gave me the shot and I fell asleep. The shot hurt in the hospital, but the shot Dr. M. gave me yesterday in his office did not really hurt much. Yesterday, when Dr. M. had to give me a shot for my ear, with that big needle, I thought it would hurt a lot. That is why I screamed and yelled and made a big fuss.

Psychologist: You argued for half an hour, till you, the doctor, the nurse, and your mother were worn out. But if you would have *trust* in your doctor, you would have saved everyone a hard time.

Johnny: I didn't see the needle but I thought it was like the nurse's needle in the hospital. I was afraid of that big needle going into me.

Psychologist: The doctor doesn't put the whole long needle into you. The needle is just the small part; the rest of the thing is the part that holds the medicine. When he gets the point of the needle into you, he pushes the medicine in through the small opening in the needle.

Johnny: Does the needle have an opening at the tip?

Psychologist: Yes, there is an opening inside the needle and if you relax instead of tightening up, the needle goes in easier and hurts less. When I have to get a shot I usually think of something else or recite a poem I have memorized. You can hypnotize yourself by saying anything you want to get your mind off the subject, or counting, or thinking of something else, or saying to yourself that it doesn't really hurt that much. Just keep your mind off the shot. It only takes a few seconds. When you count three backwards it is usually over.

Johnny: Oh, I thought the whole thing was pushed into you together with the needle at the beginning.

Psychologist: If you have trust in your doctor and believe in him, you will not be afraid. Dr. M. doesn't lie. It may hurt a little, but it isn't that bad.

Johnny took his second shot without a fuss.

Any experience a child has in a hospital or clinic will affect his future fears and attitudes when undergoing medical treatment. Previous pleasant experience with a certain nurse or doctor will give a child reassurance and ease his anxieties.

A child who is seriously ill needs the assurance of familiar surroundings and the presence of parents more than ever. Yet that is the time when she may have to be hospitalized and be cared for by strangers, not knowing what will happen to her.

Eight-year-old Gail was brought to the hospital with a fatal disease. Her doctor suspected leukemia and referred the case to a children's cancer center. The child sensed the worry of her parents and was very apprehensive about what would happen to her. When she was brought into the hospital room her parents were permitted to come in with her and stay in the room. She had brought along her favorite stuffed toy. Her mother helped her undress and put on her night gown. The chief of staff came in with the resident, nurse, and volunteer worker.

Dr. Good: Hello Gail. Welcome to our hospital. I want to introduce myself and the people who are all here to help you and to make you comfortable. I am Dr. Good. I will be coming in to see you at various times and you can discuss anything you want to know with me or any of these other people. This is Dr. Aaron. He is the resident physician and you will see a lot of him because he lives in the hospital. This lady is Miss Joy, your nurse; Miss Hazel, her assistant; and Mrs. White, the volunteer lady who comes around to read to you, talk to you, or just to keep you company, so that you don't get too lonesome. Remember that we are all your friends and don't be afraid to tell us about anything that bothers you or ask us for anything you want, and we will try to get it for you, if we can. Any time we have to give you some medical tests or treatments we are going to explain to you exactly what we have to do, whether it will hurt or not, and why we have to do it.

When they left the room Gail's mother said, "See, Gail, I told you that the people are all very nice here in this hospital and they will try to do everything they can help you and make you comfortable." Soon a lady came in with Gail's supper. She had a hamburger, a baked potato, some peas, and a glass of milk. For dessert she had some chocolate pudding. It was all very good. The doctor's warmth and friendliness gave Gail and her parents some reassurance and quieted some of their fears and apprehensions.

After eating her supper, Gail said to her parents, "Mommy and Daddy, I am not afraid to stay here. Go home now and eat your dinner, too. Jacky and Grandma will be waiting for you. You know that I can call you on this phone any time I want to. You can call me, too. Don't worry, I will be all right. The people here are nice and will take care of me. If I push this button the nurse will come right in to ask me what I want."

The small child is especially fearful of separation from his mother when he is hospitalized. He is afraid of being hurt and forgotten. The nurse must therefore act as a friend and mother substitute, to give love, comfort, and security to him, not just to inflict pain. When painful treatment is required, he should be told what will happen to him, a short time beforehand.

The nurse must be warm and sympathetic toward the child, tell him it is O.K. to cry, and stay with him a little while after the treatment to comfort and console him.

The nurse must also discipline the child by setting limits, so that he knows the rules of the hospital and what he is allowed to do. By treating him like a normally healthy child she takes some of the burden off the parent who may feel guilty about disciplining a sick child, and may feel that he should be given extra privileges. When the child is permitted to become the boss, he may turn into a confused tyrant, burdened with making decisions that may bring about insecurity in him and hardships for everybody. The nursing staff should be stable and consistent in their discipline and ways of handling the child, so that he knows what to expect.

The nurse must be in constant attendance when a patient is dying because he must not be left to die alone. Parents should be informed when the end is near. The doctor should also be called to help the patient die comfortably or to attempt to prolong life, if he decides that is the thing to do at that moment. The nurse should not be alone with a dying patient. She needs the support of others at that time. The relatives of the dying patient will feel relieved by the reassurance that the doctor is in close contact with the attending nurses, so that he does what is necessary and also that the patient does not die alone.

THE SOCIAL ATMOSPHERE IN THE HOSPITAL

The social atmosphere in the hospital affects everyone in it. A hospital is a social structure that provides a role for everyone in it except the role the patient should take. The hospital chart showing the pecking order of the personnel has no position for the patient's role. The nurse has all kinds of authorities over her and she may receive conflicting orders from some of them which may provoke anger and anxiety in her. Unconsciously she may pass on her resentments to the helpless patient (Stainbrook, 1970).

The importance of empathy and easy communication between doctors and patients cannot be overemphasized, for they serve the most vital psychological and emotional needs of the patient and supersede all other factors in the hospital set-up. No matter how skillful and knowledgeable the doctor may be, if he lacks the human qualities of warmth, care, and concern; if he fails to treat the patient as a person instead of a case or number, he cannot be considered an adequate and mature professional man.

A report of patients' reactions to hospital care (Drake, 1968) stressed, above everything else in hospital stay, the great importance of the human qualities expressed by the doctors and nurses. Those who complained about poor treatment by the hospital personnel said that the doctors and nurses "just didn't care about patients as people. It was always the disease process or hospital routine that was important." The patients indicated that doctors and nurses didn't have time to talk to them or to reassure them at a very difficult time in their lives.

Although there were complaints about hospital food, hard beds, unsanitary conditions, and noise in the corridors, none of those factors could compare in importance with the patients' longing for kindness and consideration from the doctors and staff.

The complimentary remarks about good treatment in certain other hospitals praised the doctors who were attentive and who took time to explain procedures they were about to undertake. They also noted the friendly atmosphere of the hospital which reassured them at a time when they were undergoing great anxiety.

Some doctors cite overwork as the reason for paying little attention to the emotional and personal needs of their patients, but Drake indicates that the doctors' attitudes may be a way to deny death. He says, "We wonder if in many cases this is not a convenient cloak covering a hardened, perhaps defensive attitude toward death and pain" (Drake, 1968).

Drake quotes a five year study of a university affiliated hospital, by a Yale University pediatrician and a sociologist who write, "The physician focused his interest on physical disease. . . He was usually not concerned with personal and social influences in relation to the disease . . . the problems of the patient were viewed in a physiologic or 'mechanistic' content" (Duff and Hollingshead, 1968).

Clinic patients often complained about the need to wait many hours in unpleasant waiting rooms before they were seen for a five minute examination. Such procedure shows indifference and lack of respect for the patient as a person whose time is also important.

THE NURSING STAFF AND THE PATIENT

What is the place of the nurse in helping the dying child and his parents? The nurse must emulate the interest and concern expressed by the doctors in order to establish an atmosphere of warmth, kindness, and know-how in the hospital and clinic. All other personnel are influenced by the nurse and absorb her manner of handling patients and parents. The nurse has to help build the morale of the hospital workers as well as contribute to the peace and serenity of patient and parents in every way she can.

Because the nursing personnel spend more time with the patient than anyone else, their attitudes and actions are vital to the health and happiness of the patient. A hospital atmosphere of acceptance, friendliness, and concern, established by the doctors, must be reflected in the conduct of the nursing staff, in order to bring about a climate of service and security, hope and comfort. Their attitudes and behavior are of inestimable influence in helping patients and parents live through the tremendous ordeals they must face through a long and lingering illness. The conduct of the nursing staff can be frightening, painful, and emotionally traumatic to the child and his parents; or it may be a source of soberingly enriching and maturing experiences to all concerned, as they contribute to a better understanding of the true meaning of life and death.

By her actions and attitudes the nurse sets an example for the rest of the hospital personnel to follow. Often a mature and understanding nurse may influence and help young doctors and interns by the way she handles patients and solves problems. If she uses finesse and tact, many of them will unconsciously turn to her for guidance and advice. The nurse is the physician's delegate to deal with patients, parents, and relatives. She has close contact with all of them and can be of great help and comfort to them in times of stress and despair.

What can the nurse do? The nurse must always remember that she is caring for a *living patient,* not a dying one. As long as the patient is alive every detail of care and help are of utmost importance. Don't give the patient up for dead as long as he is alive and conscious The nurse's cheerfulness and active interest in making the patient comfortable and content at all times has deep meaning in making the patient feel he is still alive and valued as a person. The nurse must show respect for the patient and compassion for his pain and suffering by doing everything she can to give him relief and assurance. The child should be made to feel that the nurse is his friend and should not be afraid to express his needs and feelings. As the nurse develops rapport with the child he feels free to communicate with her more easily and may confide his deep fears and anxieties to her.

"The support of the physicians and nurses is much more important than anything that can be done for the patient" (Elmore and Verwoerdt, 1967). Many ill patients have an altered sense of time. "Anxiety and psychological upset tend to hasten death." Fatally ill people are often unable to cope with everyday life. Nurses must show acceptance of impatience and frustrations about little things in the patient, because the sick person is always on edge so that his fears and anxieties make every little thing loom large. The nurse should consider the importance of all these details to the patient and try to attend to them, because as long as the patient is concerned about the little things, he has not given into depression and indifference about what may happen to him later.

The Nurse's Own Attitude Towards Death

The nurse's own attitude towards death is vital. It affects her ability to give adequate physical and emotional care to the patient.

If she accepts death as part of life and doesn't deny death, she can face the child and his parents with strength and fortitude. If she denies death and runs away from it, because she cannot face it, she will deal with death by running away from the patient, and *the dying patient will know it.* She will then invoke the greatest fear the patient has, *the fear of abandonment.*

The nurse must accept the fact of death and resolve her own fears before she can help the child and his parents. However, in many hospitals, death is purposely hidden and either not discussed, or is dismissed after brief mention.

Some institutions are now having conferences and discussions in order to help medical students and nursing personnel achieve a better understanding of their own feelings about the meaning of death and dying. Only through such self knowledge will they be able to care for their patients in a more mature and acceptable manner. Drs. Kazzaz and Vickers (1968) of the Fort Logan Mental Health Center, Denver, Colorado, state that "psychiatric nurses aides, and social workers show denial, separation anxiety, and unresolved feelings that severely inhibit their growth and effectiveness as therapists." These doctors state that "only with ongoing programs aimed at realistic understanding and acceptance of death can ward personnel be helped to overcome . . . the strong cultural thrust toward denial of aging and death."

The program includes staff participation in psychodrama on the meaning of death, attendance at an autopsy and at seminars on religion and psychiatry. As the members of the staff began to gain insight into their own feelings about death, they were better able to communicate honestly with their patients. Instead. of being evasive, the staff learned how they could approach the patient on his own terms of handling his feelings about death. The patients' responses varied from "denial, projection, and wishful thinking to final acceptance of the inevitable." Drs. Kazzaz and Vickers found that after the training given doctors and nurses in working out their feelings toward death, and increasing their knowledge about the patients' feelings, the staff attained considerable ease in working with patients.

A study of pediatric house officers' reactions to caring for children who are dying, indicated that the staff experienced anticipatory mourning along with the child's parents. The doctor hesitated to tell the parents about the fatal prognosis and tended to withdraw from the patient (Schowalter, 1969).

Dr. Schowalter describes a program to provide systematic child psychiatric consultation about the emotional aspects of hospitalization conducted by the Ward for Older Children of the Yale-New Haven Hospital. Three weekly meetings are held by the psychiatrist and ward social workers. One meeting is with the patients from twelve to seventeen years old. When a death has occurred on the ward it is not hidden but it is discussed at the meeting. Another meeting is with the floor nurses. They decided it was more honest not to close the children's doors when a dead patient is wheeled off the floor.

The third meeting was for fifteen to twenty persons who work with adolescents in the outpatient clinic or on the ward, such as the chaplain, teacher, staff child psychiatrist, child psychology fellow, medical students, house officers, nurses, social workers, and the medical director of adolescent services. They discussed the tendency of parental guilt for the fatally ill patient to be projected unto the ward personnel, the value of listening as well as talking, the need for one doctor to be designated to communicate with the patient and parents, and the dangers of the staff's withdrawing from the patient. "It is natural for the healer to mourn the loss of the patient and of the illusion of his own omnipotence" (Schowalter, 1969).

Dr. Elizabeth Ross (1969) organized a seminar at the University of Chicago on death and dying for medical students, doctors, nurses, and theology students of all denominations. A dying person volunteers to act as a teacher by frankly discussing his personal feelings, hopes, and despairs with a psychiatrist and a chaplain, as he nears his own death. This seminar serves as therapy for the patient as well as a learning experience for the medical personnel, who listen in behind a one-way glass partition and afterwards discuss the interview. Dr. Ross says, "It's amazing that so many physicains and nurses never really discuss what death means." She observed a great change in the attitudes of those who attend the sessions regularly and she has come to realize that the participants in the seminar must work out their own feelings concerning death before they can learn from the patient.

THE NURSE AND THE SUICIDE PATIENT

How can a nurse help a patient who is contemplating suicide? A nurse must understand her own feelings about suicide before she can best help a suicidal patient. "An alert nurse may be able to detect the signs of an impending suicide and initiate action to provide the necessary assistance for averting tragedy" (LT Pollock and LTJG Trostman, 1970). The nurse should have assistance in sharing this responsibility with someone else. Many nurses don't know how to handle a suicide patient.

The nurse should try to communicate with the patient and not be afraid to use the word *suicide.* Encourage him to talk about it instead of avoiding the problem and trying to cheer him up. He may drop hints that he does not want to go home, that he has sleeping pills but does not sleep, he may show a sudden reversal in behavior, be delusional and confused, state that he can't go any longer, that he has no friends, complain of failure and inability to function, enter the emergency room with an unexplained wound, and say that the nurse is the only one who really cares about him (Pollock and Trostman, 1970).

The discussion with the nurse interjects a sense of reality to the patient. She must be able to listen, show interest and empathy. She should let him cry and express his feelings of anger, hopelessness, and helplessness. She should try to discuss with him better ways to cope with his problems. "Most suicidal patients have a great deal of ambivalence and the suicidal state is limited in duration" (Pollock and Trostman, 1970.)

Nurse Must Give Supportive Care

The need for unhurried nursing care and personal attention to dying patients in order to relieve their feelings of loneliness and abandonment is stressed by Carol Ron Kneisl, R.N. (1967). She says that staff members often limit their contact with the patient in order to avoid unanswerable questions and to decrease their emotional involvement with the patient. This, together with rotation of staff, results in superficial relationships and communication with the patient. She suggests the selection of limited personnel who have the ability to be warm, supportive, and good listeners. Such a staff is especially needed, because, she explains that "when dying is prolonged, family members tend to visit less frequently even though the patient indicates he values their presence."

But even the friendliest of nurses cannot always be near the dying patient who wants her at his bedside when he is aware of the shadow of death lurking above him. The fear of dying alone, with no one near him, contributes to the thought of being abandoned. It adds to the loneliness and bitterness of dying without the presence and comfort of loved ones near by.

"Until recently, it has been the custom in various countries to have a relative constantly attending a dying person, so that somebody was always present with him to the end in order to offset his loneliness" (Hackett, 1969).

"It is a Jewish duty to visit a sick person if such call is likely to give comfort to the sufferer, the visit to be followed by prayer. It is the Jewish duty to remain with a dying person until his last moment" (Rabbi Leo Jung, 1943).

No one knows the moment of his death. No one wants to die alone. As long as someone is near him, the sick person feels he will be saved. When help is near, hope stays with him. So a dying person should never feel that help is far away and he may die before they reach him. He should die in the arms of someone he loves or someone who gives him faith in a future world if his religion teaches him such faith and trust.

CARE AT HOME OR HOSPITAL?

Is the hospital the best place for a dying child? When should a dying child be required to pass his last days in a hospital and when should he be allowed to die at home in the arms of his family? Is the hospital *always* the best place for a dying child? Is it always the best arrangement for the *family* of the dying child?

Hospitalization for the child means increased dependency, depersonalization, and regimentation. He finds himself in a strange environment at a time when he desperately needs the familiar surroundings of his home and the love and protection provided by the presence of his parents, the assurance and comfort of his own bed and home.

In the hospital a child loses the identity as a person — he becomes a patient among many other patients. At home, he is a beloved member of his family, where he feels safe and wanted. He doesn't feel abandoned or forgotten, for someone is always near him. The familiar surroundings of the home give the child assurance that he is taken care of. He can "feel at home." How good it is to have your own roof over you, and your own loved ones at your side! There is always someone who is near. Whenever he opens his eyes he sees them and does not feel alone.

For the family, running back and forth to the hospital is destructive of strength and independence. Parents may feel deprived of the opportunity to care for their child when they must stand aside while hospital personnel take charge. They must follow the rules and routines of the hospital.

At home, they can adjust their activities to the individual needs and desires of their child. If this takes too much of their strength they can employ help in the house. It would cost less than hospital care. It would give parents as much time to be with their child as possible; to share the short time with each other to the fullest. It could leave memories never to be forgotten.

To want to have the dying child at home, the parents must be able to accept the fact of the fatal illness and not deny that death is near. They must want to share every precious moment with their child while he is still alive.

If the parents need to avoid the responsibility or feel unable to face the ordeal emotionally, physically, or efficiently, they will have to send the child to the hospital. But if they have the strength, the desire, and the courage to keep the child at home, they may find it to be an enriching, maturing, and meaningful experience. The moment of death is not as important as the measure of life given the child while he is still with us.

Parents may need to accept the fact that the child may die when there is no doctor around to "save the child." They may thereafter blame themselves and feel guilty, when in fact, their doctor could do nothing to prolong life in a meaningful way. Doctors are not gods and can only do so much. They are limited in their power to help and to heal. To prolong life in a meaningless suffering, unconscious existence, is of no value to anyone. A person should be allowed to die in dignity, peace, and possible serenity. In most private hospitals today, there is no doctor available when he is most needed, and a patient may be completely alone when he is dying.

Under what circumstances should the decisions be made whether to put a child, who has only a short time to live, in a hospital or to keep him at home?

There was the case of a 14-year-old girl who was beginning to fail from a progressive muscular wasting disease. The doctor sat down with the family and discussed how the case could be handled. The doctor writes, "We could put her in the hospital and with heroic measures continue her life a few more weeks; or we could treat her at home, keep her comfortable, and in the closeness of her family, await the end. This latter course was chosen. To my surprise and gratification it all seemed to go so easily. The family was emotionally united and closer than ever; the mother in describing it to me later made it sound close to a religious experience. I too felt included in the family cohesiveness" (Dr. X., 1970).

"Looking back, I compare it to all the hospital deaths I have participated in: The long waits in stark halls or in uncomfortable chairs by the bedside, the terrible hospital sounds, the uneasy trips down to the cafeteria for a somber cup of coffee, the fuss and bustle of technicians drawing blood or nurses starting I-Vs'.

"I surely don't mean to say that all dying children should be kept out of hospitals; certainly that is the place for many for a variety of reasons. But where the course is inevitable and the means to keep the patient comfortable are available, what's so bad about dying at home?" (Dr. X., 1970).

Hospitalization is an anxiety-provoking experience for all of us and especially for sick children who yearn for their mother and father. If we can ever avoid it by letting the child die a natural death of a hopeless disease, in the peace and quiet of a loving home, with members of his family near by, we should consider abiding by such a choice with the guidance, cooperation, and approval of their doctor.

Feifel and Jones (1968) questioned people about their choice of the place to die. The majority said they preferred to die at home rather than in a hospital, because of its familiarity and comforting features.

MAKE THE MOST OF THE PRESENT

We only exist in the NOW, the Present, for no one knows what is in the future for him. The past has a strong hold on us, but we must not constantly look back to what existed in the past, good or bad. If someone dies, we cannot make him live again by returning to the past ourselves, or by staying in a dead present while time roles on in reality. If we insist on living in the past, we are as dead as those who have really died. Only our biological body lives on.

No one lives forever, but we repress our fear of death by denying that it will ever happen to us; or if it will happen, death is such a long way off, that it is not worth thinking about so we push it out of our mind. If we tell a teen-ager that smoking will take away ten years of his life, he laughs, for the end of his life seems too far away to make any difference. *Now,* the *present,* is the most vital and meaningful time to him. And perhaps he may be right about thinking that the present is all we really have, especially in this atomic age. Of course, we should tell him that the smoking is affecting him *now,* every cigarette, to a certain degree.

But let us especially talk about the meaning of the present, not when we think death is far away, because we do not know the day we will die, but when we suddenly learn that we, or especially our child, has a malignant disease. Then death stares us in the face and we cannot ignore it. Some people will immediately try to avoid the death by avoiding the sick person and thus deny death by abandoning the dying. This is actually what is being done to a greater or lesser degree, by relatives, doctors, and other medical personnel. This brings about the greatest fear and the greatest pain of the dying person, the fear of being abandoned while he is yet alive. What we should do, if we have courage and understanding —

if we truly have love for the person and *think about how much he needs us,* rather than of our own loss — is to *see how precious the present is and try to make every moment count!* Those who avoid facing the present, because of their fear of the future, are losing precious, valuable, never-to-be-forgotten experiences of human encounters.

A child is normally outside playing with his peers, or is going to school and being absorbed with his own interests and hobbies, so that parents really never get to know their child. But when illness suddenly strikes and they spend much time together, they may suddenly gain deep insight into his personality, as they share their thoughts and feelings openly and sincerely.

The *now* is more precious because time is limited — time is running out. *Today is more dear because there may be no tomorrow.* The present is like the precious life-sustaining water to be treasured and used and valued with wisdom and watchfulness, by those lost on the vast ocean or on a desert island.

How meaningless and futile and self-defeating it is to try to deal with death by running away in order to avoid it; by not facing the dying person, when we should really do the opposite; when we should use the precious time of life while it is yet available, while it is yet with us, while it is yet *present.* The preciousness of the present is ever with us. Let us use it well before it is gone. Let us concentrate on the PRESENT MOMENT in all we do to make it meaningful and enriching in what we do with our *time,* because *time represents life* to all of us. It is especially valuable in the way we use it in human relationships. When we become aware that time is running out, because someone dear to us has a very serious and perhaps fatal disease, we must try to share the time we have with the dying person in happy, *creative living.*

With children, the present is especially the most meaningful and the most important. "Younger children seem to be more concerned about *feeling safe,* about being with a trusted person and free from pain than they are about actual survival" (Smith and Schneider, 1969).

Dr. Verwoerdt (1965) says that "Children's time scale is composed of smaller units than adults. . . Children live from one day or week to the next, while adults look ahead months or years. . . Day by day living offers the child a refuge relatively free from fear of impending death, and he thereby maintains the possibility for limited planning and action.

"Taking on a different time scale enables the patient to look forward into the future, not months but days. This relieves anxiety and creates a situation in which hope can be reactivated. By living day by day, good prospects become real possibilities."

If parents and medical personnel continually keep up a warm and close relationship with the sick child, showing that we care about him and his comfort, that we are ever aware of his needs, that we are constantly in communication with him and have not avoided him, he will be able to put himself into our care with confidence that we know what to do and will do it; that we will not let him down in hopelessness, indifference, and neglect.

In a TV program discussion with parents of children who were dying of a fatal disease, many of them said they had finally learned not to avoid the child or the reality of his condition, but to concentrate on the immediate present and try to make the most of it — to enjoy the child day by day. They had learned to think of the child's needs rather than their own sorrow. Some of the mothers said:

This child needs us, why are we being sorry for ourselves?

————————

Think of your child's welfare and her well-being day by day. It is very constructive. You would be surprised how helpful it could be.

————————

We continued as we did before, reading together. She would sing her favorite songs. We made tape records and played it back to her.

————————

People told me that I was strong. I didn't know it. I'll never again be afraid of anything that will happen to me. You can only live today to the fullest.

————————

It brought us close together. He needed to talk. We really understood the meaning of love.

————————

I can now speak without bitterness. It brought my husband and me closer together. We shared the child.

————————

The present is the most real and meaningful to all of us. When a child is dying of a fatal illness we must especially make the most of every moment of life for the child and for the relationship with us. Make every moment count in the enrichment of sharing and togetherness, of communication and companionship, of love and trust, faith and hope, with thankfulness for the precious years we shared with each other.

SUMMARY

Physicians and psychologists are now trying to overcome the taboo about discussing death and dying, and to face the reality of death. More medical and other personnel are now trying to deal with the emotional problems related to the situation of a child who is dying of a lingering fatal illness, like leukemia. In the hospital setting, the social atmosphere as well as the medical treatment must be given serious attention.

Beginning with the child in the hospital, we find that his greatest need is trust in his doctor and the other personnel. The doctor sets the pattern of care and concern as he creates the atmosphere that surrounds the child. He must try to see the child often, rather than avoid seeing him, make him feel that he really cares about him and is available to him at all times, in order to keep him comfortable and happy. The doctor must be professionally competent and emotionally mature so that he may contribute to the emotional support of the child and his family.

The child's faith in the strength, knowledge, and friendship of his physician, whom he can trust, who is consistent and reliable, will have tremendous therapeutic significance in easing the child's fears and pains, and in assuring him that his illness is no one's fault, and that it is not a punishment for something wrong he thinks he has done. Open communication between the doctor and the patient and explanation of necessary treatment, will contribute to understanding and cooperation, and will allow the child to take an active part in the management of his illness.

Children must be prepared in advance for a basic hospital experience. Hospital personnel must be constantly alert to the needs and comforts of the child, in an effort to treat the whole child and not just focus on the illness.

The social atmosphere in the hospital affects everyone in it. The nurse must emulate the interests and concern expressed by the doctors in order to establish an atmosphere of warmth, kindness, and know-how in the hospital and clinic. Her own attitude toward death must be accepting of its reality so that she does not abandon the dying child when he most needs her, but instead supplies him with supporting care and comfort. She herself must be able to accept the reality of death and face it.

Hospitalization is an anxiety-provoking experience for all of us and especially for the sick child who yearns for his father and mother. If we can ever avoid hospitalization for a child who has a hopeless disease, by letting him die a natural death in the peace and quiet of a loving home, with members of his family near by, we should consider abiding by such a choice with the guidance, cooperation, and approval of his doctor.

Children's time scale is composed of smaller units than that of adults. If we help the child feel safe, his fears of impending death are minimized. We should make the most of the present time while the child is still alive, and think of his welfare day by day as we share the precious moments together.

REFERENCES

Drake, D. C.: Doctors, nurses lack empathy, former hospital patients say. The Philadelphia Inquirer, June 9, 1968, pp. 1-2.

Duff, R. S. and Hollingshead, A. B.: Sickness and Society. New York, Harpers, 1968.

Elmore, J. L. and Verwoerdt, A.: Psychological reactions to impending death. Hosp Top, 45:35-36, 43, 1967. Abstracts, Mod Med, (March 11), 1968, p. 145.

Feifel, H. and Jones, R. B.: Perception of death as related to nearness to death. Proc, 76th Annual Convention, Am Psycholog Assoc, San Francisco, September, 1968.

Friedman, S. B., Chodoff, P., Mason, J. W. and Hamburg, D. A.: Behavioral observations on parents anticipating death of a child. Pediatrics, 32, 610-625, 1963.

Gellis, S. (Ed.): Year Book of Pediatrics. Chicago, Year Book.

Green, M.: How to help the child who is facing death. Pediatr Herald, 8(2):p. 1, 5, 1967.

Hackett, T. P.: Current approaches to the care and understanding of the dying patient: Overview of a conference. Arch Foundation Thanatol, 1(3):109-111, 1969.

Jung, L.: Essentials of Judaism. New York, Jewish Congregations of America, 1943.

Kazzaz, D. S. and Vickers, R.: Helping the geriatric staff face conflicts about death. Roche Report: Frontiers of Hospital Psychiatry, 5(20), 1968, pp. 1, 2, 11.

Kneisl, C. R.: Dying patients and their families: How staff can give support. Hosp Top, 45:35-36, 43, 1967. In Staff support for the dying and their families. Abstracts, Mod Med, March 25, 1968, p. 117.

Lascari, A. D., Evans, A. E., Howell, D. A. and Easson, W. M.: How well prepared are you for death in the young? Patient Care, 4(10):01-106, 1970.

Lourie, R. S.: Emotional problems of prolonged and terminal illness. Feelings and Their Medical Significance, 4(1):1-4, 1962.

Moser, R. H.: Impending death and the new ethics. Arch Foundation Thanatol, 1(2):10-13, 1969.

Pollock, L. S. and Trostman, C.: Suicide nursing — observation and prevention. U. S. Navy Medical Newsletter, 56:26-27, 1970.

Robinson, M. E.: The pediatrician and the dying child. Arch Foundation Thanatol, 2(1):13-15, 1970.

Ross, E. K.: Interdisciplinary seminar on death and dying at the University of Chicago. Arch Foundation Thanatol, 1(2):37-38, 1969.

Rothney, W. B.: Emotional problems detected in many hospitalized children. Pediatr Herald, 11(4):1, 1970.

Schowalter, J. E.: Who helps the young doctor to mourn? Arch Foundation Thanatol, 1(3):112-113, 1969.

Smith, A. G. and Schneider, L. T.: Helping the family cope with impending death. Clin Pediatr, 8(3):131-134, 1969.

Stainbrook, E. T.: Conversations with a psychiatrist. C.B.S. Television Lecture, September 12, 1970.

Verwoerdt, A.: Communication with the fatally ill. CA, 15(3):105-111, 1965.

Werner, S. G.: Teen-agers reveal attitudes on living with chronic illness. Pediatr Hearld, 11(4):6, 1970.

Weston, D. L. and Irwin, R. C.: Preschool child's response to death in infant sibling. Am J Dis Child, 106:564-567, 1963.

Dr. X.: The open line. Pediatr News, 4(6):26, 1970.

Chapter V

WHAT TO TELL THE DYING CHILD

NEW YEAR'S EVE

"If you're waking, call me early — call me early, mother dear,
For I would see the sun rise upon the glad New Year;
It is the last New Year that I shall ever see —
Then you may lay me low i' the mold, and think no more of me.

"To-night I saw the sun set; he set, and left behind
The good old year — the dear old time — and all my peace of mind;
And the New Year's coming up, mother, but I shall never see
The May upon the blackthorn, the leaf upon the tree.

"I have been wild and wayward, but ye'll forgive me now;
You'll kiss me, my own mother, upon my cheek and brow?
Nay, nay, you must not weep, nor let your grief be wild;
You shall not fret for me, mother; you have another child.

"If I can, I'll come again, mother, from out my resting place;
Though you'll not see me, mother, I shall look upon your face;
Though I cannot speak a word, I shall hearken what you say,
And be often and often with you, when you think I'm far away."

Alfred Tennyson
NEW YEAR'S EVE

Beth Knows She Is Dying

IN *Little Women,* by Louisa M. Alcott, Beth
knows that she is dying but does not at first want to tell the sad
news to her family. Finally Jo realizes it and Beth tells her it is
true. Sharing their sorrow brings the two sisters closer together in
love and tenderness. Beth feels relieved of her secret and asks Jo to
tell the family; but the family, too, finally see that Beth does not

80

have long to live. They fill her room with sunshine and brightness and spend much of their time with her, as they carry on with their work while sharing their interests with her.

Beth was looking at her so tenderly that there was hardly any need for her to say, "Jo, dear, I'm glad you know it. I've tried to tell you, but I couldn't.". . . Beth tried to comfort and sustain her, with her arms about her, and the soothing words she whispered in her ear.

"I've known it for a good while, dear, and, now I'm used to it, it isn't hard to think of or to bear. Try to see it so, and don't be troubled about me, because it's best; indeed it is. . ." Beth could not reason upon or explain the faith that gave her courage and patience to give up life, and cheerfully wait for death. Like a confiding child, she asked no questions, but left everything to God and nature . . . She could not say, "I'm glad to go," for life was very sweet to her; she could only sob out, "I try to be willing," while she held fast to Jo, as the first bitter wave of this great sorrow broke over them together . . . "the hard part now is leaving you all. I'm not afraid, but it seems as if I should be homesick for you even in heaven."

Many medical authorities today believe that children who have a fatal illness are aware of their condition. Earlier children's literature supports this belief. The conspiracy of silence concerning death did not exist in the lives of children in the 19th and early 20th century. Children's experience with death was common and children's literature and textbooks contained many stories and poems that reflected the sadness and grief of people when a death occurred in a family or village, for death was a reality in all their lives.

The poem, "New Year's Eve," by Tennyson, shows that the child knew that she was dying and wanted to enjoy every moment of life while she had it. It was the beginning of a new year and she believed that she would not live to the following year. Just as today, some children believe that sickness and death are punishments for bad conduct, so children of earlier times blamed themselves when sickness struck them. Parents too, thought that death was a punishment for some sin they must have committed. In this poem the child says that she has been "wayward," but that now that she is dying her mother will forgive her. She consoles her mother that she has another child and therefore need not grieve for her.

This child's idea of death is that only the body dies, but the spirit lives on. The finality of death is inconceivable; it just takes on a different form. She says she will visit her home and listen to her mother talking, but will be unable to speak to her or make her presence known.

Many of the poems and stories in children's early literature express a religious faith in God and in a future spiritual world. Their rural background makes them aware of nature and that they are a part of the unity of the universe. The literature shows the comfort that comes with faith in a future life, as it becomes absorbed from their environment where life repeatedly renews itself.

A study of the way death is handled in children's literature should prove helpful to us today in how to deal with the problem of death and dying. Should a child with a fatal illness be told about the diagnosis of his disease? The question of letting a child know about the seriousness of his sickness is basic to the entire way he is handled by his parents and the medical personnel.

Waechter (1971) reported a study of parents' attitudes about telling their children of the seriousness of their illness as reflected in the TAT test. Some parents felt that the child should know about his illness and be allowed to talk about it openly. Other parents felt strongly that the child should not know. He should not be allowed to hear the words *cancer* or *leukemia,* but must be told that his illness is temporary and he will get over it. Other parents asked for assistance in dealing with the problem of telling the child (Waechter, 1971).

The first consideration must be the wishes of the child's parents. If they insist that the child must not be told anything at all about his condition, the doctor must approach the entire relationship with the child and his family, the nurses and the hospital personnel, in a way built upon lies and subterfuge.

It is necessary to accept parents' wishes to keep the facts of their child's fatal illness from him, if they insist. But after they have overcome the initial shock themselves, they may be told that professional research and experience indicate that it is better not to lie to the child; that he usually senses the seriousness of his condition anyway, and he wants to talk about it; that the older child knows he has a serious illness but may want to protect his parents by not telling them that he knows. He should be told that his parents do know about his condition, and it is better to be able to communicate with them and share his feelings freely and honestly.

The parents of a 10-year-old boy did not want him to know that he had a fatal illness. After his death, when his best friend told them that a few months before he died, their son confided to him that he had leukemia and expected to die soon, the parents regretted that because they had tried to keep their son's illness a secret and would not talk about it, he had been forced to die alone (Lascari, Evans, Howell, and Easson, 1970).

When a child finds that parents or doctors are lying to him, he loses confidence and trust in them. This may contribute to a deep sense of anxiety, loneliness, and feelings of alienation, at a time when he most needs their assurance of love, interest, and concern.

Physicians, psychiatrists, clinical psychologists, clergymen, and nurses, who are specialists in the field of managing dying patients and their families, participated in an intensive conference on problems concerning death and dying (*Patient Care,* 1970). The discussion included problems of managing the dying child and the teenager, and how to provide emotional support to them and to their families.

To Tell or Not to Tell

Experts disagree about the way to handle the problem of whether or not to inform a dying child of the diagnosis of his disease. Some believe that the child should be spared this knowledge; others believe that a child eight years or older should be informed about the seriousness of his condition, while a third group believe that his questions should be answered honestly, but no information should be volunteered. The answers should depend upon the child's age, his concepts of death, and his emotional maturity.

Those authorities who say the child *should not be told* about the fatal prognosis of his illness believe that the information would be so traumatic as to overwhelm him. It would also prevent him from using denial as a protection. Some say that the process of trying to protect their child from this knowledge makes the parents feel that they are doing something to help him, so are contributing to his welfare.

Those who believe that the child *should be informed* about his condition say that otherwise he is more disturbed about the secrecy going on all around him than by the actual knowledge of the facts when parents and medical personnel use subterfuge to misrepresent the seriousness of his sickness. Secrecy separates the child from those who are most important to him and affects the openness of his relationships, leaving him lonely and frightened. They feel that the child wants the opportunity to discuss his fears and concerns which may be more terrible than the facts in reality; to ask questions that may overwhelm him; and to feel reassured that there will always be a bridge of understanding between him and the adults upon whom he depends. Of course, he must be assured that there is much that can and will be done to control his illness, if he has leukemia, and that research is constantly continuing to seek a cure for it. Hope must ever be maintained and never be abandoned.

Those authorities who believe that the child's questions *should be answered honestly,* in accordance with his level of understanding, but without their volunteering information, think that this method gives the patient the opportunity of deciding whether or not he really wants to ask for the information. They say that the diagnosis should not be forced on the child but information that he specifically asks for should be answered honestly but in simple terms.

Most children never ask directly if they are going to die, though they frequently act fearful and apprehensive. In any event, the child should not be told outright that he is going to die, or how much time he still has to live. If he does ask this question, he should be told that he has a serious illness, but that there is always hope, and no one truly knows exactly when another person will die, but sooner or later everyone must die.

The preschool child thinks of death as the temporary separation from those who love him, and that it is a reversible process. He is mostly concerned about fear of suffering physical pain associated with medical treatment. The grade school child thinks of death as separation from loved ones and going to heaven. He must be assured that he will never be abandoned. Frequent visits to the hospital by friends and relatives, and keeping the child in the home as much as possible, will prevent anxiety and give him reassurance that he will not be abandoned.

The adolescent understands the reality of personal death and views it as a punishment for some transgression. The thought of his personal death fills him with tremendous bitterness and despair, for he has not yet had a chance to live and he thinks it is not fair to be cheated out of life while others go on living. "Why me?" he asks.

Child Senses his Fatal Prognosis

Although the physician may not tell the child directly that he has a fatal disease, in a number of non-verbal ways the child senses his fatal prognosis. Some doctors who have treated a large number of dying children feel that, without being told, most of them know their illness might be terminal. The doctor must then accept the child's awareness of his condition and not try to pretend that it is otherwise.

Although most authorities and hospitals have a policy of never directly telling a child that he has a fatal illness and will probably die, most of them *imply* that the child knows his condition and wants to feel free to talk about it without fear of disapproval. Listen to the child. If he wants to talk about it let him feel free to speak without fear that his questions will be turned aside or avoided. Children know when parents and physicians are honest and sincere.

Natterson and Knudson, (1960) studying fear of death in fatally ill children and their mothers, state that the greatest causes of distress manifested in hospitalized fatally ill children were fear of separation from the mother, fear of traumatic procedures, and the fear brought about by the death of other children in the hospital. They represented separation fear, mutilation fear, and death fear. The fears were related to the maturation of consciousness according to the child's developmental age.

The fear of separation was most severe in the younger group, from ages 0-5; the reactions to procedures were most intense in the age group 5-10 years; and the reaction to the death of another child in the hospital was strongest in the age group of 10 years and over. The authors suggest that fear of separation, fear of mutilation, and fear of death, follow a maturational pattern.

If a child wants to discuss death with doctor or parents, it can be done without indicating that you are talking about him.

The fear of separation is deeply instilled in all of us, but it is especially strong in children. The child is not so much afraid of dying as of being alone, separated, abandoned, lost. The threat of losing the parent makes him want to merge with the people in his environment (Hansen, 1971). This need to cling to others, the demand for the physical presence of parents, doctors, nurses, is found in all age groups. The child has fantasies of being tiny, helpless, hopeless, filled with despair and anger. He fears being alone and has the fantasy of being rescued — the hope for a cure. He wants to be with loved ones, to be held lovingly, to be fed and cared for. He refuses to go to sleep because he is afraid it would separate him from loved ones.

The dread is in the leave-taking. To lose faith in those in power to whom the child looks to for care, protection, and support, is devastating to him and makes him feel alone and helpless. It is the journey, not the moment of death, that is so frightening to the dying child. He expresses anger and despair toward all powerful persons; towards parents, doctors, God. He feels betrayed and cheated of the unfulfilled promises of life.

That children are aware of their fatal illness is expressed in their TAT (Thematic Apperception Test devised by Morgan and Murray) stories whose characters suffered from the same illness the children had (Waechter, 1971). Their stories indicated that hospitalized children and those with a fatal illness showed more anxiety than other children. The type of anxiety usually revealed sadness, fear of separation, fear of pain, physical injury, mutilation and death. Leukemic children showed more anxiety than children with cystic fibrosis (Waechter, 1971). Their stories showed an effort at defense through denial, but revealed fear of an inalienable, hostile environment from which they were unable to escape and which they were helpless to alter. Children with major surgery noted body intactness in the characters in their TAT stories. Loneliness and death imagery were ascribed to the characters in the stories by children who had a fatal illness. Understanding and acceptance may decrease fear of discussing death.

Karon (1971) believes that there is a need for a strong, honest relationship with parents and patients. He says that the patient is not told that he is going to die, but often the child wants to discuss his condition and death and he is permitted to talk about it and ask questions in the Children's Hospital at Los Angeles. If a child over nine years old with leukemia asks if he is going to die, we tell him that some die and others get well. Telling a child the diagnosis of leukemia is not a death sentence because the outcome is not predictable. Most childhood cancer will improve with treatment. We tell the child that treatment will make him feel better; that we will try to help him and we will never abandon him, says Dr. Karon. We employ psychological testing to help determine when to tell the child who is over nine years old.

Dr. Jerome L. Schulman (1970) of Children's Memorial Hospital, Chicago, says, if the child does ask if he is going to die, tell him, "You have a very severe illness, but we will do everything possible for you." The child should know that he has a very severe illness, what its name is, what the manifestations are, and what the treatment is to be. He should have frequent opportunity to raise questions and they should be answered completely (Schulman, 1970).

You Cannot Fool the Child

Most professional people who are working with children who have fatal illnesses, stress the fact that you cannot fool the child about his condition; that he dies a thousand deaths if he has to cope with the conspiracy of silence. Children in the hospital are aware of the doctor's attitudes, the tests, and the examinations. From the changes in their parents' conduct which showed tension and anxiety, the children concluded that they had some serious illness. "I knew I had some serious illness, the way my parents were acting. My mother was crying; I saw about leukemia on TV."

Children always know when a certain subject is taboo and parents do not want to talk about it. It used to be about sex. Today, death is still a taboo subject. The child notices that his parents are in great distress and are avoiding the subject that is most vital at the moment — the question of what is wrong with the child. This cuts off communication between parents and children and places all of them in an embarrassing, difficult, and dishonest situation that only leads to anxiety, frustration, and separation. Sometimes the child thinks he must protect his parents by pretending he does not know how sick he is. This does not help anyone. There must be honest communication to build a bridge of closeness, mutual understanding, and sharing.

Children become suspicious when they are suddenly given more attention than usual and are treated with special consideration and favors. Extra presents, new clothes, Christmas in July, high marks in school that they don't deserve, can only mean that they are going to die soon and everyone wants to be good to them. It is much more reassuring to the child when he is treated according to the usual pattern of discipline and attention he is accustomed to. Spoiling a child when he is sick only tends to frighten him, makes him feel insecure, and sometimes makes a tyrant of him when he thinks he can control his parents with unreasonable demands.

By not indulging the sick child in the hospital he is prepared for the normal discipline and routine when he goes home. There he must follow the regular family program of school, homework, meals, bedtime, and other activities that he must share with siblings. Unnecessary privileges and lack of normal discipline given to the sick child is bad for him and harmful to his siblings. If he gets too much attention with special gifts from relatives, the younger siblings may become jealous; the older siblings may become anxious and worried about the patient, and this may affect their schoolwork and other normal activities. Parents should be praised for following normal activities in the home.

If parents won't tell, children find other ways of getting information; they turn to other patients and doctors (Vernick, 1971). Mr. Vernick, a clinical social worker, tells about his therapeutic program in a hospital ward for leukemic children. He was in charge of the social activities that kept the children occupied and active. "Children can label each adult. They size up people who do communicate with them. They except the physician to level with them even if parents won't. Kids test me. In separate groups for teen-agers and younger children we had group discussions with the doctors about leukemia. The discussions were taped and the children would re-listen to the tapes. Also the parents could listen to the tapes and learn what questions children ask and how the doctor answered them; learn of their worries, fears, and hopes. They wanted to know how long they would have to stay in the hospital, about the change in their physical appearance, loss of hair and other changes; about remissions, and about when they could go home" (Vernick, 1971).

The children are never really told directly that they are dying, but they are given the opportunity for free and open discussion without being afraid that they will be rejected for asking questions. We should be open for communication and let the child decide what he wants to talk about. Prognosis and survival in leukemia is still unpredictable as much research is in progress and patients usually live much longer than before. Teenagers want to know about their future, whether they will be able to get married, and if their sickness will affect their future children. We must also remember that children often let us know *how much they don't want to know about their sickness.* Denial, too, has a place in the service of the sick child who is dying (Vernick, 1971).

THE HOSPITAL PROGRAM

The old image of a sick child lying passively in a hospital bed and receiving only medical treatment and meals does not represent the picture of the child today who has to spend a long time in a progressive, modern, psychologically oriented hospital. There you find a social and educational program that provides active participation in all sorts of group learning, and play activities to match with their strength ability. The goal is to help the child live as normal a life as possible.

Pat Azarnoff, M.Ed. (1971) coordinator of activities at Children's Hospital, Los Angeles, describes their program and states that very few children need to lie passively or just watch TV. Their purpose is to keep the child mobile. Through play, children become more relaxed and less fearful. The child activity programs includes toys, equipment, games, and a special place to play. Even in the outpatient pediatric clinic the children who have to wait are engaged in play activities. This also gives parents an opportunity to discuss matters with the staff.

Toys are played with even when an oxygen tent has to be used. If a child is so weak that he has to lie still, his favorite stories can be read to him, or his favorite records played for him.

Children have living pets. When a weak child woke up she reached out to pet her hamster and it made her smile. When there is a pet animal in the room it becomes a topic for conversation between parents and patients.

Siblings are allowed and encouraged to visit their hospitalized sister or brother. They must not be kept in the dark about the sick child in the family, but must know what is going on. When not told the facts, their imagination has been found to be worse than reality. Being with the patient, seeing him, playing with him, and communicating with him as they share time and talk together are rewarding and meaningful experiences for all of them. It is natural and possible for children with malignant diseases to play. It is good for siblings to know that a sick child, though limited in some ways, still has the desire to laugh and talk, and play when he is strong enough. At other times they can sit together and play quiet games or listen to records. When siblings know the facts it gives reality to the situation and is far better than letting their imagination run wild with fear and confusion, is the opinion of psychologist David Rigler (1971).

Siblings may become disturbed and need counseling. They want to know if the disease is contagious; whether they will get cancer, too, and if their future children will get cancer. Siblings suffer, too, and some of them feel guilty. Some complain of feeling rejected by parents because they are so preoccupied with the sick child that they have no time for them. A number of the siblings developed headaches, depression, persistent abdominal pain, started to wet their beds and to lower their school marks.

The Place of the Teacher in the Hospital

Schoolwork is a normal part of the hospital program for the leukemic patients in the Children's Hospital in Los Angeles. The role of the teacher is very important (Shulman, 1971). The child needs to participate in some purposeful activity. The teacher confers with the child's school to find out what his class is studying. She helps him with the schoolwork so that he will be up with his class when he returns home. Children welcome books and the teacher. It bridges the gap between home, school, and hospital, and helps the child concentrate on normal activities. It gives the parent an opportunity to get involved in helping the child with his lessons. Sometimes a mother, who has some special knowledge such as art or music or story telling, can interest a group of children in the hospital to participate in some project in art or music or dramatics.

Of course, the teacher has to understand the child's medical condition. Sometimes she acts as a play therapist and helps the child express his feelings through play and imagination. Sometimes she is a comforter and sits near him and comforts him when he is sad or in pain, or fearful of some anticipated medical procedure. Sometimes he is too tired or weak to be bothered with lessons. She may then read him a story or play a record that he likes. Sometimes she may just sit with him quietly and hold his hand. At all times, the teacher is a great and understanding friend, nice to have around, and is always welcome, says teacher Barbara Shulman (1971).

Other activities include eating together at a large table, by all the children. A child might be brought to the table in a wheel chair. Eating then becomes a natural, shared social situation where children can converse and be together.

Osler's Care of a Dying Child

He visited our little Janet twice every day from the middle of October until her death, a month later, and these visits she looked forward to with pathetic eagerness and joy. . . . Instantly the sick room was turned into fairyland, and in fairy language he would talk about the flowers, the birds, and the dolls. . . . In the course of this he would find out all he wanted to know about the little patient.

The most exquisite moment came one cold, raw, November morning, when the end was near, and he brought out from his pocket a beautiful red rose, carefully wrapped in paper, and told how he had watched this last rose of summer growing in his garden and how the rose had called to him as he passed by, that she wished to go along with him to see his "little lassie." That evening we all had a fairy tea party, at a tiny table by the bed, Sir William talking to the rose, his little lassie and her mother in a most exquisite way . . . and the little girl understood that neither fairies nor people could always have the color of a red rose in their cheeks, or stay as long as they wanted in one place, but that they nevertheless would be happy in another home and must not let the people they left behind, particularly their parents, feel badly about it; and the little girl understood and was not unhappy (Cushing, 1940).

SUMMARY

Whether to tell or not to tell a child that he has a fatal illness depends upon a multitude of complicated questions. The decision reflects the attitudes and ideas of the doctor, the parents, and the patient. It permeates the entire program and atmosphere of the clinic and the hospital. There is really no simple answer, because every patient is different and every case is unique.

But, through experience and research we have acquired some common considerations and facts to guide us.

Although no hospital informs a child directly that he has a terminal illness, neither do they deny it directly. It is believed that the child does sense the seriousness of his illness in most cases, and he usually wants to feel free to discuss it to the extent of his own personal need to know. We must always be open to communicate with him when he is ready and wants to talk. His greatest fear is that of being separated from us and abandoned. It is important that we assure him that we will always be near him; that we will make every effort to help him and care for him to the best of our knowledge and ability; that we will never let him down nor suffer too much pain. We must always treat him with love, hope, and kindness.

In treating a child with a malignant illness, the medical, psychological, and social approach must be based on the concept that *we are caring for a living child, as long as he is alive,* until his last breath. Every second of *the now* is important. Every person lives moment by moment! No one knows what the next moment will bring.

Those who are responsible for the care of a fatally ill child must not try to avoid or abandon him because they are afraid to face death. They must learn that death is part of life and accept it. They must show him care, consideration, and kindness, and be with him until the last moment of his life to help him die in comfort.

To let him die alone negates everything that was done to help him live. We must help him face his own death by facing it with him with love, tenderness, support, and devotion. That Osler had deep understanding and empathy with the dying child is portrayed in a mother's account of how he cared for her dying little daughter.

REFERENCES

Alcott, L. M.: Little Women. New York, World, 1946.

Azarnoff, P.: Childhood cancer emotional consideration. Symposium sponsored by the American Cancer Society of Los Angeles County and the Children's Hospital of Los Angeles, Los Angeles, January 8-9, 1971.

Cushing, H.: The Life of Sir William Osler. London and New York, Oxford University Press, 1940.

Hansen, H.: Childhood cancer emotional consideration. Symposium sponsored by the American Cancer Society of Los Angeles County and the Children's Hospital of Los Angeles, Los Angeles, January 8-9, 1971.

Karon, M.: Childhood cancer emotional consideration. Symposium sponsored by the American Cancer Society of Los Angeles County and the Children's Hospital of Los Angeles, Los Angeles, January 8-9, 1971.

Lascari, A. D., Evans, A. E., Howell, D. A. and Easson, W. M.: How well prepared are you for death in the young? Patient Care, 4(10):91-106, 1970.

Natterson, J. M. and Knudson, A. G., Jr.: Observations concerning fear of death in fatally ill children and their mothers. Psychosom Med, 22(6):456-465, 1960.

Patient Care: The paradox of death and the "omnipotent" family doctor. Patient Care, 4(10):(entire issue), 1970.

Rigler, D.: Childhood cancer emotional consideration. Symposium sponsored by the American Cancer Society of Los Angeles County and the Children's Hospital of Los Angeles, Los Angeles, January 8-9, 1971.

Shulman, B.: Childhood cancer emotional consideration. Symposium sponsored by American Cancer Society of Los Angeles County and the Children's Hospital of Los Angeles, Los Angeles, January 8-9, 1971.

Tennyson, A.: New Year's Eve. In Harris, W. T., Rickoff, A. J., and Bailey, M. (Eds.): Fifth Reader. New York, D. Appleton and Co., 1879.

Vernick, J.: Childhood Cancer Emotional Consideration. Symposium sponsored by the American Cancer Society of Los Angeles County and the Childrens Hospital of Los Angeles, Los Angeles, January 8-9, 1971.

Waechter, E. H.: Childhood Cancer Emotional Consideration. Symposium sponsored by the American Cancer Society of Los Angeles County and the Childrens Hospital of Los Angeles, Los Angeles, January 8-9, 1971.

Zeligs, R.: Children's attitudes toward death. Ment Hyg, 51(3):393-396, 1967.

Chapter VI

THE PARENTS OF THE
FATALLY ILL CHILD

THE physician must concentrate his support on the child's family when he has established the diagnosis of a child's fatal illness. He must inform the parents about the child's condition without trying to avoid this unhappy confrontation. This is a very difficult duty. The doctor must perform it honestly and sincerely, with kindness, sympathy, and understanding. It is best to *talk to both parents together*, so that one parent will not have the heartbreaking task of telling the other one. When they are together, they can gain strength and comfort from each other.

The doctor should take the parents into a quiet, pleasant room and in a patient, unhurried manner explain the child's condition to them. He should not leave them right after telling them the shocking news, but must stay with them, continue talking, and try to explain anything he thinks they might want to know at that time, although their minds may really be too confused, then, to enable them to clearly take in the entire situation. The same questions will be asked a number of times throughout the child's illness, and he must be prepared to answer them with patience and kindness in layman's language so that they have some understanding of what he is talking about.

Every parent reacts to the tragedy of his child's illness in a way that is consistent with his own personality make-up. But when parents are informed of the tragic diagnosis of their child's illness, they are usually so overwhelmed that they really do not follow the explanations given by the physician, so it is best not to go into too much detail at the beginning. Later, the physician should be ready to answer many questions that parents repeatedly ask. Information about a child who has leukemia should be given so that parents are able to care for him with intelligence and under-standing.

Give Parents Facts to Strengthen Hope

Along with the diagnosis, the doctor should give them any possible facts he can to strengthen their hopes and give them emotional support. He should explain that the "child will not suffer a painful death, that a cure may be found, and that the time he has left will not be a hopeless series of tragedies" (Lascari, Evans, Howell, and Easson, 1970). He must tell them that he is not giving up hope but will continue to do everything that can be done for the child.

Explaining to the parents why certain treatments and tests are performed and why certain drugs are administered, will help them feel better satisfied that the child is being cared for properly and that he will not suffer unnecessary or extreme pain. During the process of the child's illness parents should be encouraged to learn what is actually going on from time to time.

Parents must be assured that the child's illness is not their fault and that no one could have prevented it. They should be advised that the child is receiving the proper medical care by trained specialists. Taking the child to more doctors in the hope of receiving a more favorable diagnosis should be discouraged, but if they insist on another opinion, their physician should assist them in making arrangements for consultation with another specialist.

When parents ask how long the child has to live, they should be told that no one can really predict this, for the duration of the illness is highly speculative. Predicting the time of death will tend to banish all hope.

When a child does die, parents should be reassured that he suffered as little as possible. If he dies in his sleep, it is less traumatic for the child and for his family. Then they feel that he fell into a quiet sleep and slipped away into a peaceful end.

Young parents may ask the physician if they should consider having another child. He should explain to them that there is no reason why they should not have another child because leukemia is not inherited nor contagious. If there are siblings he should stress the need for continued attention to them so they do not feel they are being neglected while the parents are completely preoccupied with the sick child. The doctor can suggest ways in which the parents can learn to live with the situation and what they can do to contribute to the emotional health of the sick child and also to his siblings.

The sick child should not be pampered or spoiled but should be given the same amount of discipline as before his illness. This will contribute to his feelings of security and also help avoid resentments of siblings about any special treatment of the patient.

The child should be made to feel that the parental role in caring for him is considered important by the medical authorities and it should not be undermined. Nurses can be particularly helpful in guiding both parents in effective participation in caring for their child.

Parents Help with Care of Child

Sometimes the home care of a sick child may require painful treatment by the parent. The child may respond with expressions indicating that his parents hurt him because they hate him. This can be very disturbing to the parents. The doctors and nurses can help by explaining to the child that just as they have to hurt him sometimes in performing medical treatment, so the parents may have to do the same thing to the child when he is being treated at home, but it is still better than having to go to the hospital for such care. This can help the child understand that his parents do love him but are just following the doctor's orders in giving them the necessary treatment.

The Rainbow Babies and Children's Hospital at Western Reserve University Medical Center in Cleveland includes facilities to enable mothers to remain with their hospitalized children. Parent participation is stressed. The mother is encouraged to feed and bathe her child, take his temperature, give oral medication, and learn to administer treatments that must be continued later at home. A six year study of the effects of early childhood separation from their mothers showed that every child exhibited conspicuous reactions to separation, regardless of whether the mother-child relationship was close or distant, whether they had been separated before for hospitalization, and regardless of the length of hospitalization.

Letting the parents help with the care of the child in the hospital can be constructive to most parents, because it makes them feel that they are part of the team working for their child. When the medical and nursing staff assume total responsibility, parents may feel that their child has been completely taken away from them. They may respond with hostility and anger at the hospital staff. Anger against the staff by a parent may also represent a reaction to the crisis rather than a personal feeling of hostility. When parents are allowed to help under cooperative supervision, they feel that they are doing something for their child and tend to establish rapport and understanding with the staff.

The hospital staff's understanding of the parents' feelings can be helpful and very meaningful. Parents who are allowed to participate in the care of their child usually have a feeling that they have done everything in their power to help their child. They are grateful for the opportunity to be with him and share the time with him as long as they can. They should be encouraged not to withdraw from him, but to maintain friendly relations with the child and to be warm and supportive. This is his greatest need. They must be consistent in their conduct toward him in order not to arouse fears or anxieties.

The City of Hope Medical Center provides free care for children with terminal illness. The need to preserve crucial parent-child relationships when the child is hospitalized is stressed by Dr. Robert Rosen, Chairman of the Pediatric department (1971). Most parents want to know what caused the illness, why it happened to their child, and how long the child has to live.

Most mothers are encouraged and able to participate in the total care of their child, but under strict supervision. The mother does not sleep in, but in all other ways she is included in the hospital program. She is there to provide tender loving care for her child as she ministers to his physical needs, bathes and dresses him, selects the menu, and feeds him if necessary. The arrangement is a real help to the hospital as well as to the parent and patient. The child feels loved and reassured when his mother is with him and is taking care of him. She finds comfort in knowing that she is needed and useful to her child and that she is not abandoning him. It gives her dignity and self esteem to be a member of the hospital team serving her child.

A supporting mother is also admitted and helpful in the treatment room, where the child may have to undergo painful bone-marrow tests and various treatments. There exists a continuing mother-doctor open-door policy. It is the parent's prerogative to interview the doctor and know what is going on, especially when the situation is serious. There is a dual viewing of microscope as the doctor explains the findings in a layman's language and makes the disease meaningful to the mother (Roscn, 1971).

Most children are in remission or well enough to remain at home during the greater part of the treatment. It is therefore necessary for the parent to understand about the disease and to be able to carry out the doctor's instructions. Hospitalization is reserved for serious relapses and for times when necessary treatment cannot be given at home. During remissions the child is checked in the clinic once or twice a week. Mothers are taught by the physician to be responsible for the treatment of their child, to give simple nursing care, and to telephone the hospital between clinic visits for instructions, if symptoms of toxicity appear. The mothers who help with the care of their children in the hospital are usually more competent on taking care of the child when he is home (Bozeman, Orbach, and Sutherland, 1955).

Parent participation in the care of the child during hospitalization represents a tremendous improvement in the psychological and mental health of mother and child. Formerly, and in many hospitals today, mothers felt deprived of many opportunities of expressing their maternal functions of feeding and caring for their child, when provisions for feeding, clothing, discipline, and play, were carried on by the hospital personnel without her participation. This sometimes resulted in rivalry between nurses and mothers for the possession of the child. Strict visiting hours caused grief and separation anxiety in parents and children. When parents stay with the child and care for him, tearful separation problems are resolved as parents come and go with little restriction.

THE ROLE OF THE SOCIAL WORKER

It is the function of the social worker to help parents cope with the diagnosis and problems of fatal illness in their child. Parents' reactions to the diagnosis that their child has a dangerous disease is shock, followed by denial, anger, then guilt and depression. It is the job of the social worker to help the parents cope with this problem and to gain effective functioning of family cooperation and care. She must interview the parents in order to assess their needs and resources and obtain information about their emotional and psychological needs (Issner, 1971). Many practical problems of everyday living and family functioning are discussed and efforts at solutions are made. Problems of money, transportation, care of other siblings, and time for household duties are dealt with. The social worker needs to listen, comfort, support, and advise the parents as she helps them face the periods of hospitalization, remissions, and the final death of the child.

Experiences with Parents' Groups

To give emotional strength and courage to parents who are suddenly confronted with the devastating news that their child is suffering from the serious illness of leukemia, the social service department of the Children's Hospital in Los Angeles organized discussion groups for parents of leukemic children. About ten or twelve parents met once a week, under the division of psychiatry, to discuss emotional feelings related to the diagnosis and perhaps imminent death of their children. The parents needed to be given the choice to come, so an orientation meeting was held where parents could sign up if they were interested in attending. There were twelve weekly sessions, led by the social worker. After eight sessions the attendance decreased; also when the child was in remission and doing well, the parents did not come.

Many parents wanted to learn about the disease. They did not like to bother the doctor about many things they wanted to discuss and found it easier to bring up questions in the group, so they had one meeting with the doctor, where they could speak up without hesitation. "It is easier here — I feel more free to talk here," a mother said. They had more time to talk when the children were not waiting. Emotional problems and hostile feelings were ventilated and shared.

Parents who experienced a newly diagnosed case of leukemia in their child underwent emotional shock. At the first meeting they responded with disbelief and denial and avoided talking about their feelings. By the third session the parents started to feel more comfortable in the group and began to reveal their reactions. It took only one parent to start talking about her feelings and others followed. They expressed their anger and feelings of guilt; they shared their sadness and heartbreak.

Throughout the different sessions the parents were encouraged to talk about any problems they had to deal with. How should they discipline the sick child? What should they tell the siblings? What should they do about siblings who feel neglected and deprived because the mother spent too much time with the sick child, when he is in the hospital or when he is at home during remissions? What should the teacher say to the classmates about the sick child when he is away from school and when he returns to school? How should parents help the patient meet his peers when he returns from the hospital and has undergone physical changes due to the disease and medication, such as loss of hair, increased weight, and other handicaps? Some peers will tend to tease the sick child and bring him to tears; others may cut off relationships with him. What should they say to a sick child who asks what happens to little children when they die?

The discussions concerned ways of coping with grandparents, relatives, and neighbors. The place of religion in their lives received attention. Some became more religious; others blamed God and asked how he could do this to them; while still others looked for different kinds of religious activity.

In some cases the strains of marital problems came to the surface causing a breakdown of communication. There were some evening meetings so that fathers could also attend. Discussions helped share feelings and experiences during relapses, including elements of hope.

The discussions gave the social worker and medical personnel a clearer understanding of the social and emotional problems connected with the case of a child who is suffering from a fatal illness. "We don't have all the answers. The parents' reactions at the end can help us" (Knapp, 1971).

By meeting with other parents and talking with them, most parents gain a supportive feeling. Some mothers expressed feelings of guilt for wanting to spend less time with the child in order to get some relaxation from the constant strain and the underlying anxiety that was always with them. The "I'm not alone" realization helped them to bring out forbidden thoughts and to dispel negative, angry, and hostile feelings, as they shared common heartaches. "When I come here I feel I can breathe fresh air and sleep better. Talking to the group helps me."

Some parents wanted to talk to those mothers whose child had been sick for a year, in order to know what to expect later. They wanted the assurance that the child would not suffer much pain later. The purpose of these group meetings was to serve a mental health function by sharing feelings with others in a similar situation. A sorrow shared is a sorrow halved. It was a step toward acceptance without guilt. Yet, in spite of this effort in preventive breakdown in mental health, fifty percent of all families who had lost a child with leukemia, needed psychiatric help after the death of a child (Knapp, 1971).

THE TRAUMATIC IMPACT ON PARENTS

Anyone who has experienced a serious earthquake has not only been terribly "shook up," but lives in constant anxiety that any moment another quake will suddenly shake them because after-quakes are sure to follow. The sudden diagnosis of a fatal illness in a child can be compared to the experience of being in an earthquake. The shock leaves parents in constant fear and foreboding of things to come. They are constantly awaiting the final blow. They never know the moment when it will strike them down. There is no happy ending. "The course of childhood leukemia under treatment is extremely variable and cannot be predicted in advance for any single child" (Bozeman, Orbach, and Sutherland, 1955). The remissions and relapses that occur during treatment make each experience a harrowing event for the parents, who live in constant fear that the threatening loss has become actual.

The psychological impact on mothers, whose children had cancer, was studied through personal interviews (Bozeman et al, 1955). Upon first hearing the diagnosis the mothers expressed anger, guilt, and self blame. They also blamed the physician for the destruction of hope for recovery. Their sole wish was to prove that the diagnosis was wrong, because *this could not happen to their child.* Hospitalization of their child would prove they were right and the doctor was surely mistaken, they believed.

But hospitalization implied separation which was frightening to both child and mother. "I hold my girl in my arms in the wards wondering if she will die tonight. How can I tell whether she will die tomorrow or not?" (Bozeman et al., 1955). This fear of final, irrevocable separation was manifested in mutual clinging of mother and child, with repeated questions of when the child would be discharged from the hospital and allowed to go home.

When the diagnosis was finally accepted and treatment started, the parents made every effort to learn as much as they could about the disease. Some mothers finally accepted the reality of the situation while others continued to deny the diagnosis until the terminal illness made denial impossible. Denial was especially found in mothers whose children had responded well to treatment and had been able to spend considerable time at home, free of symptoms. But most mothers never gave up hope that a cure might be found to save their child.

The most frequently expressed needs of the mothers were "tangible services," temporary escape from the oppressive awareness of the illness and approaching loss, and emotional support to bolster their functioning in the face of the horror of the situation (Bozeman, et al, 1955). All children in the group studied continued under medical treatment although this imposed such burdens as financial expenses, care of the other children in the family, and difficulties of transportation of the patient to the clinic.

The parents were almost unable to bear the continued anxiety. They needed to escape from the implication of the illness, through some diversion and to relationship with other people, where they could achieve emotional support. The mother had a need to talk about her feelings, to be assured that there were people ready to help her whenever she needed aid, and to comfort her. She appreciated the support given by friends and relatives. All fathers helped their wives in meeting some of the practical problems. Several fathers initiated diversions by insisting that their wives participate in social activities. However, a number of fathers became more disturbed about the child's illness than did the mother, especially when the patient was a girl.

Most of the maternal grandmothers could be depended upon for tangible service to the mother, but only a few gave her emotional support. Some grandmothers became so emotionally upset by the child's illness that the mother had to care for them in addition to her problems related to the sick child. Some mother's sisters gave her emotional support and help. Mothers called upon friends and good neighbors for assistance and emotional support, more often than upon family members. Most of the mothers gave up participating in social activities and in entertaining friends in their home.

The role that religion played in the emotional support of the parents varied. Some became more religious while others were angry at God for not restoring their child to good health. The chief value of religion was the hope of its possible help in saving the child's life (Bozeman et al., 1955).

Following the diagnosis many mothers showed disturbances in eating and sleeping. They became nervous and irritable with the other children in the family and could not function well in their household activities. An understanding of the emotional and circumstantial problems of parents brought about by the un-expected and prolonged fatal illness of their child should be helpful in guiding the medical, nursing, and social service personnel in their work with both parents and patient.

To study the emotional conflicts in mothers whose children suffered from leukemia, the Thematic Apperception Test was given to nine such mothers. The test is made up of nineteen pictures on cards and one blank card. The mothers were presented with twelve pictures and asked to make up an imaginative story about each picture. Their stories revealed their constant awareness of imminent death and anticipated loss and separation, and indicated that a part of themselves was dying (Orbach, Sutherland, and Bozeman, 1955).

The feeling tone expressed "unhappiness, sorrow, acute despair, and intense feelings of loneliness." Emotions reflecting inner devastation, rage, turmoil, death, anticipated loss, separation, murder, and suicide were projected into the cards. Rivalry with nurses for the maternal care of the child suggested the reactivated rivalry of the mother with her own mother, who denied her warmth and emotional support, stemming from her past developmental experiences. "A woman yearning for a supportive relationship from her own mother, which is denied her, may at the same time be bitterly hostile toward other women who she fears will deprive her of those maternal functions that are rightfully hers" (Orbach et al., 1955).

The mother's relationship with her own mother affects her relationship with her own children, and the meaning of the child in her life. The sex of the child plays a part in its meaning to her. Mothers clung to their sons far more than to their daughters, while fathers showed much more concern for their daughters. Some mothers, in their need to reverse the past, expect the child, usually of the same sex, to play a reparative role to compensate her for past disappointments in her own childhood. The child's fatal illness prevented her from doing this and resulted in profound anger and rejection of the child in fantasy.

The parent-child relationship is also represented in the mother's relationship with the physician. He symbolizes the parent who protects the lives of his children. The unconscious belief in his power to abolish the illness made some of the mothers of children with leukemia feel that he was endowed with a terribly malignant power that would not allow him to cure their child. The physician must therefore not only treat the child but must also try to establish supportive relationships with the parents in order to soften the blow, by letting the parents know that he deeply understands their grief and anguish. He must understand their unreasonable antagonism and hostility, at the diagnosis, and not be offended, because it is equivalent to the loss of the child. He must sympathize with parents in their need for some hope for the child's recovery.

The social worker must play a supportive role and help the mother solve tangible problems. She must guide her in many ways dealing with the situation as it affects her daily responsibilities and functioning as a mother, wife, housekeeper, as well as the parent of a fatally ill child. Everyone connected with the care of the sick child must reach out with warmth, friendliness, understanding, and concrete acts of kindness to help the parents and involve them in the care of their sick child, in every possible constructive way, in order to help minimize the terrible emotionally traumatic blow caused by the prolonged illness and death of a child with a fatal illness, such as leukemia (Orbach et al., 1955).

SUMMARY

The physician must concentrate his support on the child's family when he has established the diagnosis of the child's fatal illness. He should take both parents together into a quiet room and in an unhurried manner, give them the facts, but maintain some hope. Let them ask questions; explain that the illness is not inherited, that it is no one's fault and could not have been prevented, and that they should not blame themselves for anything. He should suggest ways of living with the situation that will best contribute to the child's emotional health and also to the care and consideration of siblings and the parents themselves. They should neither pamper the child nor make him feel unloved and abandoned. The mother should be permitted to help in the care of her child in the hospital. This contributes to the emotional health of both mother and child, and is also of service to the hospital. There should be an open-door mother-doctor policy where she can feel free to come to him at all times, to discuss the condition of her child, as she learns about the disease and the course it is taking.

Social workers at the hospital help parents cope with their emotional, social, and practical problems. Discussion groups for parents of fatally ill children, led by social workers, gave parents supportive feelings by meeting together and knowing they were not alone in their sorrow. They discussed their feelings of sadness, their problems concerning the care of the sick child during remissions at home and school, the care of siblings, taking the child to the clinic, and the practical and emotional support needed. They asked questions about the details of the disease of the doctor when he attended the meeting.

The traumatic emotional impact on mothers of fatally ill children was studied by the use of the TAT test. It showed that their stories revealed awareness of imminent death, feeling tones of sorrow, despair, and loneliness. The research reflected the mother's need for tangible and emotionally supportive help. Most of the mothers failed to get emotional support from their own mothers. A mother's own developmental experience affects her feelings about her children. The fathers were more concerned about their daughters who were ill, while the mothers clung more to their sons. The doctor symbolizes the father image. The social worker must play a supportive role to help the mother with her problems. The final loss of the child caused lasting emotional disturbance in the mother.

REFERENCES

Bergman, A. B. and Schulte, C. J. A., (Eds): Care of the child with cancer. Supplement to Pediatrics, Am Acad Pediatr, 40:(3 Part III), 1967. Proceedings of a Conference Conducted by the Association for Ambulatory Pediatric Services in Conjunction with the Children's Cancer Study Group A on November 17, 1966, at the Children's Orthopedic Hospital and Medical Center, Seattle, Washington.

Bozeman, M. F., Orbach, C. E. and Sutherland, A. M.: Psychological impact of cancer and its treatment. III. The adaptation of mothers to the threatened loss of their children through leukemia: Part I. Cancer, 8(1):1-19, 1955.

Issner, N.: Childhood cancer emotional consideration. Symposium sponsored by the American Cancer Society of Los Angeles County and the Children's Hospital of Los Angeles, Los Angeles, January 8-9, 1971.

Knapp, V.: Childhood cancer emotional consideration. Symposium sponsored by the American Cancer Society of Los Angeles County and the Children's Hospital of Los Angeles, Los Angeles, January 8-9, 1971.

Lascari, A. D., Evans, A. E., Howell, D. A. and Easson, W. M.: How well prepared are you for death in the young? Patient Care, 4(10):91-106, 1970.

Murray, H.: Thematic Apperception Test, Manual. Cambridge, Harvard University Press, 1943.

Orbach, C. E., Sutherland, A. M. and Bozeman, M. F.: Psychological impact of cancer and its treatment: III. The adaptation of mothers to the threatened loss of their children through leukemia: Part II. Cancer, 8(1):20-33, 1955.

Rosen, R.: Childhood cancer emotional consideration. Symposium sponsored by the American Cancer Society of Los Angeles County and the Children's Hospital of Los Angeles, Los Angeles, January 8-9, 1971.

Chapter VII

WHEN THE END IS NEAR

THE hardest part of all, is when death's shadows fall. When the illness has reached the terminal stage the parents should be notified that death is near, but they should be reassured that medical treatment is being continued and the doctor is not abandoning the patient. Pain will be controlled and the child will not suffer or die in agony.

When the child is put on the critical list he is moved into a separate room in the hospital. He may be put into an oxygen tent there. The parents stay in the room with the child. There should be *absolutely no whispering* in the sick room. This is frightening to the patient. "Whispering in the presence of a dying patient is a cardinal sin," says Dr. Hilton Read (1970). "If you're going to talk about the patient with the nurse, go as far away as possible. Never whisper near the patient or in his room. The dying patient has an accelerated perception and whispering even in the presence of a comatose patient can be a most traumatic experience. The patient knows you're saying something bad about him; otherwise you would say it out loud" (Read, 1970).

Relief of pain or some reassuring words that make him feel you care about him will be a great help to the patient. When a teenager was crying, a social worker held her hand and cried with her. "You really care about me," the girl said, and she was comforted. Aloofness of personnel or parents suggests abandonment to the dying child at a time when he most needs closeness, kindness, and comforting. Never leave a dying patient alone for a moment. The fear of dying alone may bring terror to him in his last moments, when he needs you most.

It is the nurse who is most often present when the patient is dying. The feelings in the helping person is very important. Nurses, doctors, and all hospital personnel must be aware of their own feelings about death. Taboos about death, such as touching a dying person, and other fears and superstitions should be dispelled. Emotional escape must be understood and overcome, as the helping personnel learn to accept death as a part of life and deal with it on a mature and reality basis. When the patient feels that he is not alone, but that he is still important as a person until the very end, it helps him die in dignity as a human being, respected and loved until his last moment of life.

When the child is low, yet aware, change the atmosphere; relate to him in some way so that he may feel your presence. He may want you to play a favorite record, read a story to him that he likes to hear, or he may just want you to sit near him and hold his hand, so that he feels you are near him. Children tend to know when the end is near. Yet, until they are comatose, they are not accepting of death.

If the child should happen to die in the hospital when the parents are not there, they should not be notified by phone that he is dead. They should be called and told that the child is very low and asked to come to the hospital. When they arrive, the doctor should take them into a quiet room and tell them that the child died peacefully. If they want to see their child they should be brought into the room and allowed to see their child before he is taken away.

Parents do not want the child to suffer any more. Most parents accept death as a release, after a child has suffered through a long illness. Parents have usually gone through the mourning period during the child's illness when they realized he was suffering from a fatal disease.

THE DIFFICULT TIME OF DEATH

The minutes following the actual death are usually the toughest for the doctors as well as the family. What can the helping people at the hospital do for the parents at the moment of death? Stay with them. Say something that expresses your real feelings and they will know it, even if you just say that you are sorry. Touching is important and meaningful. Put your arms around their shoulders. Let them express their grief in their own way. Accept and encourage emotional release through talking, crying, remembering certain meaningful or endearing incidents, or in any other way they express their feelings. Repeat again that everything possible was done for the child. Assuage any guilt feelings or regrets parents may express.

Some parents will turn to religious beliefs; others may blame God and be angry for what they believe he has done to them. Don't argue with them about anything, but accept them in every way. Be loving rather than logical. The doctor should assure the parents of his availability to be of help to them in any way he can. In the City of Hope Medical Center, Duarte, Cal., many parents expressed support and sympathy for the doctors and nurses. They were thankful for everything. The child's toys and things were left in the hospital for the other children.

When a child has been diagnosed as having a fatal illness and his parents finally accepted the fact that their child will die in the near future, they begin to mourn in anticipation of their loss. This is a normal protective device that prepares the mind for the realization of the final reality without being completely overwhelmed. Although they have cared for the child lovingly and faithfully, emotionally they have begun to pull themselves away, in preparation for the final blow.

Often, the illness of the child becomes the focus of the family's attention. With the child's death the family is relieved of the pressure, but may be overwhelmed with guilt at the realization that the ordeal is finally over. It is in a sense also a relief that the child's suffering is over and the parents' vigil is finished. But if the parents never believed that the child would die, the reality of his death may be a traumatic shock to them.

The physician can help the parents redirect their energies back to the family and to assume normal activities after the mourning period, without feeling guilty that they and their other children have accepted the death and have resumed daily routines of living.

HELPING SIBLINGS ACCEPT THE CHILD'S DEATH

What should parents tell their children when their sibling has a lingering illness? When a child has been diagnosed as having a fatal illness, his preschool siblings should be told that he is ill and in the hospital. Older siblings should be told, in most cases, what the illness is, its course of development, and that it is a very serious disease, but the doctors are doing everything they can to help the child. The siblings should be allowed to visit the patient and to play games with him. This will help eliminate fears and fantasies and build up continued close relationships as they share time together.

During remissions, when the patient is at home, the siblings will get used to the fact that he needs special attention and medication at times. When he is better, the normal family routine will go on. Gradually, as they see him at home and in the hospital, they learn to accept his illness, and like the parents, the older siblings may pre-mourn his death.

When death does come parents should explain to the siblings that the child received the best care and did not suffer too much. A quiet, calm, direct explanation will reassure the siblings that a person can have a loss, be saddened by it, but can and must learn to face and accept it as a part of life.

Nevertheless, the death of a child still has a traumatic effect on his siblings as well as on his parents. "The traumatic effect of the death of a parent or sibling in childhood is always followed by profound and complex psychological reactions which may and often do permanently distort further maturation of personality" (Moriarty, 1967).

The way the parents themselves react to the loss will be absorbed by the children. When the parents are helped to accept the death, the siblings will be able to face it with more courage and understanding.

A child may react to the death in ways different from that of adults. He may go out and play and act like nothing has happened. He has to use denial until he is ready to cope with the reality of the situation. "The appearance of easy acceptance . . . to the loss, by a quiet child is often illusory" (Auster, 1964). A child may also go into a depression by a death in the family.

We should not underestimate the siblings' sense of loss, grief, and bewilderment. Parents should not avoid speaking about the child who has died, but should mention him in a natural way in everyday conversation. Otherwise they are denying the death and fostering the same denial in their children. When parents are ready to accept the reality of the death, their children will be able to accept the fact that death is final and their sibling will not return.

The atmosphere in the home should be free and open so that siblings can discuss the illness and death without fear of it being a taboo subject. Otherwise they may suppress feelings of fear and guilt that their death wishes caused the death of the departed child. They should be told the cause of death and that it was no one's fault.

The siblings may begin to fear that they or their parents might die. Explain that the disease is not contagious or hereditary, if that is true, that normally children grow up to be adults and parents usually grow old and have many years yet to live.

If a child dies of cystic fibrosis, the most common lethal genetic disease of children in the United States, transmitted as an autosomal recessive disease, other children in the family may be affected and become very fearful that they, too, might die. Parents must then see that they get a thorough medical examination and let the doctor explain to the older child what his condition is. If the child is free of symptoms, the doctor can reassure him; but if there are symptoms, the doctor can explain his condition to him and keep him under surveillance, with regular check-ups and any necessary medical care needed.

"We need to intensify rather than lessen our efforts to understand the psychosocial aspects of death, loss and bereavement in cystic fibrosis, an area to which, unfortunately, not as much attention has been paid as would seem warranted" (Lifschitz and Goldberg, 1969).

The siblings should be encouraged to participate in the funeral and cemetery services, but should not be forced to view the body. It is better to have the casket closed. It is vitally important *to have the family stay together.* The children should not be sent away from home during the mourning period and even later. Parents cannot afford to be so absorbed in their own grief as to forget the effect of the loss on their living children.

Grief may be expressed differently in adults and in children.

It is important to recognize and respect the child's own way of expressing his feelings and not to misinterpret or criticise him for his way of dealing with death. The child may be suppressing his feelings and his fears. It is important that the surviving children be allowed to discuss their feelings about the death of their sibling freely and openly, otherwise their fears and anxieties may be hidden beneath a surface of silence and continue to disturb them unless they are brought to the surface and clarified. The child must not be denied the help and support that he so desperately needs.

Closeness to the reality of death may cause the siblings to fear they will die soon, too. Young children may be very confused about death and they "often believe that their parents were somehow responsible for their sibling's death and may also *cause them to die*. Although many parents are shocked by this, it is only by open expression of this notion that the child can win reassurance from the parents, and find himself able to cope with it.

"Young children who feel unsure of their relationship with their parents, who have difficulty in expressing their feelings, and who are sensitive and vulnerable to stress, may show signs of disturbance for an extended period . . . difficulty in going to sleep, nightmares, fears, clinging to parents, or a regressive return to immature behavior . . . Without professional help many children develop a serious emotional illness which persists to adult life" (Robinson, 1969).

A family follow-up eleven months after the death of their child indicated that "a few of the siblings developed nightmares and difficulty with schoolwork, or were distressed about questions from classmates. One younger sister of a patient developed an obsession with her sibling's toys. This child was being taken for monthly blood counts at the insistence of the mother" (Oakley, 1965).

Sometimes a child may feel that the parent would have preferred his death instead of his sibling's death. He may feel that he must personally make up to the parent for his sibling's death by living his brother's life as well as his own. John Kennedy really wanted to be a scholar but felt that he should become president because his older brother, who had died, would have aspired to that office. Perhaps Robert Kennedy had the same feelings about John.

Children must learn that their parents mourn the death of their sibling. The parents should acknowledge the pain of their loss and also encourage their remaining children to do this. Parents who are able to accept and express their own feelings of grief and also to support the emotional needs of their surviving children will be able to cope with their loss.

The conspiracy of silence about the death of a young child or the still-birth of an expected infant can be very traumatic to the older pre-school child. He is not indifferent to the absence of the younger or expected child. The parents must explain to the child that the sibling was too sick to live and will not come back; that he has died. "The parent's ability to verbalize this loss informs the child that this event is not so overwhelming that mention of it must be avoided" (Weston and Irwin, 1963).

The child may repeat the words of the parent that says the sibling has died and associate it with the absence of the sibling, without having a complete understanding of death. But the concept grows with time, if he is allowed to verbalize it and accept it as an explanation of the absence. The child must be assured, definitely, that anything he did or thought was not the cause of the illness or death of his sibling. The parent must then reassure the child that *his own body is in good health and that he will not die.* If he should happen to get sick or become very fearful that he might die, a thorough examination by his pediatrician can reassure him about his health.

"The parents' ability to talk about their feelings of loss, grief, anger, and disappointment helps the child accept these feelings in himself" (Weston and Irwin, 1963). The parents must not use this child as a substitute for the one who has died. Also, if another baby is born into the family, it must be made clear to the siblings that this is an altogether different person and is not the dead child reborn and come to life again. The idea of resurrection is based on the primitive belief that the dead will rise again. Whatever the parents' religious belief may be, they must make clear to their living children that a new baby is not the old baby reborn. Only in that way can they clarify the meaning of death to their children.

Now, let us bury the dead and go on with life and living. By example, the parents must set the pattern for the children to emulate. In every way the family must support each other in recognizing and accepting the death of the child, in carrying on the process of living and loving, with attention focused on the present and future, on the right to carry on all normal activities of daily living, without guilt or remorse, but rather with faith and joy in God's many blessings. This can be accomplished when parents separate themselves from the dead, who needs them no more, and concentrate their love and work on the living, for *life* must go on.

THE FAMILY FOLLOW-UP

The period from the time of diagnosis until the death of the child is a time of great emotional upheaval in the parents. They are under much stress and anxiety, as they wait in dread and fear for the final blow, for the moment when their child will be taken from them by death.

When the end comes, the hope is gone and the fear is gone. The battle is over. There is a sadness, a let-down, as grief and mourning set in. The death of the child must not be the end of the relationship with the family. They need help in accepting and adjusting to their loss. Grief must be acknowledged and shared. The doctor must let the family know that he will always be available to talk with them, otherwise they might hestitate to bother him. If he calls a week later and asks them to come in to see him, they will feel that he really cares and has not forgotten them.

The hospital arranges an appointment with the family a month later. When the primary shock is over they want to talk. The parents are still confused. They cannot believe that the child really died. They go through the stages of shock, denial, and depression, especially around the holidays when they are more aware of the missing child. They want to visit the children's hospital agian. It helps them verify that it really happened. It helps them face reality. They may need to come back a number of times and talk to the doctor or the staff of the hospital. It may be three months later, six months later, or even a year later. Some mothers will volunteer their services to the hospital.

There is a need to meet with the parents periodically to see how they are reacting and to help them; a need to have free and fearless discussion and to answer any questions that remain in their hearts and minds. The parents must be repeatedly assured that what happened was no one's fault and could not have been prevented; that everything possible and known in modern medicine was done for their child; that the child was not allowed to suffer too much and he died in peace (Oakley, 1966).

There is a need to watch for depression and organic symptoms of grief months later, especially when the initial reaction has been mild. Sometimes a whole year passes before the effects of the grief and bereavement shows up. Every effort must be made to avert and prevent the severe emotional problems that may arise years later.

Sharing the sorrow can be of great help. Caring counts. Only *when other people care,* can sadness and happiness in life be meaningful and supportive to the human spirit. Only when the bells toll for everyone can mankind be comforted and know that we all belong to the human race and that death is part of life, for everyone.

THE LAZARUS SYNDROME

When a child has a lingering illness that is usually fatal, his family, having no hope for his recovery, may begin to mourn for him too early in advance. In their minds he is already dead, so that they separate themselves from him emotionally before he actually dies. They may give away his clothes and toys and not even come to see him in the hospital anymore.

How does the child respond to his dying and to his separating family? The seriously ill child senses that his family is withdrawing from him emotionally as well as physically. He tends to withdraw from his social environment and concentrate on his own illness and fears. As he becomes more and more isolated, he feels alone, unwanted, forgotten and abandoned. When death seems imminent he, too, begins to separate himself from his family and directs his attention to his loneliness and his dying.

How does society treat the dying child's family and his relatives? During the child's illness, the family and relatives have been going through social isolation from friends and neighbors who expect them to live in constant sadness and depression. They do not like to associate with people who are involved with a dying child and avoid them as much as they can. It makes them feel too vulnerable, too aware that death is part of reality and it makes them afraid; they want to deny death and push it out of their minds.

Society should not expect parents to live in constant grief. Acceptance is part of mourning, too, and life must go on. People should try to help parents find normal social outlets and encourage them to participate in usual social activities without criticising them or making them feel guilty. This is good for both the family and the child. He will not feel so guilty when he knows that he is not causing his parents to give up all their social activities. They can be more relaxed when they come to see him and tell him what they have been doing, and perhaps bring him a souvenir of the event or some other gift. It does no one any good to have the family give up all contact with the social world and it may really harm the child, his family, and society.

Religious and other organizations might take an active part in helping the family find relaxation and recreation in an effort to live as normal a life as they can. This does not mean that the parents will reject their child, but they could still plan their time with consideration for both themselves and the child.

The prognosis in medicine can never be predicted one hundred percent. It sometimes happens that the child does not die. What happens if he survives? He will never be the same person that he was before his illness. This is called the Lazarus Syndrome, as if like Lazarus the child has arisen from the dead. The family may not know what to do. Emotionally they have already given him up for dead and have separated themselves from him. They have already made other plans and arrangements to live without him. He does not come back as the same child with the same position in the family (Easson, 1970).

The child who recovers has to move back into his family as a new member who has risen from the dead, and they have the emotional task of adapting to him as if he was an unwanted stranger. Sometimes the rejection by his family makes him so completely unwanted that other living arrangements must be made for him.

Doctors should always hold out some hope that the seriously ill child may not die. Parents should be encouraged to live with some hope and not to separate themselves from the ill child while he is still alive. The child should still be considered a part of the family until the very end.

ON REPLACING A CHILD

When a child dies, a sibling may feel that his parents would have preferred that he would have died instead of his brother, because the child who died was their favorite. They may even verbalize this wish and cause the sibling to feel rejected and unwanted. Or they may unconsciously reveal this thought by calling the sibling by the dead child's name. The living child will sense the parent's wish and try to be like the dead child in order to be loved and wanted. This child can never dare to be himself.

Such parents need counseling. They must be made to realize that the life of one child has nothing to do with the life of another child. Both could have lived and both could have died. Life and death are in the hands of the Creator and is beyond our understanding. All that the parents can do is to try to give the remaining child their love and care, and be grateful that they still have another child. If they do this, the child will know it and feel secure and loved.

Parents have a deep sense of loss when their child dies. They feel punished and somehow responsible for the death. They blame themselves for not giving the child enough love, care, and attention, although this may not at all be true. They feel the loneliness and emptiness, the guilt and deprivation. They miss the child in everything they used to do together.

If only they had another chance they could do a better job in bringing up their child! They decide to replace the emptiness by having another child either through pregnancy or adoption.

They adopt a child of the same age, sex, and coloring as their dead child, and give it the same name. In their mind the dead child has come to life again. It may be the unconscious belief that the dead are reborn and live again, found in the ideas of children and the religions of some primitive peoples.

The parents expect the replaced child to act like the one who has died (Kalish, 1969). Any deviation from this expectancy is met with disapproval by the parents. The child begins to feel that she cannot be herself. Who am I? She begins to question her own identity. She feels loved only as a living substitute for a dead child whose image has taken away her own. She loves her parents but feels that she cannot be her true self because she is just a symbol for their dead child.

Such parents need counseling, preferably before they adopt another child. No person can take the place of another person who has died. But the emptiness of a loss can be filled through reaching out to help and serve another child who needs and wants loving parents, and who can enrich their lives through mutual love and happy warm relationships and experiences.

Before parents who have lost a child consider adopting another one, they must first get over their mourning for the dead child and accept the separation as final. After they have recognized the reality of their loss, and their grief has subsided, they can consider taking another child into their hearts and home. If they make such an important decision it should have as its purpose the desire to contribute to the life of another human being. The focus should always be on the child, not on themselves. Their need will be served as they serve the child. The parents should never think of the adopted child as a replacement. This is a different child. They have mourned and they have separated. They must look ahead and not behind.

It is better to select a child who is different from the dead one in many ways — in age — looks — coloring — personality — and perhaps even in sex. Of course, this child should be given a totally different name than that of the dead child. The parents should never make a comparison between the adopted and the dead child, or indicate that the adopted child is a replacement.

If the parents decide to have their own child they must not think of the new-born as a replacement but as a totally different person in his own right.

SUMMARY

Older children should usually be told what their sibling's illness is, but younger children should be told that the child is ill and in the hospital. Children should visit their sibling in the hospital. The death of a child has a traumatic effect on the siblings. They absorb the way their parents react to the death and parents can do much to help them cope with the situation. Parents should continue to speak of the dead child in normal natural conversation, and encourage the siblings to talk about him freely. They should be made to feel free of guilt and told that the illness was no one's fault — that it is not hereditary, and that they expect the rest of the family to live a long and natural life.

The siblings must be told about the death of a young child or the still-birth of a newborn in the family, otherwise the conspiracy of silence may make them insecure about their own lives.

When a child dies, the siblings should participate in the funeral services and should not be sent away during the mourning period or even later. The parents should accept the siblings' way of expressing grief, even though it may be different from their own way of mourning. Young children who are vulnerable to stress may show signs of disturbance by having difficulty in going to sleep, having nightmares, clinging to parents, and regressing to other immature behavior.

The parents' ability to express their feelings of loss and grief helps the siblings to accept those feelings in themselves. They must learn that their parents mourn the death of their sibling, but have to accept it, and go on with life with courage and purpose.

After the death of the child there is a follow-up by the doctor and medical staff of the hospital, during which the parents revisit the hospital. They are encouraged to talk to the personnel and doctor, to discuss what had happened to the child, and to bring to the surface any thoughts and feelings that bother them. They are then reassured that everything was done to help the child and that the disease was not caused by them or anyone else. They are told that they have suffered enough and should now face the present and participate in the good things of life with enjoyment and without guilt.

They have done all they could for the child, now they must live and care for their living children, spouse, and relatives and resume their normal routine of daily living. This does not mean they didn't care. It means that they have accepted what they could not prevent, and must now concentrate on the present and future with hope and acceptance. Life must go on for the living. "Into each heart some rain must fall."

REFERENCES

Auster, S. L.: Seventeenth annual meeting of World Federation for Mental Health. Medical Tribune, September 2, 1964.

Easson, W. M.: The Dying Child: The Management of the Child or Adolescent Who Is Dying. Springfield, Ill., Charles C Thomas, 1970.

Kalish, R. A.: The effects of death upon the family. In Pearson, L. (Ed.).: Death and Dying. Cleveland, Press of Case University, 1969.

Lifschitz, M. and Goldberg, I. K.: Avenues of thanatologic research in cystic fibrosis. Arch Foundation Thanatol, 1(2):23, 1969.

Moriarty, D. M. (Ed.): The Loss of Loved Ones: The Effects of a Death in the Family on Personality Development. Springfield, Ill., Charles C Thomas, 1967.

Oakley, G. P., Jr.: Family follow-up held essential after death of leukemiac child. Research and Reviews, 1965, 5, 47. In Pediatric Currents, 15(6):23, 1966.

Read, H.: Utilizing allied health personnel in the management of death. Symposium. Patient Care, 4(10):81-87, 1970.

Robinson, M. E.: When a child dies. In Kutscher, A. H. (Ed.): But Not to Lose. New York, Frederick Fell, 1969.

Weston, D. L. and Irwin, R. C.: Preschool child's response to death of infant sibling. Am J Dis Child, 106:564-567, 1963.

THE HANDICAPPED OR DISABLED CHILD

THE living organism is constantly on guard to protect itself against injury or illness. The fear of becoming handicapped is surpassed only by the fear of death itself. A child who loses a part of his body or becomes functionally handicapped in some way, goes through a tremendously traumatic experience and is never really the same person for the rest of his life.

How the child meets a catastrophic illness depends upon many factors. The way he is treated by medical personnel, the preparation for the procedures he must undergo, the help he is given to work through his grief and mourning for his loss, his personality and self image, his relationship with his parents, siblings, and peers, all contribute to the degree with which he is able to meet and cope with his disability.

THE NEED TO EXPRESS GRIEF
FOR A HANDICAP

There is a need to express grief for a handicap due to a catastrophic illness. Grief is the normal emotional response to the loss of a part of the body, of a capacity or function, or even of a possession (Aldrich, 1967). It is natural to experience mourning and depression when a part of the body is lost through surgery or accident. Actual mourning takes place when an arm or a leg is lost. The severe depression that follows may bring on denial or even thoughts of escape through suicide.

The child who has a catastrophic illness and becomes handicapped must be helped to express grief over his loss. He needs to go through the experience of grief and mourning in order to accept his handicap, cope with it, and make realistic adjustments to his disability.

The work of grief includes movement from denial which follows the original shock to a fuller realization of the loss. This increasing recognition is accompanied by such physical symptoms as despair, withdrawal, hopelessness, anger, anorexia, sleeplessness, apathy, and restlessness (Missildine, 1965).

Physical responses to grief are "not only crying, but tightening of the throat, sensation of a load on one's chest, disturbance of breathing such as gulping, gasping, sighing, the feeling of suffocating; inability to eat, no appetite, food seeming to stick in the throat, frequent excitation of bowels and kidneys; either physical exhaustion or agitation" (Switzer, 1970).

Grief has long been considered comparable to depression. It may find expression through self-recrimination, feelings of hopelessness, lack of confidence in meeting problems, psychomotor retardation, generalized hostility, and even suicidal preoccupation (Missildine, 1965).

An important aspect of the natural course of grief is the initial period of shock. In normal grief, a period of depression follows shock and is in turn succeeded by gradual recovery. Recovery, however, may be delayed. In fact, the whole sequence may be interrupted if the extent of the loss is severe or if the patient is unusually ambivalent or guilty about the lost object (Aldrich, 1967).

To help a child express his grief he must be able to talk about his fears and his feelings, his ideas and concerns, with an understanding and compassionate person. He may reveal misconceptions and misinformation, fears and fantasies that are far worse than the facts and the reality of the situation. He needs to know the facts. Although he must be told the truth, along with the facts, he must be given comfort and reassurance. He must have trust in those significant authorities upon whom he depends for help and assurance. By encouraging the child to share his grief with them, they can help him accept his handicap, cope with it, and learn to make realistic adjustments to his disability.

A gradual detachment of the lost part is achieved as the grief is brought into consciousness. This process helps the child separate himself from the lost object and accept the reality of his loss. "The basic function of grief is to test reality. Its usefulness lies in the fact that the grief normally erases those attachments which otherwise might menace the individual by leaving him fixed in an illusory life" (Missildine, 1965). An absence of the opportunity to work through grief may foster sustained and depressive response. The prolonged response to the stress of illness might be overcome by more active intervention in support of the grief process.

PSYCHOLOGICAL PREPARATIONS FOR SURGICAL PROCEDURES

Children who enter a hospital for surgery are beset by a multitude of fears, such as fears of castration, of mutilation, of desertion, and even fear of death (Erickson, 1969). Such fears may be aroused by their own hospital experiences, by the attitudes of hospital personnel, and by the child's own speculation and misinterpretation of what is happening to other children around him. Screams from the treatment room or children returning from operating rooms wearing casts or covered with many bandages can terrify other patients that something catastrophic will happen to them, too. After surgery, large bandages, incisions, and stitches, tubes in their bodies, and removal of bandages or stitches are frightening to children who do not know what to expect. Knives or hypodermic needles may be interpreted by them as lethal weapons that may threaten body integrity or even life itself.

When a small child hears the words "dye injection" prior to X-ray procedure, he may fear that he is being prepared to die. Adolescents encased in body casts have expressed fear of suffocation. They also fear the electric cast cutter when it is used to cut their casts (Erickson, 1969).

The child must be carefully prepared for surgery, especially if it involves the loss of a part of his body or the loss of a function. The doctor should explain to the child and to his parents why the surgery is necessary, exactly what the procedure will be, what to expect in terms of risk and pain, and how long he will have to remain in the hospital. He must be prepared for the outcome if amputation is needed. He must be assured that the sick part will be handled with respect and dignity, and that it will be replaced by a healthy substitution in the form of a prosthesis. The child should be encouraged to feel free to ask any questions he wants to, in order to alleviate any fears built up through fantasies, misinformation, and superstitions.

A child's reaction to a major catastrophic disability depends upon many factors. If he is an adolescent his earlier years have already helped form his self image and personality. If he has a great need for independence and is interested in physical and social activities, a situation of helplessness and dependence upon others may be greatly feared. But the child who wants to withdraw from a world that he finds difficult to face, may wish to be a helpless invalid so that he may feel more safe when he is taken care of by others (Aldrich, 1967).

The impact of an amputation or a facial deformity can be completely devasting to some people, so that they may withdraw within themselves and not want to go any place or see any-one. Blindness may cause complete hopelessness, withdrawal, and depression, making the person give up trying to adjust to the handicap. But if the person has had the deep sense of security, the feeling of being loved by his family and friends and being respected by others for his positive personality and character, he may have the strength and courage to develop the confidence in his ability to cope with life's demands and adjust to his disability.

Adolescents usually find it tremendously difficult to face a major disability because they are at the age when they are confronted with many uncertainties about their entire future. This is a period when decisions must be made that will affect their whole life. The meaning of sex, the choice of a mate, the importance of a career and a job, all loom ahead. The sudden, unexpected onslaught of a major disability can flatten all dreams, hopes, and ambitions and fill the future with darkness and futility.

PATIENT'S PERMISSION FOR SURGERY

Should unwilling patients be forced by physicians to undergo surgery? What is the responsibility of a doctor who has a patient with a malignant disease that requires the amputation of a leg in order to try to save a patient's life? A 16-year-old girl suffering from osteogenic sarcoma, a bone cancer which spreads quickly through the body, refused to have her leg amputated. Her mother concurred with her daughter's decision. Some physicians from a city hospital appealed to the court for an emergency order to operate. The judge appointed an independent surgeon who said that the girl's chances of survival without the operation were two to three percent while it would be twenty to thirty percent with the operation.

The girl testified in court that she would rather take her chances without the operation; that if her leg would be removed she would be a charity case the rest of her life. She said that she wouldn't be able to enjoy life, get married, or even afford an artifical leg, and her mother agreed with her. The judge said that the court would not superimpose its will on unwilling people, and while the prospects were sad, bitter, and tragic, he would not grant the order to amputate; that he was not going to play God.

Another case was that of 15-year-old Richard who had injured his leg during a football game. The wound became cancerous and the doctors told Richard that his leg would have to be amputated in order to save his life. A week passed before Richard was seen again. He had run away from home rather than have his leg cut off. When he came back he said that he had changed his mind and decided to go through with the operation. Richard had to surmount the shock of losing his leg. He had to learn to accept the reality of his handicap before he could cope with it and adjust to it. He had to accept the fact that he would have to wear an artificial limb the rest of his life. After the surgery, Richard, wearing an artificial leg, was sent to a special school for handicapped children. Knowing that other children had suffered a similar fate and that he was not the only one with a handicap helped Richard accept his disability.

THE CHILD'S FEELINGS TOWARD
BEING HANDICAPPED

The child gets his self image, his feelings of worth and value, from the way his parents treat him. He absorbs their attitudes and accepts them as his own, for how else can a child learn who he is and what kind of a person he is? The child's feelings about his being handicapped is influenced by the way he is treated by his parents, siblings, relatives, teachers, schoolmates, peers, friends, neighbors, and the strangers he may meet in public places.

The child who is born handicapped has never known what being normal means. His special life style is immediately prescribed by his limitations, whether they are physical, mental, or emotional. Today, much effort is being made to help such children develop their potentialities to their full capacity. However, the purpose of this chapter is not to deal with the problems of the exceptional child, but with the child who becomes handicapped due to an accident or a catastrophic illness.

How does a child who is struck down by such an insult to his health and well-being react to the situation? A child who becomes orthopedically handicapped may respond to his disability in many different ways. This depends upon his family's neurotic structure, the type and extent of the disability, the sex of the child, the age of the child at the time of the onset, the use the child and the family have made of the disability as the focus of other problems, and the pain, anesthesia, restriction of motion the child is subjected to, and other factors (Missildine, 1965).

The child who cannot face the reality of the situation may use denial as a defense mechanism. This is very difficult to keep up because it can contribute to a withdrawal into fantasy and away from reality. It may cause the child to see the world in a distorted state and become increasingly more maladjusted to his physical and social environment.

A very bright and attractive eleven-year-old German girl who had come to the United States, seemed to have unusual difficulty in learning the English language. The teacher discovered that the child was very hard of hearing. When she spoke to the father, who was a physician, he denied the existence of the disability. After much difficulty in convincing him that the child should have a hearing aid in order to be able to succeed in her lessons, he reluctantly allowed her to be fitted with an aid. The child learned fast and blossomed into a happy and cheerful girl.

Many such parents attempt to manipulate the environment by not mentioning the deformity. They state flatly that nothing is wrong with the child. This tends to make the child feel guilty because his parents cannot accept his disability. He gets a distorted image of reality because it is being denied by all sorts of defenses, leaving the child confused and unable to give his best attention to his schoolwork, his relationship to people, and to the physical world in which he lives.

Many children feel that their illness is a punishment for misconduct on their part. Their parents and the community also feel that they were being punished for some sin they had committed. "Why did this have to happen to me? Why did God punish me?"

Handicapped children are in an ever-present state of depression to some degree. When the child is in the hospital or at home, especially at bedtime, he becomes lonely, anxious, and fearful. Parents who consider the child a possession and not a person in his own right and insist upon having a perfect child, will express their rejection by telling the child not to come home from the hospital until he is normal again. Such children manifest acute anxiety prior to surgery and are afraid their parents will disown them and forsake them.

Sometimes the child's depression and anxiety develops into a blandness or apathy that causes him to build a wall around himself which separates him from others. The child's preoccupation with his disease and very negative self image prevents him from relating well with others. Such children may exaggerate their handicap and become afraid to face the world, because they feel they will be looked down on, pitied, or laughed at.

Their relationship with their parents are usually strained. Parents may be blamed for putting them in the hospital where they experience separation anxiety, pain, fear of surgery, and its outcome. Some children become passive while others become demanding as they use their disability to control their parents and often stimulate guilt in them.

The children know that they will probably have to return to the hospital for care later and they face the future with feelings of uncertainty and hopelessness. They may discard a needed prosthesis because it calls attention to their disability. Adolescents who are normally unsure about who they are and what their future will be like, are much more distressed by the tremendously added burden of looking ahead to an uncertain and fearful future of a job, dating, and marriage. Some of them will prefer marriage to another handicapped partner who will not then be able to look down on them.

There are, however, strong characters who will face reality with courage and determination. They do not want pity or special treatment as they strive for independence and achievement.

Patty had to have her leg amputated when she was 13 years old because she had developed cancer. At age 17 she described her feelings and experiences. Once a week she had to report to the hospital for chemotherapy. She looked ahead to the time with dread because of the pain and side effects, such as losing her hair and other reactions to the medication. She has a prosthesis, but she wore pants instead of dresses most of the time so her handicap wouldn't be noticed.

Patty wanted to be treated as an equal without being coddled or given special attention. She said, "People, parents, doctors, nurses, didn't feel sorry for me or express sympathy, so I felt that I could talk to them freely at all times about my problems." In peer relationships she was accepted by her friends in the elementary school, but in high school her friends tended to drop off and did not invite her to parties or give her any attention.

PARENTAL ATTITUDES TOWARD THE HANDICAPPED CHILD

The child's feelings about being handicapped are greatly influenced by the way other people, and especially his parents react to his disability. If they react with repugnance, he will regard his deformity in the same way. If they show pity, sympathy, or overprotection, he will learn to expect those attitudes from others and feel inferior and degraded (Missildine, 1965).

The parents' response to a child's handicap is the most important factor in reflecting his own self image and in the methods he will use to cope with his disability.

All parents do not have the same attitudes toward parenthood. Some mothers may not look forward to child-bearing and child-rearing with self-confidence in their ability to perform well, nor with a belief that having a child is necessary for self-fulfillment. Other women may be more interested in a career rather than in the home responsibilities entailed in bringing up children. Those mothers who enjoy the feeling that they are indispensable to the child may change and become less emotionally involved, permitting the child to reach out to others and become more independent of her. Other mothers do not enjoy the child's dependency and encourage him to reach out toward independence as soon as possible.

But a child who is handicapped in infancy, and is therefore more dependent than the normal child, may invoke guilt feelings in his parents about his special needs. If the child also happened to be unwanted in the first place, due to financial or marital difficulties, or other family problems, a catastrophic illness of the infant may call forth conflicting emotions in the parents and may reactivate other partially unsolved problems. The parent may attribute the cause of the disability to punishment by God for some imagined sin or to negligence. The blame may also be placed on someone else, such as a member of the family, a neighbor, the doctor, the inheritance of so called "bad blood" from the spouse's family.

The parental denial of the handicap, based on unreality, can only bring grief, disappointment, failure, and bitterness (Missildine, 1965). Instead of such denial, the mother should encourage the child to develop and use the potentialities that he has, to their fullest possibilities. Denial is a trap that can only lead to disaster, as reality must take over in the end.

The mother's need to assuage her conscience by overprotecting the child causes him to become an extreme burden to her, so that she herself may become emotionally disturbed because she is unable to live a life of her own. Such overprotection may limit the child's efforts to reach out toward growth and independence and cause him to become increasingly frustrated, angry, and discouraged. This "mutually inhibiting parent-child symbiosis" (Call, 1963) is harmful to both the mother and the child, for both of them need to become independent persons in their own right.

The parents of a cerebral palsied child had difficulty in perceiving the child's handicap as well as in understanding what his actual abilities are. Psychological as well as other infantile dependencies must be resolved in order to free the mother from the unnecessary burdens of attending to every imagined need of the child, and permit him to gain the self confidence and courage to reach out into the world of reality and develop his own personality, independence, and talents. The parent must learn to give the child the confidence and faith in himself to achieve this growth.

A series of discussions with four groups of parents of cerebral palsied children indicated that the parents focused their attention on the child's defect rather than on the whole child, as an individual. They felt no need for psychological help and were not motivated to change their attitudes and ideas. When their child was separated from them and sent to a nursery school the parents were surprised to see how much the child was able to learn and how many things he had in common with other children.

Special effort must be made to help the handicapped child participate in a real world of activities and social contacts. He must be given equal opportunity with normal siblings to explore his physical and social environment — not to sit alone doing nothing, but to play with toys, move about as much as possible, keep actively interested in worthwhile activities; develop interests and hobbies, and make friends with other children. This may involve extra effort on the part of his parents to make arrangements for such activities, but the energy expended in this direction will contribute to the development of a healthy and happy child and will result in a more accepting and happier parent.

In the family group, the child should be considered on an equal plane with the other members when it comes to discussions and decisions about family affairs. Every effort must be made to help the child overcome the limitations of his handicap by treating him with respect, as a normal person in all areas in which he can achieve and function on an equal level. This will help give him a self image of a worthy and able person even though he does have a handicap. Other children will tend to adopt the attitudes and actions of the child's family. They will learn to express less prejudice towards him as they accept him as a person equal to others.

If we give the handicapped child enough self respect and feelings of being loved and wanted, he will be able to withstand the prejudice and hurt of stupid and ignorant people who may try to belittle him and put him down. Others do not have to pretend that the handicap does not exist, but they must accept it for what it is, in a matter-of-fact way and help the child when it is necessary, without compunction or embarrassment, pity, or denial, for no one is perfect, and no one is superior in his humanity. "The gods bestow not equally on all, the gifts that men desire."

HOW TO HELP PARENTS OF HANDICAPPED CHILDREN

When a child is born with a disability or becomes handicapped through illness or accident, parents respond with shock, disbelief, anger, despair, and grief (Call, 1963). What can professional people do to help parents meet this crisis effectively?

Parents need to be assured that they have the right to grieve. After their mourning, they must accept the reality of the situation and deal with it constructively.

When a severely mentally and physically handicapped child is born, parents must decide whether to take the child home or institutionalize him. Most parents face this situation with guilt and anguish, for there is no satisfactory answer. Doctors can only describe the situation as they see it from long experience, but the final decision must be made by the parents themselves.

A mother who had raised her mongoloid child at home, who had grown into his teens, said that her greatest fear was that he would outlive her and then there would be no one to take care of him. She said, "I want to outlive him by just one day, so that I can know a single day of freedom."

A father describes his agony and overpowering feelings of guilt as he tried to decide what to do. He writes that the pediatrician firmly declined to offer advice concerning their newborn mongoloid child, but that he did explain to him that many parents do make the decision to institutionalize their child; that their son would grow up among children like himself, not aware that he is different. He said that it was better to experience heartache now than to know a cumulative, greater anguish later on. Taking the child home would trap the family in "an irreversible situation" (Bard and Fletcher, 1968).

The parents decided to put the child in an institution when their doctor told them that the child would be vulnerable to severe heart ailment, digestive and respiratory troubles. His life would probably be short and mental development would be arrested to age two or three. Children in the sanitarium are kept warm, fed, and sheltered; medical emergencies are met, but no operations or miracle drugs are used to prolong life. The father writes, "On the trip home, I prayed for my child's death, cursing and damning myself as I did . . . A few hours later I received a phone call that my child had died" (Bard and Fletcher, 1968).

To let a newborn child, who is severely mentally and physically handicapped, die a natural death, from a life-threatening disease, rather than using life-saving measures, is another heart-breaking decision for parents to have to make. Lawson (1968) reports a study of Australian parents who were confronted with the need to make such a decision. He tells about parents of 20 newborn children with severe physical or mental defects who developed a life-threatening complication such as meningitis, who were asked if they wanted life-saving measures to be used. In all cases but one, the parents hoped for a peaceful death for their severely handicapped infant. In six cases the parents stated directly that they would prefer their infant to die. Five sets of parents favored implementation of life-saving measures, and eight were against active intervention. The six sets of parents re-interviewed four years later expressed their original feelings that it was better for the infant to die. There was no apparent connection between the views of the parents and their religion.

Religious leaders were interviewed on the subject. The Catholic Church felt that ordinary but not extraordinary treatment measures are indicated to keep an infant alive. The view of the Hebrew faith was that every effort must be made to keep the infant alive. Most parents prefer that their severely handicapped infant die peacefully but would rather not be responsible for the decision. Lawson (1968) says that rather than have parents live with the guilt of making such a decision, two or more doctors of consultant status should state what they recommend, but if the parents find the withholding of treatment unacceptable, the physician has no choice but to make every effort to keep the patient alive.

The birth of a child with some handicap may so overwhelm the parents that they do not know how to approach it. But when the physician talks to the child and handles him with gentleness and tenderness, and the parents see how the child responds, it starts them on the road to understanding that loving the child will call forth love from him, for every child can sense through his body whether he is loved or unwanted. This gives the parent the right start in accepting his child (Hebeler, 1970). Encouraging communication between the parents and their handicapped child is very important for their future relationships. It will make the child feel free to speak up without fear when he needs them most.

Parents must realize that a child is not a possession but a person in his own right. They should not be overwhelmed about what the neighbors or relatives will think or say. It may be a misfortune to have an imperfect child, but it should not be thought of as a disgrace. This can happen to anyone. No one is immune. Accept it with dignity but not with shame.

Parents must be helped to accept the child as a person who has the same feelings, interests, intelligence, and ability to learn that other children have. They should neither focus on the handicap nor deny it. They should rather accept the handicap, try to *see the whole child,* and evaluate all his positive potentialities. Every person must accept his own strengths and weaknesses and put his assets to good use.

If the parent thinks of the child as a cripple, he will reflect this image to the child. If he will think of the child as a person and believe in him, the child will believe in himself, with confidence and self esteem. This is a challange for the parent to act as a mature person who neither rejects his child nor overprotects him so that he may become a helpless, overly dependent, infantile, human being, for such overprotection will limit the child's growth and self respect and dwarf his personality.

Give the child faith in himself. Encourage him to reach out and achieve his goals. Do not do anything for him that he can learn to do for himself, no matter how difficult it may be. When there is a need and a goal, with encouragement the child will find a way. Parents should also explain to the child's teachers, siblings, and friends, what he is able to do for himself, and that he should be encouraged to extend himself to the limits of his capabilities.

Stories of handicapped people, like Helen Keller and many others, who have overcome their handicaps, have proven that in every person there exists deep, unexpected, hidden potentialities that can be developed when there is self confidence, courage, and effort. It is up to the parents to give the child this encouragement. And every success will lead to the self confidence and effort that leads to further successes.

There is always the problem of dealing with people who do not understand how they should act when in the presence of a handicapped person. When friends and relatives seem uncomfortable about the child's handicap, stare, or ask questions, parents may become annoyed and angry, but they must learn to have patience with people who really do not know how to act in such a situation. Parents can prepare the child to deal with such people by explaining that they do not understand and do not know how to act. The child must learn not to expect them to understand; to make them comfortable by talking openly, in a matter of fact way, about the handicap as a part of the conversation, and thus put people at ease. If he accepts it as a reality, they too will accept it.

If the child realizes that most people mean well, but may sometimes be tactless in an inexperienced situation, he will accept them for what they are and not let their behavior bother him. The important thing is for the child to accept his handicap himself, so that he does not withdraw from society but is able to face people and make the best of the situation. After a while they will forget his handicap as they get to know him as a person with all the good qualities he has developed.

SUMMARY

The living organism is constantly on guard to protect itself against injury or illness. A child who becomes seriously disabled through a catastrophic illness goes through a tremendously traumatic experience. The way the child is treated by medical personnel, the preparation for the procedures he must undergo, the help he receives in working through his grief at the loss of a part or a function of his body, his personality and self-image, his relationship with his parents, siblings, and peers, all contribute to the degree with which he is able to meet and cope with his disability.

The child must be helped to express grief over his loss. He needs to talk about his feelings with a compassionate and understanding person. As the grief is brought into consciousness, a gradual detachment of the lost part is achieved. The basic function of grief is to test reality and learn to accept it.

The child who enters a hospital for surgery is beset by a multitude of fears. He must be carefully prepared for what will happen to him. He must be encouraged to ask any question about the procedures that he is concerned with, in order to alleviate any fears built up through fantasies and misinformation.

The impact of an amputation or facial deformity can be completely devastating to children, and especially to adolescents. Deep love and family security can contribute to the child's courage and confidence in coping with his disability. A child's reaction to a sudden serious handicap will be influenced by the extent of his disability, the pain and restrictions caused by it, his family structure, the sex of the child and his age at the time of the onset.

Both the child and his parents may try to meet the problem of his handicap by the use of denial. Such defenses only create confusion and contribute to misinformation about the real world. The parental denial of the handicap can only bring grief, disappointment, failure, and bitterness. Parents and child may feel that the disability is a punishment for some sin they have committed. The parents' response to a child's handicap is the most important factor in reflecting his own self-image and the way he will cope with his handicap. The child may become depressed; his relationship with his parents may become strained.

Some children will use their disability to control their parents; others may face reality with courage and determination. They will strive for independence with all their strength and will call forth hidden resources to help them overcome their handicap.

When a newborn child is born with a defect, parents should be taught to focus on the whole child instead of on the handicap. The physician can help parents accept such a child by treating him with tenderness and affection as he handles him and talks to him. They must learn not to worry about what others will think, accept the child for what he is, and give him help in being confident and resourceful in coping with his disability. The child should be given self-esteem to be able to face the outside world with courage. The most important thing is for the child to accept his handicap himself and learn to live with it.

REFERENCES

Aldrich, C. K.: Emotional problems in catastrophic illness. Reprinted from the Symposium on Catastrophic illness: Impact on families: Challenge to the Professions. Cancer Care, Inc., National Cancer Foundation, New York, 1967.

Bard, B. and Fletcher, J.: The right to die. Atlantic, 221(4):1-4, 1968.

Call, J. D.: Emotional problems of handicapped children and adolescents. Feelings and their Medical Significance, 5(3):1-4, 1963.

Carr, A. C.: A lifetime of preparation for bereavement. Arch Foundation Thanatol 1(1):14-16, 1969.

Childhood cancer emotional consideration. Symposium sponsored by the American Cancer Society of Los Angeles County and the Children's Hospital of Los Angeles, Los Angeles, January 8-9, 1971.

Erickson, F.: Hospital setting can hold terrors for ill children. Pediatric News, 3(5):6, 1969.

Green, M. and Solnit, A. J.: The vulnerable child syndrome. Pediatrics, 34:58-66, 1964.

Hebeler, J. R.: Multi-handicapped children stir parental rejection and anger. Pediatric News, 4(7):23, 1970.

Lawson, J. S.: Ethical problems associated with management of congenitally handicapped newborn infants. (Royal Children's Hospital, Melbourne, Australia). Aust Paediatr J, 4:186-192, 1968.

Missildine, W. H.: Emotional responses to handicap in children. Feelings and Their Medical Significance, 7(1):1-4, 1965.

———: Socioeconomic and emotional factors influence prophylaxis of recurrent fever. Pediatr Currents, 20(1):1-3, 1971.

Moore, T. D. (Ed.): Ethical Dilemmas in Current Obstetric and Newborn Care: Report of the Sixty-Fifth Ross Conference on Pediatric Research. Columbus, Ohio, Ross Laboratories, 1973.

Switzer, D. K.: The Dynamics of Grief. Nashville, Abingdon, 1970.

Zeligs, R.: Children's attitudes toward death. Ment Hyg, 51(3):393-396, 1967.

Chapter IX

DEATH AND THE ADOLESCENT

W HAT is the meaning of death to an adolescent in our culture today? How does his personal experiences with death, and his awareness of death and dying as being a part of the cycle of life, affect his feelings and attitudes toward death? How is he affected by the sudden death through accidents of friends or family? How does he face and deal with the unexpected news that he has a fatal disease and his own death is imminent?

"The adolescent lives in an intense present; now is so real to him that both past and future seem pallid by comparison. Everything that is important and valuable in life lies either in the immediate life situation or in the rather close future" (Kastenbaum, 1959).

MEANING OF DEATH TO THE ADOLESCENT

Our knowledge about the maturing child in the second decade of life should help us understand the meaning of death to him, his experience with death, and his tragic need for care, comfort, and understanding, when he is suddenly confronted with his own imminent, untimely death.

The child's understanding of death grows with his physical, mental, and emotional development, from birth to young adulthood. His understanding of death is a part of his total personality and psychology. As the child grows, so grows his knowledge, his feelings, and his interpretations of the meaning of death (Easson, 1970).

The child's self-concept grows from being a part of his mother's body to being a part of his family, to the idea of his own uniqueness as a separate individual. He begins to realize that his separate existence can also result in his separate non-existence in death. To the child and the adolescent, death is not a separate concept unrelated to his age and development. It is part and parcel of what he is, how he thinks, and how he feels. His concept of death grows with his age, education, experiences with the death of members of his family, friends, and relatives, and how they themselves respond to death as a part of their own experiences with death, their culture, and their religious beliefs.

The fear of death and every effort to avoid it is a part of the living organism. Consciously or unconsciously it is ever on guard to protect itself from harm. However, to the young child, the adolescent, and the young adult, death seems very far away and in the remote future.

THE ADOLESCENT IN TODAY'S CULTURE

The adolescent in today's culture is faced with many problems of living, as he separates himself from the family unit and reaches out toward independence and self-fulfillment. Physically and emotionally he encounters many changes he must deal with in order to establish himself as a self-supporting adult with skills that will help provide employment opportunities and economic independence, and social activities that will lead to a choice of a mate, marriage, and a family of his own.

Although growing up entails many problems, it also invites opportunities for numerous interests, goals, and achievements. Life beckons with many rich possibilities in our modern culture of scientific knowledge and public education. The youth today has many stimulating attractions to investigate. He also has many confusing and complicating decisions to make. He has civic responsibilities to meet in a world where military service might still be a requirement that hangs over his head, for he may have to serve his country, whether such duties fit into his character and personality, or not.

But whatever the problems of living in our culture at the present time are, it is a time when the normal, healthy young person is looking forward to life and growth with hope and glad anticipation.

However, many of the developmental stages may be

accompanied by maladjustments and activities that may lead to destruction of health and even of life itself. Of course there is always the chance of accidents or fatal illness that may strike young people at any age and snuff out their lives prematurely, before they have had a chance to meet life's challenges and to enjoy the pleasures and profits of growth and maturity.

Experience with death is traumatic at all ages, but at adolescence the individual is especially vulnerable, for at that period our youth are beset by many anxiety provoking problems of living and growing.

A DEFINITION OF "ADOLESCENCE"

To understand the meaning of death experiences to the adolescent and how such experiences affect his life, his growth and development, we must first get a true picture of what we mean by the term "adolescent" in our culture. We need a more clearly defined image of the growing, developing, maturing individual in the second decade of life. This decade covers a rapidly changing period of biological, intellectual, educational, social, and cultural growth that underlies the individual's entire future.

The adolescent youth wants to be recognized and respected as an individual in his own right and to be able to make his own decisions about the way he dresses, his curfew time, his choice of friends, school program, and other activities.

The tendency to classify all youth in this decade of life in one age group, under the title of teenager or adolescent, has led to much misunderstanding. There would be less confusion about our understanding this decade of life better, if the stages of growth were more clearly defined. This period needs to be divided into smaller, more specific developmental units. There should be a detailed, concrete description of each stage of development, with a special name for each stage.

Easson (1970) divides the developmental ages of the individual in the second decade of life into *early adolescence,* from 10 to 14 years old; *mid-adolescence,* 14, 15, and 16; and *older adolescence* or *young adulthood,* 17 to 20 years old. He clearly differentiates between the maturational development of the three groups. Our failure to make this differentiation has contributed to our misunderstanding and mishandling of our teenagers.

The present writer will discuss the adolescent's experience with death from the point of view of the developmental stages of the three age groups.

The Early Adolescent Period

The writer has long felt the need to focus greater attention on the early adolescent youth, ages 10 through 13, in order to understand that age period better. If there has been real understanding between the parent and child before adolescence there will be a better chance for understanding and accepting them later. Wise parents recognize and accept harmless trends of the times that really will not make any difference in the future life of young people, like hair styles and dress that give them the security of belonging to their own generation.

The early adolescent period is a time of great change in the life of the developing individual. He has many new things to learn at a time when he is very unsure about his own identity and self image. Death anxiety is increased at this critical time of life (Alexander, Colley and Adlerstein, 1957).

During this early adolescent period the youth is not really ready for independence in thought and action, but he feels he must leave the security of the home and step out into the social world. He seeks security by belonging to his peer group. He becomes less dependent upon his family and more dependent upon his friends for emotional support and a way of life. But, although he gives up parental direction for group direction, in reality *he is in the group but not of the group,* for his interest is "almost totally self-centered and narcissistic" (Easson, 1970).

Without thought or analysis he may accept and absorb his peers' culture; their ideas, their ethics, and morality. He participates in their activities without really understanding what he is doing and why he is acting in ways that are strange and confusing to his parents and teachers. His sense of loyalty and moral values set before him by his parents are abandoned while he absorbs the standards and values of his peer group, regardless of reality and the consequences of his conduct. "When he feels especially unsure and inadequate, he may bolster up his self-image by becoming negativistic to all his parental standards . . . to dissociate himself from his religion and his culture" (Easson, 1970).

Parents, teachers, and society as a whole are bewildered by the seemingly senseless things some of these young adolescents are doing; by their use of dangerous drugs, shop lifting, and law-breaking in general. Parents feel hurt to see that their child, who they thought had always been so loving, loyal, and obedient, seems to have forsaken them and their teachings, as he blindly transfers his loyalty to his peers.

Of course, this is not true of all young adolescents. A closer examination of those who completely rebel against their parents, may indicate that there has been an underlying degree of alienation, where the child has actually separated himself by withdrawing into himself, spending much time alone in his room, and not communicating with his family very much. Such a child is especially vulnerable to the strong influence of his peers.

Identification with the peer group is a temporary stage of development and the eventual achievement of identity comes from older people who are important to the young adolescent.

But can his peers really stand by and give the young adolescent help and support when he is involved in deep and serious troublele? How do the peers of the dying adolescent react to the knowledge that he is struck down with a fatal disease? His peers are reaching out toward life with all its rich potentialities of love and liberty, growth and fulfillment. The idea of death is far, far away in the dim future. Time is of the essence and death is a vague shadow far beyond the horizon. When death does come, suddenly, out of the future into the present, his friends will have no business with it. They will avoid it like the plague. Peer groups of young adolescents tend to turn their backs on one of their members who is struck down with a fatal illness. It makes them feel vulnerable themselves at a time when death knocks at their peer's door.

Faced with Impending Death

How does the adolescent in the second decade of life face and deal with the unexpected news that his own death is imminent? The need to belong to a peer group as a step toward independence and growth to adulthood comes to a shocking halt and reversal when the young adolescent is suddenly faced with the unexpected reality of his own impending and untimely death.

Still deeply imbedded in his personality, as a part of his early training, are his parental ideals and values. Although he tries to repress the standards of his parents, he unconsciously feels guilty about not fulfilling their expectations about school achievement, home responsibilities, and social behavior. When illness or accidents do strike, he may feel that he is being punished for his disobedience or disregard for the rights of others. He expects punishment for his misconduct.

Accidents and trauma cause most deaths to teenagers. Violence is all around us. The news media play up crimes in the streets, murder, mutilation and death in our cities, war and destruction in the world. Many adolescents fear a violent death (Johnson, 1968).

Our teenagers recklessly risk their own and other people's lives as they drive their cars without respect for traffic laws or the rights of others. In their excitement they dare to challenge danger and death, so they involve themselves in more accidents than any other group. When they cause injury or death to others by ignoring parental guidance, participating in illegal activities, such as breaking traffic laws, speeding, drinking alcohol, or taking dangerous drugs, they feel responsible and fearful about what they have done. If their own mutilation or imminent death is the consequence of their conduct, they feel guilty and may become deeply depressed.

The dying child begins to question his own conduct in rejecting the standards and ideals of his parents. Crossing the bridge from parents to peers, with all the confusion and unreasoning conduct, causes pain and guilt feelings in the youth. His parents have been hurt by his rejection of them and their values. His peers have deserted him. Now he must become a dependent person again. Now he must turn to his parents for care and consolation. He is filled with guilt and remorse. He feels that he is being punished. He is angry, desperate, furious, bitter, and utterly helpless in the face of death. Why me? he asks. The punishment is greater than the crime! What has he really done to deserve this death sentence?

The shock and disbelief of this young person when he learns that his own death is imminent is tremendously overwhelming. He is in every sense the living, maturing, growing, blossoming child when untimely death casts his shadow on him and marks him for his own. Nipped in the bud, before he has begun to live, before he is allowed to grow to maturity, the darkness of death falls upon him.

The tremendous sadness and heart break of it all is that death claims the child when he is at the peak of his growth, when he is full of life. When life calls to the adolescent, "Come hither, come hither," when love lingers in his heart and stirs it with longing and living, with creating and producing; when life is at its very pinacle, then death dares to deny life's longing; then death cries, "This is for others – this is not for you!" When the blossoming child is reaching out for self-fulfillment, for the completeness of his maturing personality, comes a blight that says, "No, no, this is not for you!"

How does the adolescent feel when he learns that he is dying of a fatal disease, that his life is being nipped in the bud by the cold fingers of death, stopped in the midst of growth, stopped with no fulfillment of the promise of youth? How great is the heartbreak – how deep is the wound – how desolate and dark is death at his door!

Shock and surprise, anger and rage, despair and denial, overwhelm the young adolescent as he anticipates his own imminent death. Fear and hopelessness envelope him and he may go into a depression and revenge himself by rejecting parents and all medical personnel. His sense of guilt makes him feel that he is being punished for rebelling against the authority of parents and the establishment, in an effort to become an independent person. Yet he feels that this sentence of death is too harsh and too cruel; that only an unforgiving parental authority or Deity can mete out such extreme punishment. "His resentment deepens his guilt and accentuates his depression" (Easson, 1970). He feels rejected by parents and society and an unforgiving God.

During his illness, his growing need to become an independent person may still make him defy parental and professional warmth and care, although in reality he longs for loving attention, comfort, and concern. "The bitterness of the young adolescent who is dying causes more problems to his family and to the treating staff than the feelings of any other patient who is facing death" (Hamovitch, 1964). He feels lonely and alone as he faces his oncoming death. Only a deeply understanding older teenager can establish a close and helpful relationship with such a young person.

How Parents and Professionals Can Help

What can parents and the professional teams do to help the young person face his future with strength and fortitude? Parents and medical personnel can help the adolescent who has a fatal illness by giving him every opportunity to talk about his feelings. "Ventilation," the freedom to express all his feelings, is a great comfort to the patient and promotes intelligent management of the case. The patient who feels that he is not alone, that he is still among the living, is less likely to lapse into depression and will channel his energies into productive activity while there is still hope (Brauer, 1970). All patients dying of cancer rarely abandon hope (Kubler-Ross, 1969). Hope must never die too far ahead of the patient (Aronson, 1959).

Parents can try to help the young person understand that his illness is not a punishment and it is no one's fault. It is a matter of chance and could happen to anyone. We do not know all the answers about the cause and cure of fatal illness, but doctors and scientists are constantly working to gain knowledge that will save lives that are threatened by certain diseases.

Parents can accept their child's anger and rejection, depression and defeat, without returning such feelings. They must make him feel that they love and accept him with all their heart. They should not avoid him but should be available to him when he needs them most. This is also true for the professional team. The dying adolescent must be helped to die in the presence of loved ones, of people who do indeed care about him. He must feel loved and accepted. As he grows weaker he will be able to accept loving care without feeling that his independence which he has achieved as an adolescent, is being threatened or disrespected.

We must all learn to understand how such a child feels who is forced to face his own untimely death with all the agony that it entails. We must learn to understand how he thinks and feels about his dying, so that we may be better able to help him. We must know that he wants to talk; he wants to have someone with him and near him. He wants to know that the significant people in his life do care about him. He wants to be assured that they will not forsake him as long as he lives; that they will be with him until the very end, to give him courage, to comfort him, and to give him the security that comes with the feeling of being loved and cared for.

What can the professional staff do to help both patient and parents? Do not expect logical or reasonable reactions from family or patient, but accept them with understanding and fortitude. Encourage the parents to help and participate in the care of the patient. Make them feel that you are not displacing them in the care of the child, but that you are including them on the team that is working for the welfare and comfort of their child. Always show respect for the parents as people whose dignity and self esteem must be fostered and upheld.

Let the patient look forward to your presence with faith and not with fear. Explain the treatment procedure to him and give the reasons and expected results of such therapy. If the patient is disfigured by drugs or surgery, do everything possible to help him look presentable and to enable him to care for himself as much as possible without having to depend upon others. Do not forsake or avoid the patient; do not make him feel alienated, and *do not let him die alone.* Always emphasize the present. Let him feel free to talk and always be ready to listen. Do not act like you are in a hurry, no matter how busy you may be. Help avoid pain and try to make the patient comfortable, but do not overdrug him. Do not use heroic means to prolong life a few more hours or days, especially if the patient is in a coma or in severe pain. To prolong the agony of death helps no one. Let the patient die in peace and be with him until his last breath.

Mid-Adolescence

When the teenager reaches mid-adolescence, at ages 14, 15, and

16, he has achieved self-identity and has become an individual in his own right, for the first time. He does not accept his peers' ideas without thought or analysis, but he reexamines them more critically, compares them with his own values, and acts according to his own standards. He is no more dependent upon them for a way of life. He can think for himself and can make his own decisions, without acting impulsively and irresponsibly. He enjoys this feeling of self-esteem and self-confidence in his increasing power to face problems, make personal decisions, and achieve mastery in many situation.

Instead of being completely self-centered, as is the early adolescent, this older youth has a more clearly defined and accepted self-image. He knows better who he is and where he stands, so that he does not have to concentrate on himself all the time. He can reach out to other people with interest and concern. This is the emotional preparation for marriage later, and for parenthood that requires sharing, giving, and caring. This maturing youth is looking ahead to life's fulfillment with all its exciting potentialities of family and human relations, of creative self-expression in work and social activities.

How utterly stunned with anger and disbelief is he, when the dread news falls upon him that an early unexpected death is his portion. Death promises only defeat to this newly competent adolescent. He will not accept this sentence of death! He denies this bitter potion, this devastating destructive force that will snuff out his life just when he has begun to live; just when he has found himself to be an adequate young adult who can function as a participating and contributing member of society. It can not be true! There must be a mistake. Death is not for him. He has not lived yet. He is not ready to die!

A tremendous sadness overtakes him. Where there had been pride and progress, hope and achievement, there is now only fear and frustration, anger, bitterness, and defeat, as the dread of death looms before him, no matter how much he tries to deny it. He must finally recognize and accept his fate. Depression and hopelessness envelope him as his strength turns to weakness and his independence and mastery turn to dependence and despair.

Being at the height of emotional awareness, he is also able to sense the sadness and heartache of those who love him the most.

He may try to protect his family by not telling them that he knows what lies ahead for him. They, too, may try to keep him from knowing the truth. But such seemingly hidden secrets do not work well in either case. The dying young person usually has insight about his condition.

It is not constructive to build a wall between himself and his family. The time that is left is precious and should be cherished. It should be enriching to all of them. As they spend time together, as they share deep thoughts and feelings, as they seek understanding of what is happening to them, of the meaning of life and death, they experience deep mutual awareness of who they are and what they mean to each other.

Because this mid-adolescent is respected as a person in his own right, who has arrived at a certain degree of maturity, he can accept loving care without feeling downgraded; he can reach out for comfort without feeling that he has always been weak and helpless. The sharing and the caring, and the deep meaning of their precious moments together will enrich the present and leave valuable memories to comfort and console family and friends when death takes its toll and departs.

The Older Adolescent or Young Adult

The older adolescent or young adult, ages 17 to 20, has achieved more maturity and may be carrying the adult responsibility of a job and even the responsibility of marriage. He feels that he has arrived as a participating citizen of his community. He is interested in what is going on in the outside world as well as in his own personal life, knowing that what happens in society affects his life, too.

Just when he has arrived at the stage of adulthood toward which all growing, developing young people strive, towards achievement and success, if serious sickness strikes him, he is shocked beyond belief. He is reaching out for mutual love and well-being. Life seems to be so full of a rich and exciting future, of love that is meaningful, dependable, strong, and vital. He is alive and in love with the world, happy within himself, and rich in the joy of his well-being. Suddenly, out of a clear blue sky, dark clouds appear and his life becomes stormy and threatening. Suddenly, death that seemed so far away becomes imminent. His life is soon to end!

Anger and heartbreak overtake him. He cannot resolve the hopelessness that follows his shock and disbelief. To die before having really lived! His anger and bitterness and despair is sometimes displaced upon the shoulders of the medical team and also upon his own family.

But after he learns to accept the inevitable, he feels the sadness and distress of his parents, as they feel for him and begin to mourn their loss of him. He learns to accept their love and concern and comfort. They can now share their thoughts and feelings in quiet discussion, in the wonder of the meaning of it all. If they have faith in their religion, in the acceptance of the inevitable, they can now accept the belief that God in his wisdom has purposes of his own and they must have faith in what is beyond their understanding. And so death comes, leaving a deeper understanding of the meaning of life and love and human relationships.

SUMMARY

Our knowledge about the maturing youth in the second decade of life should help us understand the meaning of death to him, his experience with death, and his tragic need for care, comfort, and understanding, if he is suddenly confronted with his own imminent, untimely death.

The child's understanding of death grows with his physical, mental, and emotional development from birth to young adulthood. His concept of death grows with his age, education, experience with the death of members of his family, friends, and relatives, and how they themselves respond to death as a part of their culture, and their religious beliefs. *Time* in the life of an individual affects his attitudes and awareness of death. The adolescent concentrates mainly on the present without giving much thought to the past or the future.

The adolescent in today's culture is faced with many problems as he reaches out toward independence and self fulfillment. He has many opportunities to look forward to a happy future with hope and glad anticipation. However, some of his developmental stages may be accompanied by maladjustments, destruction of health, and even of life itself. Experience with death is traumatic at all ages, but at adolescence the individual is especially vulnerable.

Easson divides the adolescent period into three groups; early adolescence, mid-adolescence, and older adolescence or young adulthood. The early period is a time of great change. The young adolescent has many new things to learn. He is very unsure of himself and his own identity. In his struggle for independence he gives up the standards of his parents, joins his peer group, and absorbs their culture, their ideas, ethics, and morality.

Death anxiety is increased at this critical time of life. If this youth is threatened by impending death, his peers will turn away from him. To them, death is a vague shadow beyond the horizon. It makes them feel vulnerable themselves when death knocks at their peer's door.

Accidents and trauma cause most deaths to teenagers, and many of them fear a violent death. If mutilation or imminent death is the consequence of their own conduct, they feel guilty and may become deeply depressed. The dying young adolescent begins to question his own conduct in rejecting the standards of his parents. Shock and surprise, anger and rage, despair and denial overwhelm him as he anticipates his own impending death. He feels that he is being punished and is filled with guilt and remorse. During his illness, his need to become an independent person may still make him turn away from parents and professionals, although inwardly he longs for their loving attention and concern.

But they must try to help the young adolescent, by being patient with him, and by accepting his anger and rejection without returning such feelings. They should encourage him to talk about his illness and assure him that it is not his fault and it is not a punishment. They must let him know that they love him and accept him with all their heart. Parents and personnel must understand that the sick youth wants to have the significant people in his life near him. He wants to be assured that they will not forsake him, but will be with him, care for him, and comfort him, as long as he lives. They will not let him die alone.

The mid-adolescent, ages 14 to 16, has achieved self-identity. He does not follow his peers' code blindly, but has acquired the self-confidence to follow his own standards. This maturing youth is looking forward to the rich fulfillment of life's future with hope and excitement. If death suddenly strikes him he is stunned with anger and disbelief. At first he denies this bitter destructive decree, but when he is finally forced to accept his fate, a tremendous sadness overtakes him. Every precious moment must now be made more meaningful and enriching as he shares his thoughts and feelings with his loved ones.

The older adolescent or young adult, ages 17 to 20, has achieved more maturity and may be carrying adult responsibilities. He is alive and in love with the world, happy within himself, and rich in the joy of his well-being, when suddenly, death that seemed so far away becomes imminent. Anger and heartbreak, hopelessness and despair overtake him. He also feels the sadness and distress of his parents. They all learn to share their feelings in quiet discussion, until death comes, leaving a deeper understanding of the mystery of life and love and human relatedness.

REFERENCES

Alexander, I. E., Colley, R. S. and Adlerstein, A. M.: Is death a matter of indifference? J Psychol, 43:277-283, 1957.

Aronson, G. J.: Treatment of the dying patient. In Feifel, H. (Ed.) The Meaning of Death. New York, McGraw-Hill, 1959.

Brauer, P. H.: When cancer is diagnosed. Med Insight, 2(6):20-25, 1970.

Easson, W. M.: The Dying Child: The Management of the Child or Adolescent Who Is Dying. Springfield, Ill., Charles C Thomas, 1970.

Hamovitch, M. B.: The Parent and the Fatally Ill Child. Los Angeles, Delmar, 1964.

Johnson, E.: Many adolescents fear a violent death. Medical Tribune, Nov. 25, 1968, p.10.

Kastenbaum, R.: Time and death in adolescence. In Feifel, H. (Ed.): The Meaning of Death. New York, McGraw-Hill, 1959.

Kubler-Ross, E.: On Death and Dying. New York, MacMillan, 1969.

Zeligs, R.: Glimpses Into Child Life. New York, William Morrow, 1942.

Chapter X

SUICIDE AMONG CHILDREN AND ADOLESCENTS

W HAT makes a child or adolescent try to take his own life? Many authorities believe that when children or adolescents try to kill themselves they are reacting in an irrational manner. "The suicidal state does not remain in the acute phase, so that a person who wishes to kill himself is suicidal only for a limited time," says Shneidman (1968).

Jacobs (1971) disagrees with this view and tries to support his thesis that suicide attempts by adolescents represent the final step in a series of unsuccessful efforts to meet their problems of living in a positive constructive manner. He claims that their final decision is a rational choice based on what seems to them an intolerable situation, that leaves no other way out but death by their own hand.

The individual's personal qualifications as well as his environmental opportunities contribute to his ability to cope with his life situation in a favorable or unfavorable manner. Under difficult circumstances, when troubles escalate in ever increasing number and magnitude, with no seeming solution to the overwhelming pressures, the degree of frustration can reach a point beyond endurance. To escape from his terrible predicament, a youth may turn to suicide as the only way out.

Maurer (1964) found that adolescent girls disagree in their feelings about suicide as a way of meeting life's problems. Some felt that suicide was a way out while others were horrified at the idea of taking their own life. One girl said, "When the load becomes too heavy, why don't people just kill themselves and end it all?" Others said that they do not understand how a person could do such a thing and they felt sorry for such a person.

What life and death means to a person influences his attitude toward suicide. This depends upon his developmental age as well as his religious and cultural background. Young children's ideas of death differ from that of mature teenagers.

SUICIDE AMONG YOUNG CHILDREN

Suicide among young children is often due to their belief that death is temporary and reversible. In their games they often play cops and robbers where they shoot each other and then come alive again. They may attempt suicide to frighten their parents and make them feel sorry for mistreating them. They think they will then awaken and come back to life. Some child suicides may therefore be partly accidental.

Suicide rates rise with advancing age in youth. It is nonexistent in children under age five and rare in ages five to nine. However, many accidents, the leading cause of death in young children, ages five through fourteen, are probably suicide attempts that are not certified as such (Seiden, 1969), by parents and physicians who often conceal such attempts in children of this age. Currently there are about 100 suicides reported per year among children ten to fourteen years of age (Suicide in Youth, 1972).

Methods used by children under ten years, in their attempt to take their own lives include, running in front of cars, hanging themselves, putting a plastic bag over their heads, and swallowing a large number of pills.

Why do young children attempt suicide? Children's mis-understanding of the finality of death and their feelings of helplessness in a destructive environment may motivate them to try to kill themselves. The precipitating cause of a young child's effort to take his own life may sometimes seem trivial and unimportant to adults, but its importance to the child is influenced by his intellectual and maturational stage and his relationship with the significant persons in his life.

The child is limited in his ability to solve his own problems and to escape from intolerable situations. His complete dependence upon parents for loving care and guidance makes him vulnerable to feelings of hopelessness and despair, when he is rejected by them.

Dr. Reginald S. Lourie says that children repeat acts they feel will shorten life. This includes accidents, self-injury, running away, which may function as a substitute for suicide. "Almost seventy percent of emotionally disturbed youngsters hoped for their own death and more than fifty percent of well-adjusted children thought of killing themselves in order to escape from a difficult situation, gain admiration from others, or used threats to manipulate others" (Lourie, 1965).

The problem of the abused child is rapidly growing, so that authorities are working to protect the personal and legal rights of children. The solution to take children away from parents who mistreat them is not always the best answer for the child. Today, organizations are being formed to help parents understand their reasons for rejecting their children and to give them more constructive methods of dealing with their own feelings of aggression and hostility.

A child who experiences a loss of love and support may accept the self-image his disturbed parents mirror to him, and he may try to destroy himself because he thinks he is bad. Such an attempt is accompanied by feelings of guilt and low self-esteem leading to depression.

In a selected group of suicidal children, Schrut (1965) found that attempts at self-destruction was discovered by the children to be the most effective method of arousing parental concern. The children used this method to punish parents and gain their attention by awakening in them feelings of guilt, anxiety and discomfort. In this way the children were able to ward off their own feelings of helplessness, anxiety, and unworthiness and project them unto parents and society.

Separation from parents, through death or divorce, especially during critical periods of the child's development, may trigger off an attempt at self-destruction. But such events need not necessarily cause the child to resort to suicide as a solution to his unhappy situation. "It is the loss of love, of reciprocal intimacy, spontaneity, and closeness that is the key to understanding suicide" (Suicide in Youth, 1972). Children can face and successfully handle grave and difficult situations if there is a loving, trusting, dependable parent or other person they can turn to with confidence and assurance, for guidance and support.

How can we evaluate the seriousness of a young child's suicide threat? A casual, spontaneous remark about killing himself, made to a sibling or parent, because of an unpleasant or disappointing incident, need not be taken too seriously. But if the child and his family are emotionally or physically ill, and the child threatens suicide to a professional person who is treating him, the matter must be given more serious attention. Although the child under ten is less likely to be able to carry out his threat, it is a cry for help that must not be ignored. It indicates emotional disturbance and poor communication with parents and requires family counseling.

The child is dependent upon adults and cannot meet his problems alone. Fear, anger, and anxiety may cause him to seek escape from a difficult situation through suicide. If there is at least one person with whom the child can relate in confidence, he will not try to take his own life.

The suicide of a young child affects not only his family, but also his peers and teachers. When a seventh grader took his own life, his teachers and classmates were stunned and looked at each other accusingly in shocked disbelief. Even children who had had only casual contact with the boy felt guilty about his death.

SUICIDE AMONG ADOLESCENTS

What causes an adolescent to turn to suicide as a way of dealing with his problems? The child learns his way of life in the family constellation. His relationship with parents and siblings forms the pattern of his personality and gives him a way of life for dealing with people and meeting problems with courage and self-assurance. When there is not a secure and mature way of life with concrete patterns to emulate, he is filled with confusion and conflict. He may have tried such solutions as rebelliousness, withdrawal, destructiveness, anti-social acting out, and psycho-somatic illness without success. He may then come to a point where he sees no satisfactory solution to the many problems that pile up and leave him so completely cornered that he sees no way out but through suicide.

Jacobs (1971) studied the life situations of 50 adolescents who had been hospitalized for attempted suicide. His data was derived from psychiatric case reports, personal interviews of the patients and their mothers, and the analysis of diaries and suicide notes. His interviews covered suicide attempts, family relations, peer relations, attitudes toward performance in school, and career aspirations. He compared his findings with those of a control group of 31 other adolescents.

He states that the adolescent who attempts suicide reflects a long-standing history of problems from early childhood, the escalation of those problems coinciding with the onset of adolescence, the feeling that he has been subjected to a progressive isolation from meaningful social relationships, and has experienced continuous failure of available adaptive techniques for coping. His final decision therefore is that suicide is the only means out of his dilemma. He feels justified in making this so-called rational decision.

Factors that contributed to the adolescent's unhappiness were separation of parents, broken romances, residential moves, and unanticipated school changes. Broken homes, due to the loss of loved ones through death or divorce of parents, unhappy remarriage of parents, conflict with step-parents, heavy drinking in the home, having to live with relatives in the absence of both parents, and serious personal illness, all contributed to the feelings of isolation and despair (Jacobs, 1971).

Conflict with Parents

The intellectual and physical growth of today's adolescent far outstrip his emotional development. The prolonged dependence upon parental support contribute to the need for parental control. Lack of real communication between the adolescent and his parents bring about misunderstanding and conflict in the home. The youth rebels at what he considers unfair and inappropriate discipline such as criticizing him, nagging, yelling, whipping, spanking, prying into his secrets, parental mistrust, extreme withholding of privileges, and lack of approval and affection. However, when his parents fail to discourage behavior that he feels is bad, he interprets this as rejection and lack of concern about what happens to him.

Especially with stepparents, there is a feeling of being unloved and unwanted when he is exposed to constant threats of being thrown out of the house if he fails to conform to what he regards as unreasonable demands and discipline. He develops feelings of hopelessness and worthlessness, apathy and indifference.

A child's hostility towards his parents plays a central role in his suicide attempts. The attempt is usually made in his home or school and is really a cry for help. He has every hope and belief that he will be found in time and his life will be saved.

Jacobs describes the adolescent's behavioral problems that progressively lead to self-destruction if any of the stages of adaptive techniques are unsuccessful. The first approach to his problems in the family is *rebellion* against what he feels are unfair demands and disciplines used by parents to control his behavior. The youth responds to the unreasonable demands of his parents with *disobedience and sassiness.* When this leads to further estrangements and feelings of being misunderstood, he may *withdraw into himself,* become gloomy and refuse to talk. This may lead to further alienation until he feels that his only way of coping with this problem is to withdraw completely by *running away from home.*

When there is complete lack of communication in the home between parents and teenagers, the decision to run away from home is getting to be more and more common-place. This method of trying to cope with the problem of conflict with parents has been stimulated by the hippie movement. The hippie center entices the youth in the belief that it is a haven of love and friendship, but it often turns out to be a den of delinquency, of destruction of self-respect, health, and even of life itself.

The results of running away can be tragic in other ways. Hitchhiking, often used as a means of leaving home, often results in dangerous consequences and even death. There are always certain characters on the look-out for despondent or even adventurous youths seeking a ride from any stranger who is willing to pick them up. The young person may be physically attacked, robbed, sexually molested, or even murdered. A parent notifies the police that his son or daughter is missing and he may never see his child again. At a later time the dead body may be found in some isolated place.

The youth finds that these methods he used in an effort to try to solve his problems are usually not constructive and often lead him into greater difficulties. When problems begin to pile up in number and extent, in a sequential order that leads to a process of progressive social isolation, until he feels there is no way out of his predicament, he may resort to attempted suicide as an attention-getting device. When that fails to alert his parents of his need for understanding and help, he may take the final step to end his life.

Broken Homes and Stepparents

Parents who do not get along with each other may be too preoccupied with their own problems to pay much attention to their children. Working parents may be too busy with their business or personal interests to involve themselves with their children. If there is conflict between mother and daughter the girl has no one to confide in. When she gets into trouble she is afraid to tell her mother and may become desperate about her situation in school or in social situations.

Premature loss of a parent through death places the child in a quasi-spouse relationship with the remaining parent. Five times as many adolescents attempted suicide in homes where one parent died or left during the previous year.

Divorce and remarriage often results in conflict with stepparents. In a remarriage, the children must come along as a part of the packaged deal. If there is a teenager in the family, the stepparent may have no concept at all how to deal with the young person and may completely resent having him around. The boy may be jealous of the man who is taking his mother away from him. The stepfather may resent any time or money spent on the youth. Because it is a new marriage he wants his bride for himself and he desires to detach her children from her. Sometimes the daughter may have some romantic fantasies about her new father, but more often he may make advances to her and cause her to run away from a frightening situation.

A stepfather may also try to discipline these young people by physical punishment instead of respecting their age and talking things over with them in a friendly, fatherly way. The mother begins to feel guilty about her child's unhappiness but is afraid to interfere because she does not want to bring conflict into a new marriage.

Overly strict parents who have no understanding of the emotional and social needs of children are unreasonable in some of their disciplinary demands. They may insist upon choosing all their children's friends at a time when peer relations and peer loyalties supercede family loyalties. When a girl is alienated from her family, the need to confide in her "best friend" is vital. She may resort to the most extreme kind of behavior in order to communicate with her friends. Such a youth is subject to greater influence of peers when it comes to "ditching" school, smoking, taking drugs, drinking alcohol, stealing from stores, and experimenting with sex, often in ignorance of the consequences of such conduct.

To help keep the family together, parents need to spend more time in sharing family affairs with their children, in making them participating members of the family who discuss problems and make decisions about family affairs, about buying a car or furniture for the home, and about the duties and responsibilities of every member in the daily routines of the home. They should understand what is going on in the father's job or business and in the financial functioning of the home.

Parents must give their children feelings of self-esteem and encouragement. There must be a democratic climate in the home with open discussion. Whan a problem arises it must be dealt with and settled without bringing up past mistakes again and again. American children must be allowed to express their feelings and ideas freely if there is to be real communication and understanding between the generations.

The influence of the culture and the country is shown in the child's behavior. The need to express feelings and emotions is indicated in suicide rates. In Denmark and Sweden the suicide rate for adolescents is twice that of the United States. In those countries the child must control his emotions, do his best in achievement, refrain from crying if he is a boy, otherwise he is hurting Mama and is considered unlovable. There the parents create highly guilt-conscious, aggression-inhibited, dependent behavior. But in Norway, the suicide rate is only one third of that found in Denmark. The child in Norway is not required to measure up in achievement and is allowed to express aggression toward his environment (Henden, 1964).

Pressure to Achieve

The pressure of parents for successful achievement may cause much conflict between parents and teenagers. This may occur in homes where the parents have themselves achieved high scholastic success and the child is afraid he can not meet with the high expectation of his brilliant, well-educated parents, so he does not try at all. On the other hand, the parents who were poor in school or did not have the opportunity for higher education, expect to make up for their failure through their child's success so they can say with pride, "This is my son the doctor." But their son may be more interested in art, or music, or drama. He may prefer to be a car mechanic and spend countless hours working on his car. Today's youth want to "do their own thing," follow their own interests, and live their own lives. A child is not a possession – he is a person in his own right. He should be helped and encouraged in his studies, but he should not be pressured or rejected if he does not measure up in his schoolwork. However, parents should seek the cause of his lack of interest or achievement.

Also, often the school curriculum is not suited to the fast-moving needs and interests of today's world. It fails to prepare our youth for employment at an occupation that interests them and that will help them become independent, self-supporting adults. Human beings have a deep sense of curiosity and educators should find constructive ways to satisfy the normal need to know and try to find out about the world we live in.

Causes: Drugs and Death

The mob psychology of the rock music culture and its hypnotic influence on the lonely and depressed youth may lead him into drugs that finally destroy him. "Feeling helpless and betrayed, huddled together, thousands of ordinary kids are a set-up for the pusher" (Goldman, 1970). These depressed and apathetic kids, addicted not to drugs but to dreams, are reckless about dropping, popping, or smoking anything that promises a momentary high. Those who do achieve sudden fame, like Jim Hendrix and Janis Joplin, become so overwhelmed when their stardom fades into the morning of reality, they cannot face the dawn of everyday mediocrity and must continue the dream of greatness into a life that is "out of this world." Sudden suicide is the answer for them and their example may bring many followers.

The pressure of peers and the need to belong and be part of the crowd may make it difficult to resist trying, "just once," to take a pill or smoke pot, until the youth may become lost in drug addiction of all kinds. From drugs to death by suicide may be the final outcome.

Broken Romance

As the adolescent reaches outward to find himself socially, his relationship with members of the opposite sex becomes vital. It is of the utmost importance in serving the need for a close contact with another person and gaining a self image as a valued and wanted person. It is a normal opportunity for sharing thoughts and feelings, hopes and aspirations, and in many cases close physical relationships. The trend toward separation from family and closeness to a friend of the opposite sex, leading to romance and love, is the natural developmental step for every young person.

To many an indiscriminate youth, any member of the opposite sex seems desirable. Recognition by such an individual is a sign, in their opinion, of personal worth and attractiveness. A seemingly insurmountable obstacle to adjustment is too early or late sexual maturation. Body image is vitally important to the teenager. To be a tall girl or short boy may be deeply disturbing. To be popular is to be valued and loved. Self-esteem and a self-image of being loved and wanted can influence a boy or girl to do anything to keep the relationship intact. This is especially true if he is rejected or undervalued in his own home and by his own family.

He is reaching out for a lifeline to a new relationship as well as for escape from an intolerable home situation. She is also dreaming of love, marriage, independence, and a home of her own. How beautiful the future looks to her. Perhaps he is just dreaming of the need to prove his manliness, to build up his image as a Don Juan, a lover. His physical need for sex is all he seems to be concerned with. Her desire to please him is all that matters in the entire world. Also, they may both need physical closeness to make up for what they failed to receive at home. They need each other — they want each other. It is all they have and suddenly it represents their whole world.

A broken romance, due to some minor quarrel, may be powerful enough to make them feel that their entire world has fallen apart. When the need for such alliance becomes greater, because it also represents a need for escape from an intolerable home situation, a broken romance, especially if it follows unexpected pregnancy, can be catastrophic and may be the immediate precipating cause of attempted suicide by the girl.

Or should pregnancy happen to be the outcome of what to them was something they really did not clearly understand, in the first place, both young people may be utterly overwhelmed and helpless by the gravity of the situation. In their minds, suicide may be the only way out.

A broken romance can lead to suicide if it is the only meaningful relationship in the life of the adolescent. But where there is good family rapport, the youth can confide in parents and get help and reassurance.

Suicide and Pregnancy

Bryant (1971) quotes public health social worker, Audrey Weum who says, "Unwanted pregnancy is a symptom of underlying difficulty. An unmarried girl may unconsciously seek to have a baby because she has nothing else to love. Maybe she is competing with her mother or is unsure of her own sexual identity and is trying to prove her own femininity."

"One prevalent symptom of adolescent disturbance is the high rate of suicide attempts among teenage girls. These girls are often the victims of chaotic, disrupted families, condemnation, and isolation" (Schrut, 1968). The deteriorating home environment, often supplemented with rejection by boyfriends with whom the girl has become sexually involved, was a common element in suicide attempts.

Pregnancy among teenage girls 17 years old or younger, is especially likely to cause difficulty for the girl and those associated with her. Gabrielson, Klerman, Currie, Tyler, and Jekel, (1970) studied attempted suicide in pregnant girls 17 years old and younger, who had attempted suicide after delivery, during 1959-1960. This was before the existence of programs for teenage mothers, which today include unified medical care, social services, and special educational provisions. Increased suicide attempts were made by Catholics, unmarried girls, and those who suffered from complications of pregnancy and venereal disease, and who came from homes that were above the poverty level. Those who attempt suicide represent a disturbed population, a high rate of venereal disease, often associated with promiscuity, and a history of emotional illness (Gabrielson et al., 1970). This report suggests that suicide is a significant risk in the post partum period. It indicates the need for increased concern with the psychological and emotional needs of the pregnant, unmarried, adolescent girl during pregnancy and for several years after delivery.

Such mothers should be followed up later in order to help them cope with their physical, emotional, and social environment and thus reduce the number of self-destructive attempts. They should be treated with care, consideration, and empathy. They need a mature friend to whom they can turn for advice and guidance.

Mobility Contributes to Isolation

Mobility contributes to the adolescent's sense of isolation and loneliness. When he has to move from place to place, due to changes in parental separation or geographical transfers in employment, the youth has to start all over again in making social and school adjustments. Since he depends a great deal on his peer relationships, it is difficult for him to leave his friends behind and become a stranger in a new social environment, where others have their friends and cliques and do not always reach out to the new student or neighbor.

If the adolescent can turn to his family for support, he does not feel alone. But if he is already alienated from his family, separation from his friends increases his feelings of loneliness and frustration. He has no one to turn to with whom he can share his sorrows and express his feelings.

The school environment offers a social situation where the adolescent has the opportunity to communicate with his peers, and to share his thoughts and feelings with friends of the same and of the opposite sex. Being expelled from school or sent to juvenile hall, or being hospitalized because of attempted suicide, further contributes to his lack of self-esteem and to his social isolation.

Clues to Thoughts of Suicide

How can we tell whether an adolescent is contemplating suicide? What are the clues in his talk and behavior that hint at his thoughts of taking his own life? The adolescent's self-image is a fragile thing based on his treatment by family and friends. If he feels that he is a failure in school, unloved by friends and family, his low self-esteem makes him want to turn his hostility inward and kill the "bad in me." In a way, he is also flirting with death as a game, a test to see whether he will live or die. Let the gods decide! (Mattsson, 1969).

Dr. Shneidman says that most would-be suicides are ambivalent. They wish to live and wish to die at the same time. They want to be rescued, to come through the trial by fire, to have a magical outcome. If no help comes they will usually try again.

The combination of many overwhelming external and internal factors pile up in serious sequence and impinge upon the youth, until he feels completely alienated from society, alone, and without any constructive way to resolve his problems. Cornered in a crisis that has reached the stage of helplessness and hopelessness, the attempt at suicide is his last cry for help. Should this method fail to reach the significant others, his final answer may be suicide.

Adolescent suicide may also be caused by a long-standing and serious illness that has become unbearable and whose outlook is hopeless.

Early warning signs can be detected in the youth's behavior and efforts to communicate his distress and disturbance. Change in his conduct should be carefully observed. Emotionally ill persons turn first and most often to their physician, next to their psychologist and psychiatrist. A youth contemplating suicide will probably seek medical aid for functional, physical complaints not indicating a specific diagnosis. He may express such hypochondrical symptoms as unusual heart beat or pulse rate, skin conditions, or sexual changes on puberty (Ross, 1966).

The doctor must realize that there are emergency mental health problems where life is at stake. The person contemplating suicide needs immediate help. The patient is in some kind of critical impasse from which he yearns to be rescued but may be unaware of any source where he can secure help. His problems may have medical, psychological, sociological, or spiritual roots and recognizing the clue that is a cry for help may save a life and lead to the professional help he needs.

In his conversation with the doctor the youth may reflect bizarre sadistic thoughts and acts, a depressed mood, and serious thoughts about taking his own life. He may reveal deep involvement with habit forming drugs, beset by extreme family conflict, school expulsion, or rejection by his best girlfriend (Mattsson, 1967).

Fear that his patient may take his own life often creates great anxiety in the physician and he may want to hospitalize the patient in order to feel assured that the patient will be safe. But the doctor's withdrawal of emotional support when it is most needed may make the patient feel that he is again being rejected by an authoritative figure, just as he feels he has been rejected by all other significant persons in his life. This abnegation of the doctor's responsibility may actually cause the patient to attempt suicide because his doctor has also let him down (Rosenbaum, 1965). The patient needs an opportunity to talk with a sympathetic person so that he can turn his rage into words.

What is in the mind of the suicide-prone patient? The doctor should be alerted to such warning signs of major emotional disturbance as sudden, unduly troubled, withdrawn behavior, or uncontrolled conduct, such as temper tantrums, defiance, destructiveness, and assualt.

An adolescent's suicide intent may be indicated by depression and withdrawal, loss of initiative and motivation, drop in academic performance, complaints of loneliness, sadness, crying, diminished motor activity, loss of appetite, sleep disturbance, and suicidal threats (Mattsson, 1969).

He may suddenly give away a cherished possession, abandon a favorite hobby, or draw up a will. He may state verbally or in writing that he is planning to end it all. He wears a somatic mask of depression and an averted gaze. He may have mood changes expressing despondency, hopelessness, and apathy. He complains that things are different, that something is wrong in his world, in his bodily functions — that he is always tired, is afraid that he must have a dreadful disease, and he has difficulty falling asleep. He is losing weight, cannot eat, and drinks too much; or he may find solice in eating too much (Ross, 1966).

An adolescent who has or thinks he has an incurable illness is a high risk and must be watched and helped to deal with his problem in a constructive way.

Most completed suicides occur within three months after improvement sets in, when the patient has more energy to express his underlying suicidal impulse in action; whereas when he was in the depths of despair and apathy he was unable to do it.

WAYS USED IN SELF-DESTRUCTION

Clear and definite plans for self-destruction are danger signs that should alert us to take preventive measures at once. People who seriously think of taking their own lives have some specific means at hand for carrying out their objective. The plan is clear and the means are available to them when they are ready to take the final step. Pills have been collected — drugs are at hand — guns are loaded. Ropes are ready for hanging. It is now only a matter of taking the final step. Or the final decision may depend upon a popular place where others have taken their lives. Let the world know and feel guilty!

The contagiousness of suicide at certain places all over the world, usually spots of great heights, such as the Eiffel Tower, the Golden Gate Bridge, and the Empire State Building, have an almost magnetic suggestive attraction for those comtemplating suicide. It is the last cry for help. If the crowd yells, "Jump," you know that no one cares. All hope is gone. But should even one person show love and concern, there is still a chance to be saved. "No one will die by his own hand if someone invites him to live," says Dr. Stainbrook.

An analysis of suicide notes should prove helpful in gaining a better understanding of those young people who feel driven to attempt to kill themselves. Jacobs analyzed the contents of suicide notes left by some of the adolescents before attempting to take their own lives. The notes indicate that every person who attempts suicide feels the need to defend such immoral conduct, for the ethics of our times consider suicide, or self murder, as wrong and unacceptable by society.

Only about one third of the suiciders leave notes. In his note the youth tries to absolve his guilt by explaining that the situation was not of his making; that he tried to cope with his probelms, but found it impossible to do so. He rebukes society for judging him and telling him how to conduct his life, that he had no choice but to withdraw from a life where there was too much competition and trouble, with extenuating circumstances beyond his control. He cites a long history of problems that escalated, until death was considered the only solution, in a world where he never really found out what love was. He begs to be forgiven, but assures everyone that he knows what he is doing and why he is doing it.

SUICIDE RATES AMONG ADOLESCENTS

Suicide among young people is a serious problem in our social world today. The increasingly high suicide rates among adolescents is an index of their emotionally disturbing cultural environment. The rate in young people thirteen to nineteen rises with advancing age, making suicide one of the greatest causes of death among teenagers. Although the rate varies from year to year and place to place, it continues to rise alarmingly in the United States and abroad. In recent years, suicide has ranked third, fourth, or fifth as the cause of death in this age group. "It is the first leading cause of unnecessary and stigmatizing death" (Suicide in Youth, 1972).

The suicide rate for adolescent boys has always been higher than for girls, but in recent years the comparative rate for girls is rapidly increasing. "In Los Angeles County, the rate for girls increased 200-fold from 1969 to 1972, for ages fifteen to nineteen. Los Angeles is usually ahead of the rest of the country on suicide rates" (Litman, 1972).

In this age group, females outnumber males in their suicide attempts, but more males than females complete the act of killing themselves. Although 90 percent of the suicide attempts were made by girls, two and one half times as many boys as girls completed the suicide attempt (Glaser, 1970).

Dr. Mattsson (1969) studied 75 adolescents who had attempted suicide. The girls outnumbered the boys three to one in their attempts, but three boys for every one girl completed the suicide act.

"These girls generally fail in their suicide attempts, perhaps because their wish to die is ambivalent and because a sense of irreconcilable isolation and despair plays a smaller role than in older groups and in men" (Mattsson, 1969). The males were depressed while the females were hysterical, more manipulative, and less premeditated.

Methods Used in Attempted Suicides

What methods do adolescents use in their attempts to take their own lives? In almost 100 percent of the cases the girls used drugs, but the boys often used more violent methods. The boys used firearms and explosives, hanging, and drugs. Some of the leading drugs used by both sexes were a large number of aspirins, barbiturates, and tranquilizers. Other methods used included drinking bleach, inhaling natural gas, slashing their wrists, or intentionally crashing the car while driving. Some of the adolescents wanted their suicide to look like an accident. Drag racing, chicken games, and Russian roulette, may be suicide attempts in disguise (Jacobziner, 1964).

Of course, those who attempted suicide as a cry for help with the hope of being saved in time, used methods that were not immediately fatal. Sometimes, however, their hope of being found and rescued was unfulfilled and they died. Almost all those who attempted suicide desperately wanted to live. Narcotic addicts commit suicide twenty to fifty times as often as others. LSD can produce a psychosis in almost anyone, and marijuana can cause a state of panic in persons who smoke it.

The greatest number of attempts are made in spring, from April through June.

FAMILY HISTORY OF SUICIDES

Do suicides run in families? Is suicide contagious? A death in any family affects the lives, the thoughts, feelings, and actions of all its members. When it is a self-inflicted death, it can have a tremendously traumatic effect on the future feelings and behavior of all the surviving members and friends of the family.

Parental examples as a way of life may also be a way of death. In families where a parent, relative, or friend has used suicide as a method of meeting unfortunate situations, the adolescent may follow in his father's footsteps to self-destruction.

Thus, a way of life and a way of death, too, may be absorbed by the child from the family pattern of living and of dealing with problems. To have a parent commit suicide is perhaps one of the most traumatic experience a child can ever face. It will effect his entire life and may serve as an example to follow as a way of dealing with his own problems. The surviving children of suicide victims often require mental health care, and the far-reaching effects of family grief caused by an untimely, preventable death can only be surmised.

The father of John Berryman shot himself outside his son's bedroom window when the poet was twelve years old. John Berryman, Pulitzer Prize winner, professor at the University of Minnesota, father of three children, who won a national award in 1968 for his book of poetry centered on his father's suicide, entitled, *His Toy, His Dream, His Rest,* the theme of which was the suicide of his father, also followed his father's way to death by jumping to his own death from a bridge into the Mississippi River, when he was 57 years old. This was 45 years after he had witnessed his own father's suicide. Consciously or unconsciously, such experiences remain forever a part of a child's life and affect his future feelings, thoughts, and actions.

The Attitudes of Survivors in Family

The suicide of an individual hangs over the head of the members of his family like the sword of Damocles. A family member may have feelings of guilt and grief without really knowing or understanding the real cause of the suicide. If the relationship was distorted, the guilt feelings may result in feelings of depression and emptiness and persist for many years, changing the survivor's entire future, until he takes his own life, so that one suicide follows another. This may happen on the anniversary of the death or at a time of great stress and conflict.

A child who has witnessed his parent's suicide may repress the entire thing but will unconsciously be influenced by the thought and image until he is forced to bring it into consciousness in order to deal with it in its true perspective.

Many children will develop the most grotesque and distorted notions about a parent who had committed suicide. They may blame themselves by thinking they cost too much money to be supported, that they made too much noise, they disobeyed their parents, they failed in school, or other insignificant incidents that really had nothing to do with the actual cause.

When a parent does commit suicide it is important not to hide the skeleton in the family closet, but to talk to the child about it, and to explain clearly and concretely what happened and why the person took his own life. The child should be told that it was not his fault, that he was not to feel blamed, and that the parent did not know a better way to solve his problem. Discussions should follow, whether with parents, physician, or other therapists, explaining why people try to take their own life. Suggestions should be made of better ways to try to solve problems, and where to seek help when in distress.

The explanations should neither blame nor praise the dead parent. An effort should be made to understand the cause of the suicide, explain this to the child, and talk about better ways of dealing with problems, with the conclusion that there is a better way to solve them than through death.

Suicidal acts are found to create many problems among the surviving members of the family. Those whose lives are later affected run into millions. Skeletons in closets of survivors show high morbidity and mortality among family members of the suicide, much higher than among other persons (Shneidman, 1972). Some younger children have attempted suicide because of the death or attempted suicide of someone close to them. It may represent their identification with the dead person and the wish to rejoin him — a rebirth fantasy, to start over again and reunite with the mother (Furst and Ostrow, 1965).

Patients with a family history of suicide attempts or actual suicides should be carefully evaluated. Troubled adolescents with such a background represent a serious risk.

"Psychic contagion" from experiences with suicide or suicidal attempts in the family or immediate environment within the recent past may be precipitating factors in an adolescent's suicide. Teicher (1970) found that 40 percent of adolescents who had attempted suicide had a parent, relative, or close friend who had attempted suicide. In addition, 72 percent had one or more natural parents absent from the home through divorce, separation, or death, while 84 percent of those with stepfathers felt they were contending with an unwanted stepparent.

When a parent is absent from the home for long periods of time, the young child or adolescent feels he has been betrayed and deserted. The child needs his parent and is dependent upon him. He cannot face the fact that his parents are at fault in their treatment of him; instead, he represses and denies these facts and blames himself for the separation. He prefers to consider himself bad rather than to acknowledge the badness of his parents. When he reaches late adolescence, much of the hostility directed toward his parents it turned upon himself leading to feelings of depression and sometimes to suicide.

When a parent has been lost through suicide, the traumatic

effects of such a death, together with the events that preceded it, may contribute to the child's maladjustment in later life. Such experiences have been found in the history of institutionalized patients.

The adolescent needs the guidance of both his parents for his emotional and intellectual development, as he reaches out towards his future of self-dependence and adult responsibility. When the surviving parent becomes emotionally dependent on the adolescent, he may later find it difficult to make a normal separation from the dependent parent (Hilgard, 1961).

Blaming a Child for a Parent's Suicide

A parent may provoke a great deal of guilt in his child if he commits suicide immediately after he has accused his children of making him want to die. If the father takes his own life while the child is having a severe battle with his mother, the child may view the father's death as a "flight from the enemy, and his father as a deserter" (Markowitz, 1969).

The surviving parent may deny his own responsibility for the death and put the blame on the child. The entire family may be made to feel that they were responsible for the death by causing it indirectly, or by failing to stop it. They may then build up the legend of what a wonderful man the father was and deny the death as a suicide, not telling the children the true cause of death, but blaming it on some other cause. No one should be blamed for the voluntary suicide of another person. This is especially true about blaming children for the suicide of parents (Markowitz, 1969).

How long should a child mourn? Children have their own ways of expressing grief and bereavement. In the case of a parental suicide, if the grief and mourning is overextended, it can make the youth feel guilty and responsible for the death, and make it a traumatic experience for the rest of his life. Even if the parent took his own life because the conduct of his child was very disturbing to him, the youth must not be blamed. Such an act on the part of a parent is hostile and hurtful and represents his need to dominate and control others.

Every child must be accepted and respected as a person in his own right. He is not a possession of his parents. A parent who threatens to kill himself if his child does not conform to his wishes deprives his child of the right to be a person. We can only teach a child a way of life by the example we set in our daily life. Every experience the child has should be a step towards his growth in self-dependence and responsibility, until he is on his own, and is responsible to himself. Every culture has some rites through which the adolescent is accepted into adulthood and becomes responsible for himself, and for his own conduct.

A parent who takes his own life is a poor example to his child. The youth should clearly be told that he is not responsible for his father's behavior; that his father's method of dealing with a problem was not constructive and served no useful purpose. He can feel sorry, but must not be made to feel guilty about what happened. The youth's grief and mourning should be similar to that of anyone else who has lost a parent in death and has learned to accept the separation as a reality.

In every home where there has been a suicide, instead of hiding the fact in the family closet, the entire problem of dealing with the meaning of suicide should be given serious professional attention. The surviving members should be made to understand, that in practically all cases, suicide is not a mature answer to the solution of a personal problem. The causes of the suicide should be clearly and honestly analyzed and discussed. The family should then be made to understand the traumatic effect it could have upon them and they should definitely be influenced against such a procedure at any time in their lives, regardless of the circumstances. They should be trained in what to do and where to call in case such a temptation beckons to them.

PREVENTION OF SUICIDE IN YOUTH

What can be done by parents, doctors, and others to help prevent children and adolescents, who are seriously contemplating suicide, from carrying out such plans? Having someone to turn to who will accept a youth, regardless of the trouble he is in, will definitely help prevent him from taking his own life.

Rapport and communication in the home, between parents and their children of all ages, is basic to the development of stability in the home. It will prevent the alienation, helplessness, and aloneness that corner young people and may cause them to kill themselves. If a girl can come to her mother when she is in trouble; if a boy can talk things over with his father; if both parents are accepting, sympathetic, and helpful without criticizing, blaming, or belittling their offspring, he will not try to run away from life by attempting to snuff it out.

How the Physician Can Help

The physician is in a very important position to help the youth in trouble. Most people planning suicide usually consult their family doctor about vague physical aches and pains. They may seek medical attention within a short time before the suicidal act. The physician has the responsibility of detecting the would-be suicide and taking measures to prevent it. He should not try to avoid the subject but he should confront the patient directly by asking him if he has ever thought of taking his own life.

A patient with a family history of suicide attempts or actual suicide, should be carefully evaluated. If he has made a previous attempt on his life he is a great risk. The physician should talk seriously about the meaning of suicide, try to discuss the youth's problems and what he can do about them, and make him promise to call him, at any time, day or night, if he is under such great stress that he feels compelled to kill himself.

The physician must be aware of the probable common pattern of attempted suicides in adolescents, and the attitudes of non-critical acceptance and openness that will encourage the patient to confide in him. He must be very careful in considering whether he should refer the patient to a psychiatrist or psychologist, without carefully talking it over with the patient and getting him to agree to such help. Otherwise, he may feel that his family doctor, in whom he has trust and confidence, is letting him down and rejecting him.

The doctor must explain that he will stay with him and work with him, but if he wishes, a specialist who is more experienced in emotional problems of youth can be called in and may prove more helpful. However, the choice is up to the youth whether or not he wishes to have such help. If referral would make the youth feel abandoned, his doctor may himself discuss the case with the specialist who could consult with him about the best way to deal with the situation.

Jacobs (1971) concludes that suicidal adolescents usually consult a physician as a potential source of help because they feel more free to confide in and to confess to a doctor. Doctor, teachers, and peers may help prevent suicides. However, therapists are filled with anxiety and fear because of the suicidal risk, not really being able to assess whether the adolescent intends to kill himself or not. There is more to the problem and prevention of suicide than the recognition of the potential suicide. It requires intimate, continuous, and frequent contact between patient, practitioner, and family. The therapist becomes the significant other — accepting, visible, ever accessible, and purposeful (Jacobs, 1971). Meaningful social relationships must be established in order to prevent the adolescent from taking his own life.

DRUG ABUSE

Where the youth is involved in drug abuse, the family physician can offer psychological stability, non-punitive authority, and accurate information about drugs. If he can establish rapport with the patient he can arrange for treatment of drug abuse. This is one of our major problems today. Narcotic addicts commit suicide twenty to fifty times as often as others. LSD can produce a psychosis in almost anyone. Marijuana can cause a state of panic in a person who smokes it. Because a suicide threat is a cry for help, the physician must make the patient feel that something is being done about his problems. Help must be enlisted from family, friends, community resources, psychiatric social workers, religious or ethnic affiliations that will make a patient feel that people do care abour him and are going to accept and help him.

Hospitalization

If it is thought necessary to confine a patient in the hospital, it should not be done without his own permission; otherwise he may feel that his is a hopeless case — that he is being abandoned because his doctor has no faith in him and does not want to take the risk or responsibility for his life.

Suicide prevention in the hospital depends upon the awareness of the hospital personnel in evaluating the patient's attitudes, and in the physical set-up of the hospital to make every possible provision for safety. Hospital staff should be trained to recognize suicide signs in patients. If the patient exhibits severe depression and anxiety, has a low tolerance for pain or discomfort, makes excessive demands and complaints, and seems completely exhausted, both physically and emotionally, the hospital personnel need to be alerted that a suicide attempt is likely. Also, if the patient gets panicky upon anticipation of discharge from the hospital, where he feels protected and cared for, if he complains that he has no place to go to, the hospital staff must deal with the facts and see that constructive plans are made for the patient, upon his leaving the hospital.

The physical set-up of the hospital should include safety opening devices on upper-level windows and screening of stairwells. Drugs and instruments should be locked up. Other possibilities for self-injury should be considered and the patient should be watched and reassured when he becomes anxious and depressed. To have a patient kill himself while he is in the hospital is a serious criticism against the irresponsibility of the hospital management (Shneidman, 1968).

Dr. Howard M. Bogard (1970) says that two thirds of those patients seen in a hospital, following an attempted suicide are not followed up afterwards. After hospitalization for attempted suicide the patient must be followed up and given the therapy he needs. His treatment must also include counseling of his family. The risk is not over after treatment for attempted suicide. Most suicides occur within about three months following the beginning of "improvement," when the individual has the energy to put his morbid thoughts and feelings into effect, warns Dr. Shneidman.

SUICIDE PREVENTION CENTERS

Suicide prevention centers, the first program of its kind in the world, was started in Los Angeles in 1958, by two psychologists, Norman L. Farberow and Edwin S. Shneidman.

The aim of such centers it to give crisis-intervention aid to would-be suicides who phone in their cry for help. There are a number of lay volunteers, such as mature housewives, students, and others whose work is to quickly gauge the caller's life style, his stress at the moment, the seriousness of his intent to kill himself, and the need to give him immediate assistance to prevent him from taking his own life. They try to evaluate the caller's degree of lethality in order to ascertain whether suicide is imminent. They try to learn whether he has specific plans, what method he expects to use, and whether he has the means at hand to immediately carry out his plans.

Individual suicide can be prevented says Dr. Shneidman. The aim of the suicide prevention center is to prevent the caller from killing himself, by throwing a lifeline to him through continuous communication, until immediate medical attention is given him, if the threat is serious. The need for such centers arose because of the great increase in suicide among teenagers. "We are still at a loss to understand why there is such a sudden rise of suicidal acting out of the adolescents. And about all, we still seek an answer to the oscillations between suicide and homicide and their intrinsic relationship to violence in general" (Shneidman, 1967).

All suicide prevention centers do not operate in the same way. Many of them do not only try to answer the cry for help in order to save lives, but they also follow up cases and do research to determine the causes that impel young people to attempt to take their own lives.

Some authorities claim that suicide prevention centers fail to achieve their aims. "There is no evidence that any of some 120 suicide prevention centers established in the United States in the past fifteen years have reduced the suicide rate in the areas that they cover" (Kiev, 1971). Most of the calls are from low suicide risks. High risks are less likely to call.

"Only a miniscule percentage of genuinely potential suicides are ever in contact with these organizations. The acutely suicidal patient is beyond the capacity to mobilize himself to ask for help. Crisis signals must be sought and recognized before it is too late ... Untrained personnel are in no way adequate sources for solace for someone who has renounced hope. Research in depth of the individual and his development must still be our primary concern" (Friedman, 1970).

However, Friedman says that he is not suggesting the abolition of suicide prevention centers, but he feels that there is a need for greater research in this complex problem. In 1968 in search of universal detectors of the potential suicide, he and others organized the Mount Sinai Suicide Research Project at the New York's Mount Sinai Hospital. They studied about 100 suicide attempts. The program consisted of interviews, tests, and developmental histories, education and training of physicians and residents, and lectures on suicide for third and fourth-year medical students.

It is difficult to evaluate the degree to which suicide prevention centers help prevent suicide attempts by those who are determined to take their own lives. However, they must serve some people in trouble just by giving them an opportunity to talk to a sympathetic person and still feel safe by not necessarily revealing their identity, if they do happen to have such a need for privacy. Just to talk to anyone can help break that feeling of isolation and aloneness. With greater research and experience, suicide prevention centers will improve in their methods in trying to help people in distress.

ATTITUDES OF TODAY'S YOUTH

Today more young people are taking their own lives. They are influenced by their singers and leaders whom they follow. They buy their records and identify with their ideas without thought or analysis.

The poet Al Alvarez, in his book, *The Savage God: A Study of Suicide,* (1972), describes his experience, at age thirty, in attempting to take his own life by swallowing a box of sleeping pills. He was found in time, and awoke in the hospital after three days, under medical care there.

He tries in this book to make suicide understandable as a human act. He discusses the need to talk about death and about suicide. The taboo is now lifting and Americans are somewhat more willing to talk about it, he believes. "It is the only dirty little secret left. . . Death and suicide continue to be regarded as hidden subjects."

The combination of many problems Alvarez had to face made him feel that his life felt cluttered up to the point that he could hardly breathe. "You'd never guess the agony of someone who is taking his own life. . . . Those who survive the attempt try to assure themselves that they were not to blame for it." In explaining the meaning of suicide, he says that no single theory will untangle an act as ambiguous and with such complex motives as suicide. "Each of these deaths has its own inner logic and unrepeatable despair."

He discusses his friendship with the poet, Sylvia Plath, who took her own life, although "she had every unconscious expectation of being rescued."

To Alvarez, suicide includes self-destruction activities, such as drink and drugs. "It is a haunted subject, infused with sin, and fear, and death."

ADOLESCENT SUICIDE ATTEMPTS

Problems With Stepparents — Case 1

Life with stepparents is usually more vulnerable than with natural parents, since it starts out with people who have already had traumatic experiences in homes broken by death or divorce It begins with new and uncertain relationships between strangers that may create anxieties, jealousies, and insecurities.

A young child may be quiet, somewhat withdrawn, but cooperative at home, so that when he reaches adolescence and starts to act out, the parents are confused and do not understand what has suddenly come over their child. The teenage stepchild who keeps to herself and does not become a participating member of a close-knit family, will reach out more readily to her peers and adopt their ways without thought or discernment. The need to belong is so great that nothing else matters. She may reject her family entirely, to their amazement and chagrin.

A stepchild does not feel as secure and loved as a natural child.

She may feel unwanted but accepted as a part of the packaged deal in a second marriage where the children must be included. There may be mutual resentments at the need to have to live together, so problems with stepparents increase with adolescence when the child is reaching toward independence anyway.

One Sunday morning fifteen-year-old May ran away from home leaving a note that she was not happy at home with her stepfather and was going to find her real father who lived in another city. Her parents were very much disturbed and spent the entire day looking for her. She was finally found at the home of a girlfriend. May was grounded and not permitted to have anything to do with the girl who had influenced her to run away. The parents brought her to me for counseling.

I found May to be an attractive, physically developed adolescent girl with dark curly hair and big brown eyes. She was cooperative and interested in some of the clinical tests given her. She seemed to be a typical boy-crazy teenager who had fantasies and romantic ideas of love and marriage. When asked to draw a family, May drew the picture of a young mother sitting on a chair holding a baby on her lap, while a smiling husband stood close by protectively. May's Rorschach suggested that she lacked conscious control over her feelings and impulses.

Psychologist: May, why did you run away from home?

May: I ran away because I was unhappy at home. I have been getting into all kinds of trouble. I was caught shop-lifting a blouse. I really didn't need it but I thought it would be fun. My girlfriend dared me to do it. But I'm not going to steal anymore. Now I have a police record. I ditched school with two other girls. I felt so free. I used to smoke seven or eight cigarettes a day. My parents didn't know about it. It's against school laws to smoke. My dad forbids me to smoke again.

I just hate living at home. I dislike my stepdad very much. I remember disliking him when I was little, although he was good to me and bought me things. But I didn't feel loved. I want to live with my real dad. I just want to see my real dad. I was going to try to find him. He lives in another city but I don't know where. My real dad is like part of me. He helped create me.

I've just kept everything inside me — my feelings toward my

stepdad. He disagrees with everything I do. I got busted in school for smoking. My dad smokes all the time, so why can't I smoke when I want a cigarette? At home I get bad vibrations. The atmosphere is always disturbing. I feel like splitting — leaving home for good.

I was drinking last night and got busted from the people where I was baby-sitting. Their liquor that I drank didn't seem so strong. I had called in my girlfriend to stay with me where I was baby-sitting. She found some vodka in their bar and fixed me a drink. She didn't take a drink herself. I drank it without knowing how much vodka was in the glass. I was really drunk — throwing up — gingerale and vodka. I was really lightheaded — felt my legs were falling in. I burnt the top of the bar with my cigarettes. The matches caught on fire. The house was filled with smoke. The children were asleep. I threw up in the car and house on the way home. What's good for a hangover?

Psychologist: How do you feel about it now?

May: Pretty bad. Not obeying my parents. Not watching the kids where I was baby-sitting. I had no right to invite my friend into their house without the people's permission. I had no right to take their liqour and cigarettes. Now my dad has forbidden me to see my friends and grounded me. My life — I really feel like killing myself. All I can do is clean the house and do my homework. I can't even go to the shopping center alone. I'm getting all mixed up. I'll kill myself!

Everything is going around in school — pills — acid — lots of people are taking it. They smoke weed — take acid — hashish. My friends have taken Nodoz to see if it did anything. It's just a fake life — it's not reality. God, I feel that I need a smoke — nothing to do most of the time.

I was talking to my school counselor today. I'm doing all sorts of crazy and dangerous things. I am trying to get into trouble so I won't have to live at home anymore. I haven't been happy at home. All I do is keep getting into trouble so I won't have to live at home. I do things when they aren't around to blame me. If I do it — like drinking — it's because I want to do it. But I really don't want to have a bad record.

I don't care about my parents. My stepdad is all screwed up. I can still talk to Mom, but it just hurts me to talk to her. She tells me how much I hurt her. I dig on Mom. I really care about my Mom. But I really don't feel like bothering trying to understand my parents.

It's so much of a hassle living there. Whenever I get home I get all down. It's really hard for me to talk to my dad. I was asleep already when Dad woke me up and said that he would take me to Juvenile Hall in the morning because I talked with Bob. Hell, that really triggered me off. Bob came over where I was babysitting. I'm a virgin. We were just rapping. We got together as boyfriend and girlfriend.

I got caught for leaving campus at school, so I got busted. Making decisions you really have to think a lot about it. Dad is hassling me about everything I do. My school counselor told me to think of Dad as a human being, not as a father. I was afraid of him when he threatened to take me to Juvenile Hall. He wants them to frighten me. But I already have a record for shoplifting. I will just be getting in more trouble for nothing and my own parents will be the cause of it.

Psychologist: Why do you think he threatens you?

May: To try to get me to do good.

Psychologist: You do agree that he is out for your welfare — but he doesn't know how to do it?

May: I guess — but I just don't dig him.

Psychologist: You say that if you can't live with your real dad you would like to live in a foster home. Do you really feel that if you were in a foster home you wouldn't do those wrong things?

May: I do it to escape my problems. I would be much happier away from home.

Psychologist: What are some of the things your father does that upsets you?

May: He should stop hassling me about everything. He always wakes me up to yell at me. Dad gets home at about six o'clock. Every day there is always something wrong about something.

I'm so sick of taking pills. I took them for a week. You just pop a pill into your mouth. Problems at home are affecting my grades in school. Talking to my parents — getting into trouble. My friends are problems. They're not liked by my parents. I don't think of school work because of what happened. I guess I ditch a lot in school. I ditch P.E. I've asked my father to give me another chance. I've asked him a number of times and have just blown it. So he doesn't trust me anymore. In the morning, when I go to school, he watches to see if I get on the bus and don't go over to my girlfriend. At home I'm like a prisoner. I can't go anyplace. I can't see my friends. I can't use the phone or answer it if my friends call. I can't stand this anymore. I'll kill myself!

May's father, who had not the slightest idea of how to handle this girl, wanted the psychologist to give him an instant solution to the problem. Of course, this could not be done, so the father sent her away to an expensive boarding school, which he really could not afford. This suggests that the child was right about her feelings that she was not really loved, although she was given things, but was more like a boarder than a participating member of the family.

Problems with Stepparents — Case 2

Nancy, who was married at age 18 and later took her seven-year-old son to me for therapy because he was having emotional problems in school, remembers the following experience with her stepfather:

Nancy: I was terribly afraid of my stepfather. I had no privacy at all. He would go through my dresser drawers and all my things. When I was taking a shower he would walk into the bathroom and say he thought it was my mother. He would grab me and take hold of my breast.

Once, when I was twelve or thirteen years old, my stepfather accused me of being what he called a "loose girl." I was not even mature and had no interest in boys at that time. I got very angry at him and slapped him. He slapped me back with all his strength. I fell down and blacked out. When I came to, my ears were ringing and I could not see clearly. It seemed that I was in a tunnel. I tried to call a doctor I knew, but he ripped the phone out of the wall. I was hysterical. We were living in a trailer. My parents left to go to the market. They locked the trailer from the outside. I had no phone and no way to get out.

I went to the medicine cabinet and took all the pills that were there — vitamins — aspirins — and anything else I could find there, thinking they would be back in an hour. I would scare them and make them feel sorry about the way they treated me, and I would be saved. But I almost didn't make it, because they came back in two and a half hours.

I felt awful sick and told them what I had done. They didn't believe me until they went to the medicine cabinet and saw that the pills were gone. They took me to the hospital where my stomach was pumped. I was put in a psychiatric ward for 72 hours, because that was the law. There were a lot of really deranged people in that ward.

After I got out of the hospital I took the bus home. My parents didn't want me anymore. I found my clothes on the outside of the trailer. I called a friend, a fine older woman who always helped people, and I stayed with her for a few weeks. Then I got a job doing housework and found a room in a building where there were mostly old poor people. We had to share the refrigerator and the bathroom.

At night I was afraid to go to the bathroom because I didn't know the people there. I kept on going to high school. I had to buy some school supplies. I had no money to buy some food. I called my mother and asked her if I could borrow a dollar until I got paid for my job. She said she didn't have any money.

I called my grandmother who lived in another city. She was a very sick woman but very good to me at all times. I worked to earn the bus fare to her home. I hadn't eaten for several days and only had six cents, so I bought a package of chewing gum and used my last cent to weigh myself. When I got to my grandmother's house I slept for two whole days, then I was able to eat something. She took care of me, was very protective, and I continued to live with my grandmother and kept on with my high school education until I graduated from high school.

This is an example of a teenage girl who attempted suicide in order to make her parents feel sorry for the way they had treated her. She expected to be found in an hour and be revived. But she almost lost her life because the parents returned much later. Her stepfather, instead of feeling guilty, became very angry and after taking her to the hospital did not permit the child to live with them but turned her out to fend for herself. The mother was afraid of her husband and did not interfere. Nancy was lucky to have a grandmother to take her into her home and help her. Otherwise this child would finally feel so cornered that she might have seen no other way out of her predicament but to kill herself.

A Suicide Note

Teenagers who become drug addicts may feel that suicide is the only way out of their predicament. Nineteen-year-old Charles, a shoe clerk, who lived with his mother and stepfather, wrote a suicide note before he shot himself. He willed his car, clothing, stereo, etc to his friends. He wrote, "Mom and Dad, the real reason is that I don't know — but I'm sorry that your son turned into an LSD addict. I didn't think it was bad when I was taking it, but I've been getting pretty stoned lately and you just don't know what's real and what isn't real. All I can say I just had to find out for myself . . . Of course grass isn't bad — it's the acid that got me . . . But some things arise in every day living that you just don't know if it's real or really what's happening and you're lost. After you take so much of that stuff, you just don't know where you're at sometimes. You don't know if your reasoning is correct. I have thought it over many times and there really isn't anything to live for. I don't think anyone could convince me there is . . . not me anyway. So I think I'll just close with a blank statement — maybe kind of an idiotic statement, but a lot of things are crazy."

I'm signing off.

Charles

SUMMARY

Authorities disagree about whether or not a child or adolescent is acting out in a rational or irrational manner when he attempts to take his own life.

Suicide is nonexistent in children under five and rare in ages five to nine. Many young children who attempt suicide believe that death is temporary and reversible. Rejection by parents may bring about hopelessness and despair. In an effort to arouse parental concern they attempt suicide.

Adolescents who try to take their own life reflect a long standing history of problems from early childhood, isolation from meaningful social relationships, and failure to cope with the problems that cause their unhappiness. Factors that contribute to isolation and despair are conflict with parents, broken homes due to parental separation, death or divorce, unhappy remarriage of parents, conflict with stepparents, or personal illness.

Pressure from parents to achieve and a school curriculum that is unsuited to the needs, interest, and abilities of the teenager, cause unhappiness and distress. The need to escape from an unhappy home and school situation, and the pressure of peers, may lead the youth into the rock music culture, drugs, and reckless driving that further complicate his life. Broken romances, unwanted pregnancies, and the mobility of parents because of economic conditions, that lead to isolation from friends and schoolmates, may invoke thoughts of suicide in an effort to escape from intolerable situations.

It is important to understand the clues to the adolescent's thoughts of suicide in order to help him deal with his problems and prevent his attempts to take his own life. Most suicides long to be rescued and their attempts are really a cry for help.

The suicide first turns to his physician for help. He may complain about physical disorders, depression, loneliness, sadness, crying, loss of appetite, disturbance of sleep, and suicidal thoughts. Most completed suicides occur within three months of the first attempt, when the person has more energy to carry out his impulse into action.

Suicide rates in young people ages thirteen to nineteen rise with advancing age. Almost 100 percent of the girls who attempt suicide used drugs, while the boys used firearms, explosives, hangings, and drugs.

A history of suicide in the family is traumatic for all its members. It also serves as an example for other members to follow, in an effort to escape from their predicaments. Blaming a child for his parent's suicide may provoke much guilt in him and cause him to take his own life.

Suicide prevention in youth requires rapport and communication in the home, and in some cases help from the physician or psychologist. Suicide prevention centers aim to give crisis-intervention help in order to prevent individuals from killing themselves.

Society's attitudes toward suicide has been influenced by cultural and religious thought, with increasing disapproval against taking one's own life.

REFERENCES

Alvarez, A.: The Savage God: A Study of Suicide. New York, Random House, 1972.

Bogard, H. N.: Follow-up study of suicidal patients seen in emergency room consultation. Am J Psychiat, 126:1017-1020, 1970.

Bryant, P.: Youth clinic handles hush-hush problems. Los Angeles Times, San Fernando Valley Eastern Edition, Section L, October 24, 1971, pp. 1, 6.

Chesser, E.: Living With Suicide. London W1, Hutchinson and Co., 1967.

Farberow, N. L.: Bibliography on Suicide and Suicide Prevention, 1897-1957; 1958-1967. National Institute of Mental Health, Chevy Chase, Md., 1969.

Friedman, P.: Suicide prevention: A medical approach. Medical Tribune, June 22, 1970, p. 10.

Furst, S. S. and Ostrow, M.: The psychodynamics of suicide. Bull N.Y. Acad Med 41:190-204, 1965.

Gabrielson, I. W., Klerman, L. V., Currie, J. B., Tyler, N. C. and Jekel, J. F.: Suicide attempts in a population pregnant as teenagers. Am J Pub Health, 60(12):2289-2301, 1970.

Glaser, K.: Adolescent suicide: Rising problems in many areas laid to stress. Medical Tribune, Aug. 17, 1966, pp. 1, 18.

———: Suicide threats found frequent in very young. Pediatric Herald, Aug.-Sept., 1970, p. 8.

Goldman, A.: Drugs and death in the run-down world of rock music. Life, 69:32-33, 1970.

Grollman, E. A.: Religion and suicide: A study in growth. Arch Foundation Thanatol, 3(2):95-98, 1971.

Hendin, H.: Suicide: In the U.S.A. and in Scandinavia. Pediatric Herald, April, 1964, p. 5.

Hilgard, J. R. et al.: Trauma of parent loss minimized by protective factors. Feelings and Their Medical Significance, 3(6):3, 1961.

Jacobs, J.: Adolescent Suicide. New York, Wiley-Interscience, 1971.

Jacobziner, H.: Accidents and attempted suicide in children and adolescents. Feelings and Their Medical Significance, 6(1):1-4, 1964.

Kiev, A.: Suicide prevention centers fail to reach high risk cases. Roche Reports: Frontiers of Psychiatry, 1(11):3, 1971.

Levine, J. J.: Rapport needed to handle drug abuse by adolescents. Pediatric News, 3(4):3, 60, 1969.

Litman, R. E.: National leap in teen suicides due? Medical World News, 13(12):4, 1972.

Lourie, R. S.: Final decision by suicidal patient may hinge on M.D. Medical World News, Oct. 29, 1965, pp. 118-119.

Markowitz, I.: Parental loss — trauma or relief? Pediatric Digest, Jan., 1969, pp. 26-30.

Masterson, J.: Seek reevaluation of teenage turmoil. Pediatric News, 2(10):33, 44, 1968.

Mattsson, A.: Adolescent suicide. Medical Tribune, Sept. 4, 1967, p. 12.

———: Pediatrician's crucial role is stressed in heading off incipient mental illness. Pediatric Herald, Jan., 1968, p. 6.

———: Youthful suicide symptoms revealed in hospital study. Pediatric Herald, April-May, 1969, p. 6.

Maurer, A.: Adolescent attitudes toward death. J Genet Psychol, 105:75-90, 1964.

Moller, H.: Death: Handling the subject and affected students in the school. In Grollman, E. A. (Ed.): Explaining Death to Children. Boston, Beacon Press, 1967.

Psychiatrist offers explanation of varying rates in Scandinavia. Pediatric Herald, April, 1964, p. 5.

Rosenbaum, M.: Final decision by suicidal patient may hinge on M.D. Medical World News, Oct. 29, 1965, pp. 118-119.

Ross, M.: The practical recognition of depressive and suicidal states. U.S. Navy Medical News Letter, 48(5):4-9, 1966.

Schrut, A.: Suicidal children: Motivation. Pediatric Digest, Nov., 1965, p. 32.

———: Some typical patterns in the behavior and background of adolescent girls who attempt suicide. Am J Psychiat, 125:69-74, 1968.

Seiden, R. H.: Suicide Among Youth: A Review of The Literature, 1900-1967. Chevy Chase, Md.: National Clearing House for Mental Health, 1969.

Shneidman, E. S.: Essays in Self-Destruction. New York, Science House, 1967.

———: Suicide prevention: The hospital role. Hosp Pract, 3(9):56-57, 60-61, 1968.

———: Suicidal acts are found to create large problems among survivor victims. Medical Tribune, April 19, 1972, p. 2.

Snider, A. J.: Expert sees all suicide attempts as genuine. Los Angeles Times, March 24, 1968. p. 5B.

Teicher, J. D.: Adolescent suicides. Medical Tribune, Sept. 4, 1967, p. 12.

———: Suicide in youth. Pediatric Currents. 21(2):9-12, 1972.

Zeligs, M. A.: Friendship and Fractricide: An Analysis of Whittaker Chambers and Alger Hiss. New York, Viking Press, 1967.

Chapter XI

WHEN A PARENT DIES

T HE death of a parent is one of the greatest catastrophes that can befall a child and the death of both parents may be completely devastating to his entire future. The death of the middle-aged parent in a nuclear family of parents and children provokes emotional reactions that can be very traumatic. It has a profound effect on the life of his spouse and children. It brings about family imbalance that requires change and adjustment for everyone.

WHEN A PARENT IS DYING

When a parent is seriously ill or is dying, his spouse and children should be with him. They should all talk together freely and honestly about his illness and his dying, without fear, denial, or avoidance. If the family will openly discuss the approaching death and make each precious moment count, while there is still life, the trauma of the separation will be softened and accepted when the parent finally dies.

Such dialogue will give the entire family comfort and consolation, understanding and reassurance that will be of tremendous value to the dying parent as well as to the surviving spouse and children. Fears, feelings of guilt, anger, and despair can be absolved so that they will not haunt the child later and cause him to become emotionally upset and despondent. It is the unknown that is the most frightening to us. Death stirs children's fantasies with distorting and fearful ideas that could be dispelled through open and honest discussion.

These last days together can be the most enriching experiences of the child's life as he learns the true meaning of his relationship with his parent. Feelings of closeness and love that had never been expressed or understood before, may enrich the entire family and contribute to more mature values and a greater understanding of the meaning of life and death.

They should freely discuss the separation they must now accept, with the appreciation and thanks for the time they did have to share with each other, that will remain in their memories forever and guide their conduct and behavior. The pattern of the parent will be internalized within the child and be a way to light his future life.

Mr. Smith remarked, "Years after my father died, when I had a problem to solve, I asked myself what my father would do in such a case and my conscience gave me the answer."

When the patient is dying, unless he is in severe pain, he should not be drugged. He should have his family around him whether he is in his home or the hospital, until the final moment. This will fulfull his wish to have his family around him so that he will not die alone and deserted. Children will then see the peaceful countenance that comes after the struggle is over, and will remember the parent as a person in quiet repose.

> Death, when unmasked, shows us a friendly face,
> And is a terror only at a distance.
> Goldsmith

Family togetherness when a parent is dying of a fatal illness is vividly described by the wife of a 34 year-old man suffering from leukemia. The patient resented the complete wall of detachment expressed by the doctor and the hospital personnel and told them so. The wife had a bed brought into the room for herself and for fifteen months lived there with her husband. She moved her five children into a nearby apartment house and they all spent much of their time together in the hospital. She made this room a home for the entire family, adding colorful accessories and hanging family pictures on the wall. She even cooked special foods for all of them in an electric appliance. It was a struggle to fight the rigid, authoritarian hospital rules and routines, but in the end, this family profoundly influenced the medical staff in their actions and attitudes by making death and dying a deeply humanizing experience for every person involved in the hospital set-up (Driver, 1973).

Many Families Suffer Parental Loss

Our image of the American family is usually made up of a father, mother, and two or three children. We think of the family broken by death or divorce as the exception, but in reality parental bereavement is normally much more common than we generally realize.

By January 1966, 2,414,000 children under age eighteen, in the United States had lost their fathers. They comprised 71 percent of the 3,400,000 children who had lost one or both parents. Approximately 26.5 percent of the total number had lost their mothers, and 2.5 percent had lost both parents, according to the Social Security administration (Roche Report: Frontiers of Clinical Psychiatry, Oct. 1, 1969).

Divorce may affect very young children and even adolescents in a way similar to that of death. The children may react with depression, loss of appetite and weight, insomnia, nightmares, withdrawal, poor school performance, irritability, temper outbursts, and even suicide attempts (Sugar, 1970; 1972).

AFTER THE PARENT DIES

The child is shocked when his parent dies and he goes through a period of surprise, despair, and denial. He feels completely lost and abandoned. Who will take over his parent's place? Who will care for him? Who will tell him what to do?

"I have no father! I have no father! kept going through my mind, when I saw my father's beautiful, waxen face stilled in death," Rachel recalled many years later.

Some of the child's emotional reactions to the parent's death may include guilt, anger, displaced hostility, fear, a sense of loss, and of normal and abnormal bereavement (Kalish, 1969).

Children respond to the death of a parent in different ways. They may express their grief through aggressiveness, withdrawal, guilt or inward mourning. It is important that the other parent accept the child's way of dealing with the loss and make him feel accepted and loved (Birk, 1966).

When a parent is so overwhelmed with grief and unable to accept the death of the spouse as final, other significant people must help the child deal therapeutically with the loss. Pets can sometimes provide quiet comfort and understanding. The child can express his feelings when he holds his puppy in his arms. The softness and the cuddling evoke the reassurance that was his when he was cuddled in his mother's warm arms. "The child's grief, his tears, his fears, and his feelings of guilt can safely be entrusted to the pet, whose silent, non-demanding acceptance of the child's hidden emotions and his unfailing admiration and love for the child are comforting" (Levinson, 1967).

The elderly have been separated geographically as well as emotionally from their children and grandchildren in many families today, therefore their death does not greatly affect the younger generation. Only in the small number of cases where grandparents are still closely associated with the family are the children more seriously disturbed by their death. However, the nuclear family is more vulnerable and leads to greater trauma and isolation for the survivors when death strikes the middle-aged parent.

In many cases where there has been jealousy and competition between the children, either their ties become closer or their conflicts increase when they lose a parent. If the children have to be separated, placed with relatives or in a foster home, or perhaps adopted, their last link of relationships may be broken, making them feel completely alone in this world.

But in larger families that live together, where there are other significant figures like grandparents, aunts and uncles, who have been close to the child, he still has someone to turn to for comfort and consolation, guidance and advice.

Unfortunately, many families today are not close Mobility contributes to estrangement and leads to separation. We don't have kissing cousins anymore. Often, cousins do not even see each other or know each other. There may be conflicts and jealousies. When a wife cuts her husband off from his family, the children are deprived of relatives to whom they can turn for friendship, understanding, advice, guidance, and comfort. This is true during life as well as during the death of parents. We all need more people than just the immediate family to love and to turn to.

The Circumstance of the Parent's Death

The circumstance of the parent's death is important in its later effect upon the child. Death of parents caused by unexpected disasters, such as tornadoes, floods, and earthquakes, have a shocking effect on the children. In an Iranian earthquake, it was found that those children who had to take over the functions and responsibilities of a dead or injured parent were the first to recover. It was also important to have the children talk about their frightening experiences freely and openly rather than to suppress them and try to forget what happened. Wherever several members survived the disaster, it was found important not to fragment existing family groups but to keep them together when placing them in other homes.

When the death of the parent is caused by a sudden accident, the shock can be overwhelming. If a member of the family indirectly caused the accident, he may never forgive himself. The family may either blame him outright, or they may try to protect him from his feelings of guilt and transfer the blame elsewhere, perhaps on God or fate.

But when the death is a suicide, the entire family may be filled with guilt and shame. An innocent younger child, not understanding the situation at all, may secretly believe that he caused the death, either by wishful thinking or bad conduct. This event may be repressed into his unconscious and later contribute to his emotional disturbance requiring psychotherapy.

If the parent dies of a lingering fatal illness, the child who has been prepared for it may gradually learn to accept his bereavement. But if the illness is hereditary, it will cause him to fear for his own life.

The early death of a parent throws a shadow of sadness on a child. "There may be something in the child or youth that no longer grows, no longer evolves. He has lost the identifying object about which he has learned to mold his growth and behavior. The result may be a defense against the inner loss, an attempt to deny the loss, or to replace the loss" (Kimball, 1971).

Sandra, whose father died suddenly just before she graduated from high school, developed a death phobia. She said, "I cannot stand the concept of becoming nothing... After my dad died, I refused to admit that he was dead. I would talk to him in my mind. It was strange to have somebody that close die... I'm always expecting to die. I feel constantly that I'm coming a minute closer to death" (Missildine, 1971). The death of a parent makes the world seem torn apart. It is never the same again to the child. Joy and laughter does not come easily anymore. Life is serious — values are changed. So many trivial things that seemed important, suddenly become meaningless and unimportant.

The child takes his cue on how to react to the death of his parent by observing how his relatives conduct themselves, and by being told what to do. He must feel that he is a part of the family and participate in all the customs and ceremonies that are part of dealing with the death.

THE EFFECT OF THE DEATH OF
A FATHER ON HIS FAMILY

Whether the parent who dies is the father or the mother, the loss affects the family in a different way. The death of the father uproots the entire family and deprives it of emotional and financial support. A child may feel lost with no father to turn to for guidance and affection, for a masculine model to emulate, a father image to follow. The child needs and wants the discipline that sets limits. It helps him control his impulsive behavior that might lead him into trouble and sorrow. He needs praise and approval from parents, the most significant people in his life, who truly care about him and ecnourage him to strive for personal growth in character and achievement.

The death of his father influences the role the child must play in his family and society. It affects his feelings of security and worth; his self-image and sense of identity. "Who am I?" he asks. "Of what value is my life?" His self-image gives him a sense of worth and of value as a person in a social world. "What are my responsibilities to myself and what do I owe to others?" This image can only be reflected by the way others treat him — in his feelings of dependence or independence, separation or security, love and assurance, or desertion and desolation.

It requires him to make choices and decisions that he would never have to make if he had two parents to guide him, support him, and help him direct his life forward to his own growth and the opportunities open to him. His loss of self-esteem reduces his productivity and creativity.

A child needs his parents at all ages, but the age of the child, the degree of his dependency, and the need for succor and survival make a difference in how much the loss affects his life. His opportunities for parent surrogates, for people to whom he can turn, who care, who truly want him and do not make him feel that he is an unwelcome burden, will lessen the trauma of the loss for the young child.

The younger child feels deprived when he sees that his peers participate in activities that include fathers who take them on trips, go camping together, belong to Boy Scouts and Little League, and in general have a father to turn to for love, companionship, and guidance. His life is definitely affected by the loss and he envies other boys who have a father. He may ask his mother to marry again and give him a new father.

The teenage son who is confronted with his father's death has to be helped to find his rightful role in the surviving family, to understand what he owes to himself and what he owes to others — his mother, his siblings, his relatives. His mother wants him to be "the man of the house" just when his fantasies turn to building his own house. His siblings expect him to take their father's place at a time when he himself needs his father as a guide and as a mentor. "Why me?" he asks as they all try to transfer their needs upon him.

The youth needs to concentrate on his education to achieve occupational or professional training in order to become a self-depending adult. He is also at the age when he needs opportunities for social and recreational experiences that are a part of the joys of youth as well as growth toward social maturity.

These opportunities may be greatly altered by the father's death. He becomes angry and depressed. Joy and ease and freedom have gone out of his life and left only sadness and sorrow. He is filled with confusion, resentment, and guilt.

The surviving family needs guidance to help every member share in the reorganization of responsibilities that arise at the death of a father so that no child is expected to take on all the burdens and give up his own rights for self-fulfillment.

The Loss of A Husband

When the father dies the doctor can help the child most by giving first attention to the mother to restore her strength and enable her to resume her maternal role. When the loss occurs early in the child's life he is likely to suffer more from her reactions than from the death itself. A pre-school child may feel that his parent has deserted him and his surviving parent betrayed him by not preventing the death (A child's loss of his father, 1964).

When her husband dies, the wife may become overwhelmed with sorrow and helplessness. If she has been dependent upon her husband for major decisions, advice, and financial support as well as for affection and intimacy, she may feel completely lost without him. Overcome by her own grief, she is unable to help her children face the loss of their father with understanding and acceptance. She cannot assume her new role of responsibility in making decisions and disciplining her children in a constructive and reassuring manner. If she has no skills or understanding of financial matters and no means of support, she and her family will become dependent upon relatives or society.

The loss of a husband, especially among young widows with small children, has contributed to her emotional illness requiring increased medical and psychiatric treatment. The widow-to-widow program is an effort to help prevent such illness among widows, who have experienced the loss of their husbands.

The offer is usually made by a widow in the neighborhood of the same religious background and is sponsored by religious groups. Such help is accepted by some of the younger widows, especially those having children under age sixteen. These women were very eager to have someone to talk to who had experienced the same problems and learned to deal with them. They were eager to talk to an adult about their own grief and about how to help their children learn to accept the reality of their father's death. They were tied to the house and had little touch with the outside world having been occupied with the care of their home, their husband and children. The responsibility of raising their children alone without the help of their husband seemed to be an overpowering task (Silverman, 1971).

EFFECT OF THE DEATH OF THE MOTHER ON HER FAMILY

The death of the middle-aged mother of a nuclear family is tremendously traumatic to her husband and children. If she is a widow, its effect upon her children may be catastrophic and cause a complete change in her children's lives.

When the mother is ill in the hospital, the child should be brought to see her and be with her. He should also be allowed to talk to her on the telephone. This will help him know where his mother is and that she has not vanished into nowhere. It will also comfort the mother to have her children near her even if it is only for a little while.

The dying mother who has young children is filled with anguish, anger, and despair. She feels guilty because she has already abandoned her husband and children by her illness. Why did this have to happen to her at a time when they need her so much? What has she done to deserve such a punishment? What will her children do without her when she dies? Who will take care of them? Who will love them and help them and guide them. She resents the substitute surrogate who is now taking her place in the home. She is sure that she is doing everything wrong. Perhaps her husband will marry some wicked woman who will reject the children and make their lives miserable. With regression and depression come "hostility and resentment which may be directed toward spouse, children, and other relatives" (Kimball, 1971).

How does the husband feel toward his terminally ill wife? He has been dependent upon her for the care of home and children, for love and appreciation, companionship and counsel. He may react like a child would to a mother's desertion, with feelings of sorrow mixed with anger (Day, 1972).

The age of the child when he loses his mother to death is important in the way it affects his future development. "The absence or rupture of human ties in infancy can produce certain disturbances in the later functioning of the child and can impair to varying degrees the capacity of the child to bind himself to human partners later... Children who have been deprived of mothering, and who have formed no personal human bonds during the first two years of their lives, show permanent impairment of the capacity to make human attachments in later childhood... The degree of impairment is roughly equivalent to the degree of deprivation and to the age of the child. The period of greatest vulnerability is under two years of life. There will be impairment of intellectual functioning, conceptual thinking, language, and disorders of impulse control. Where there is no human attachment there can be no conscience" (Fraiberg, 1967).

When the infant or small child loses his mother he senses the change from Mother to Surrogate the moment she takes him in her arms. She offers him the bottle in place of Mother's breast, which he must soon accept in order to survive. His future development will be influenced by the type of mothering he receives from now on.

If the substitute mother gives him well-sustained, tender loving care that is also well supported by the father, the loss of the child's mother will be lessened as he develops feelings of trust and security in the mother substitute. But should indifference and neglect be his portion, he may never learn what true love is and he will be unable to express love for others. A child learns love at his mother's breast and in her arms. However, a good mother surrogate can enrich his life and soften his sorrow.

The toddler or small child who loses his mother goes through a period of mourning that is difficult to heal. The fear of separation threatens his need for survival. His mother has deserted him! Whom can he trust now? A child's face always reflects his feelings of fear or trust. And when he smiles no more, it is a sign of sorrow that has pained him. Desperately he now clings to Daddy, Sister,

Brother. He will not let them out of his sight, lest they too will disappear never to return. When someone in his family takes on the role of motherhood and gives him loving care, he learns to accept the substitute, though in his heart there will always be a scar.

The older child of three to five who can speak up, will call for his mother and ask where she has gone. He must be told the truth that Mother was too sick to live and won't come home, but Daddy, Sister, Grandmother will take care of him and love him always.

Effect of Mother's Death on Daughter

How does the death of the mother affect her daughter? The teenage girl feels her womanhood stirring within her. She dreams of bringing forth life — of birth and babies. She is therefore most reluctant to deal with death or even talk about it.

When her mother dies, the eldest daughter may have to pick up the burden of housekeeping for her father and care for her younger siblings. She loses opportunities for self-fulfillment through education and a social life with her peers. This should be her time to reach out into social activities for fun and for finding herself as a young woman. It is a time for dating and dreaming — for romance and much talk with peers of both sexes.

She needs a mother as a model with whom to discuss ideas about life and about experiences with boys, about dreams and ambitions, about the meaning of sex and how to relate to boys. When her mother dies, her daughter feels lost and alone. She does not know what others expect of her and what her responsibilities should be. What does she owe to herself and what does she owe to others?

The Cinderella Syndrome

There is a Cinderella in every family. In many families a certain child is assigned to play a certain role, like helping the mother, washing the dishes, taking care of the younger children, working to help support the family or to put a sibling through college.

When a mother becomes ill or dies, it naturally follows that such a child may take on the mother's responsibilities. This image of the mother surrogate is accepted by the family and cannot easily be erased.

If she accepts this image herself and continues playing that role, she may lose her own identity as a person in her own right and be easily taken for granted. This is especially harmful to the young daughter or aunt who has her own life to live. She must fight for her rights as a person to fulfill her own destiny without feelings of guilt; without accepting more than her part of the responsibilities which must be shared by the entire family.

She must be helped to know what she owes to herself and what she owes to others. If she continues to play the Cinderella role she may later require therapy when she finds that there has been no appreciation for her services, and for her own needs as a person, whose normal social and educational opportunities have been bypassed in order to serve others.

The Effect of the Changing Status of Women

What is the effect of the changing status of the woman on family reorganization at the death of a parent? When a parent dies the family constellation must be rearranged. The change of the stereotype and image of woman in our culture will contribute to a better balance and partnership in the family. When each parent knows the work of the other parent, if a mother or father dies, the other parent can more easily and efficiently take over the dying person's job and care for himself and the child.

From the moment the newborn infant lets out the cry that brings the nourishing breast to his mouth and makes him believe that his omnipotent magic controls the universe, to his final realization that Mother means more than milk, and his magical power over his environment is limited, he is forced to come face to face with reality.

This image of Mother, whose purpose is to nourish and to nurture, we do not want to relinquish. Women have accepted this biological role throughout history. It was a requirement for the survival of the race. But with changing times come changing roles for both women and men. The place of the woman and the man is in the home, the school, the community, and the world. Man as well as woman has the potentialities for warmth, tenderness, and nurturing. In our present culture he must be encouraged to express it, not to deny it. We disinherit man when we deprive him of his deepest and most tender feelings to express love, kindness, and grief. God gave us tears — why should we deprive men of this basic human expression?

The child would feel more secure if he had two parents to give him tender loving care; two parents to go to with problems to discuss freely and receive advice and guidance. And if one parent is unavailable or dies, the child can still turn to the living parent for comfort and control.

Woman, today, wants to be more than a service. She wants to be a person in her own right. Without sex discrimination, man can accept himself as an equal partner with woman and show her respect, consideration and cooperation as a person. He will then be relieved of all the strain that comes with the need to feel superior that the old culture demanded. This image of the equality of woman with that of man has to be established through equal opportunities for women on the same basis with men in every area of human endeavor without regard to their gender with the exception of their sexual differences in procreation.

Both men and women need to accept this new role and both will profit from it. Education should be open to women in all fields so that their talents may not be lost to society. To change the role and the status of women will take time. It requires the confidence of man in himself so that he will not need the woman to be inferior in order that he may feel superior. He can relax and be a person. He can discuss issues and problems with his wife on an equal basis without feeling it is a sign of weakness and unmanliness. Women need not hide their intelligence in order to adjust to a society and a culture that stresses the superiority of men.

Now what has the changing role of men and women have to do with the child who is losing his parent to an untimely death? The child can turn to either parent in time of need. The parent can understand the duties of the home or business and will be able to function adequately when the other parent is disabled or away. The child learns a role and develops a self-image as a person, not as a superior being because he is a male and not as an inferior being because she is a female.

Any work that contributes to human welfare is not degrading if we don't make it so. Either parent can maintain his/her dignity whether he changes the baby, washes the dishes, or cooks the dinner. Every act leads to a closer relationship with the child and helps establish trust, love, and security. In an environment of mutual respect, equality, and understanding, where there is no competition for a superior role, children will absorb the image of man and woman as persons whose value is based on their humanity and achievement, not on their sex.

PREVENTIVE THERAPY NEEDED

The death of a parent is a unique and shocking experience, especially to a young child who has had no background for coping with such a situation. Parental loss has been increasingly recognized as a significant factor in the development of neurosis and personality disorders in children, who respond with anxiety and despair to their feelings of abandonment. Some children are more vulnerable to the loss than others and need more care and concern than those who are stronger.

More attention should be given to families who have suffered such a loss and how it affected the spouse and children. Since it is known that bereavement brings traumatic consequences, preventive therapy with spouse and children should be an accepted procedure. Widespread professional programs for counseling and therapy are needed to aid bereaved families in order to prevent greater permanent trauma caused by a parent's death.

Guidance of the surviving parent should take into consideration his attitude toward the child's mourning which is slower and different from that of the parent. He should avoid minimizing the child's sense of loss, grief, and bewilderment, or denying its appropriateness. He should not refrain from speaking of the dead parent but should make natural reference to him in everyday conversation.

The parent must also be counseled against using the child as a partial replacement for the lost spouse. Prolonged bed-sharing, especailly with a child of the opposite sex, may act as an unhealthy substitute. This is an obstacle to full mourning which is necessary for achieving freedom from the dead partner. Such separation is necessary for both parent and child before independence and new natural relationships can be achieved.

REMARRIAGE AND STEPPARENTS

When a wife dies it is normal and natural, after his grief has subsided, for the husband to consider remarriage. However, he must take into account that the child's slower mourning pace contributes to poor acceptance of substitute parents. The youth may react to an unacceptable stepparent with depression, truancy, school failure, and school dropout (Kliman, 1969).

A quick remarriage to fill the empty void may result in incompatibility, especially between the stepmother and his teenage daughter. There can be conflict and competition for the father's love between his new wife and his daughter that he may not know how to resolve.

Communication and understanding between natural parents and their teenager is often difficult enough, but when there is a death and remarriage, much maladjustment and misunderstanding may arise. It is no one's fault when three strangers have to get used to living with each other in a new situation, but it is much more difficult to make the change after having had a warm family relation, that was broken by disease and death, whose scars were not yet healed. The child may deeply resent having some strange woman take her mother's place.

When a parent is suffering from a lingering fatal illness and is confined in the home much of the time, there may develop a deep bond between the parent and adolescent which will profoundly influence the future of the child and bring comfort and consolation to the dying parent.

When it is the mother who is suffering from this serious illness and is unable to carry on with her home duties, the husband and older children must take on her responsibilities. The younger child may become more dependent upon the father and upon an older sibling, while the older child may grow closer to the sick parent who is dependent upon her for care. If there has been love and understanding in the family before the illness, a pattern of care and cooperation can be established.

Fifteen-year-old Sonia said, "My mother had cancer. She was in bed for six years. There was a lot of love in our family. You could tell by the way my father took care of my mother that he loved her. I was always close to my mother. I would sit on her bed, talk to her and kiss her. I had her attention all the time. If I had any problems she could always help me.

"My mother was an easy-going, tolerant, understanding person. She had sympathy for everyone. She told me, 'If you ever did anything wrong I would forgive you before you did it.' I couldn't realize how girls could have fights with their mother. She went to the hospital many times — came back home — was sick in bed. Finally she went to the hospital and died. I had a feeling that would be the last time I would see my mother. When she died I got poor grades in school. I was sad and depressed and couldn't keep my mind on my schoolwork. During vacation I had black moods. I really enjoyed my childhood. I'm lucky I had it as a child.

"Then my father married my stepmother who is the very opposite of my mother. She is a domineering controlling woman who considers herself as the ultimate authority and no one can question her. I became extremely depressed and withdrawn. My father became worried about me. He thought that a psychologist could help me so he brought me to you. It helps me to talk to you. I can talk to you freely. You give me confidence. You make me feel as though my opinions and beliefs have value. But now, to punish me they want to take things away from me; like not going to my psychologist. My stepmother now wants me to go every two weeks instead of every week. She refuses to drive me to your office and I have to take two buses. Pretty soon she won't let me come at all. She doesn't want to spend the money, although my father works for it and wants me to come. I have to have someone to talk to who will understand my problems. When I wake up I hate to face the day — a treadmill. I feel like leaving — taking flight or striking back. My father doesn't know what to do. She fights with him, too. She is so different from my mother."

Sonia's Rorschach brought out her feelings of insecurity and deep longing for her mother; her unconscious wishes that her mother's spirit would send messengers to save her from her stepmother's harmful power over her. She said, "These are some winged men who have their arms around a woman. She is like a priestess with mystic qualities. She is in Valhalla telling them to go down to the mortals on earth and carry out her deeds. They must save the missionary's daughter who is being swept away from her father's establishment in the wilderness in Africa. These two muscular men have got her enclosed and are going to throw her in a pot — take her off to their camp ground and sacrifice her to a deity. She has got her hands raised — is imploring some power to save her. The basic thing is I see two male figures on the sides and the feminine one in the middle. They have her surrounded."

This case illustrates the consequences of a well-adjusted family, broken by the death of the mother and the effect of a quick, unwise remarriage. The outcome was a traumatic experience for the teenage daughter who felt threatened and helpless under the authority of a domineering stepmother.

SUMMARY

The death of a parent is one of the greatest catastrophies that can befall a child and the death of both parents may be completely devastating to his entire future. When a parent is seriously ill or dying, his spouse and children should be with him. They should talk together freely and honestly about his illness and his dying, without fear, denial, or avoidance. When he dies, his children will then remember the parent as a person in quiet repose.

Parental bereavement is normally more common than we generally realize. Divorce may affect children in a way similar to death. The child is shocked by the parent's death and needs special help to deal with his grief when the bereaved parent is too overwhelmed with his grief to understand the child's grief. A pet at this time may be a comfort to the child.

The nuclear family, having fewer people to turn to, is more

vulnerable to grief than the larger family. The circumstance of the parent's death is important in the way it affects the child. Sudden death, caused by disasters, accidents, or suicide, is more traumatic for the child than death caused by illness.

The family is affected differently by the death of the father than by that of the mother. With the death of the father the entire family is deprived of financial and emotional support and is disturbed by the new roles every member must play in the family reorganization. The son loses a model to emulate. He has added family responsibilities that may deprive him of financial and emotional support and opportunities for normal educational and social development. Children of different ages are affected differently by the father's death.

The death of the mother is tremendously traumatic to her husband and children. It can be very harmful to infants and younger children, especially when they do not have warm mother surrogates to give them tender loving care. The teenaged daughter may have added home responsibilities that interfere with her educational and social opportunities. She may be the victim of the Cinderella syndrome where everyone expects her to take on all the home responsibilities, without having a life of her own.

The changing status of women and men, where both find a place in the home, school, community, and world, where much of their work and contributions are interchangeable, will cause less trauma for the child, who loses a parent to death, because the other parent can perform the duties of the dead parent.

Remarriage of the spouse is normal and natural, but it must be given serious consideration, and take into account the way it will affect the children.

Preventive therapy is needed to avoid the development of neurosis and personality disorders in the later life of children who lose their parents.

REFERENCES

Becker, D. E. and Margolin, F.: How surviving parents handled their young children's adaptation to the crisis of loss. Am J Orthopsychiatry, 37:753-757, 1967.

Birk, A.: The bereaved child. Ment Health, 25(4):9-11, 1966.

Bowlby, J.: Childhood mourning and its implication for psychiatry. Am J Psychiat, 118:481-498, 1961.

A child's loss of his father stressed as a medical problem. Medical Tribune, pp. 1, 22-23, Sept. 2, 1964.

Day, S. B. (Ed.): Proceedings: Death and attitudes toward death. Batesville, Ind.: Bell Museum of Pathology, University of Minnesota Medical School, 1972.

Driver, C.: What a dying man taught doctors about caring. Medical Economics, Jan. 22, 1973, pp. 81-86.

Fraiberg, S.: Learning to be human: The Diseases of non-attachment. Current, 93(3)1-8, 1968.

Kalish, R. A.: The effects of death upon the family. In Pearson, L. (Ed.): Death and Dying. Cleveland, Press of Case University, 1969.

Keeler, W. R.: Children's reactions to the death of a parent. In Hoch, P. H. and Zubin, J. (Eds): Depression. New York, Grune and Stratton, 1954.

Kimball, C. P.: Death and dying: A chronological discussion. J. Thanatol, 1(1):42-52, 1971.

Kliman, G.: Bereaved children held in need of wide-scale preventive psychiatry. Roche Report: Frontiers of Clinical Psychiatry, 6(18):1-2, 1969.

Levinson, B. M.: The pet and the child's bereavement. Ment Hyg 51:197-200, 1967.

Many families suffer parental loss. Roche Report: Frontiers of Clinical Psychiatry, Oct. 1, 1969, 6(16):1-4.

Marris, P.: Widows and Their Families. London, Routledge and Kegan Paul, 1958.

Missildine, W. H. (Ed.): Ross Timesaver: Feelings and Their Medical Significance, 13(5):1-4, 1971.

Shoor, M. and Speed, M. H.: Delinquency as a manifestation of the mourning process. Psychiat Q, 37:540-558, 1963.

Silverman, P. R.: Facts involved in accepting an offer of help. Arch Foundation Thanatol, 3(3):161-171, 1971.

Sugar, M.: Normal adolescent mourning. Am J Psychother, 22:258-269, 1968.

———: Divorce and death have similar effect. Pediatric News, 4(2):9, 17, 1970.

———: Reactions of children to divorce. Feelings and Their Medical Significance, 14(6):1-4, 1972.

Chapter XII

A CHILD'S RELIGION AND DEATH

A BASIC part of every religion reflects man's eternal search for the meaning of life and death. Man needs religion as a way of life to give direction and meaning to his existence. It forms the foundation for bringing up his children as moral and ethical human beings.

Today, those who drop religion as unscientific and try to substitute ethics in its place are in fact replacing it with another religion. For people who believe in nothing, life loses its purpose, its meaning and direction, and there is nothing in it.

The child, like primitive man, is deeply involved with the mystery of birth and death. He has deep anxiety about death and needs clear and honest answers to his questions about its meaning. To be able to answer those questions on a religious basis, we need to understand the child's developmental attitudes towards religion as he experiences it. Different religions vary in the way they direct the child's spiritual education and in the manner they explain the meaning of life and death.

A Child's Religion Grows

The meaning of religion in a child's life profoundly influences his attitudes toward death. A child's religion is a growing thing. He absorbs the faith of his fathers, in the home, from the moment he is born, in everything he does. If he lives in a spiritual atmosphere he will be more able to accept the sacredness of life and the reality of death. Where no religious beliefs and practices are observed, the child will be deprived of growth in character and personality. He will lack the security that comes with belonging to a religious group.

We try to create spiritual values in the home and to apply them in all human relations outside the home, too. We try to help the child become conscious of nature and the wonders of the universe. When he asks, "What are we?" we let him know what religion he belongs to, but also explain that all religions teach about God and the brotherhood of men. As he grows older he is ready to learn more about other religions, but first he must understand his own religious beliefs and traditions. Otherwise the small child may get more and more confused.

The Meaning of Belonging

Human beings experience both togetherness and separation, from the time they are born until the time they die. Change is always going on and all change is accompanied by some anxiety. The infant fears separation from his mother and abandonment. Every human being carries that fear within him until he dies. No one wants to die alone. "Forsake us not," is the prayer of the old and the sick.

At the same time, every individual needs identity as a person in his own right. Separation and togetherness — identity and belonging. You can not really have identity and recognition as an individual in your own right, if you do not belong to the group. People need each other. When a crisis comes you are not alone. Who would want to build a bridge if there were no people to walk on it? Who would want to write a poem or sing a song if there was no one to listen?

Belonging involves communication. Without communication, the sounding board of one's thoughts and feelings, life loses its purpose; thoughts dry up and the individual wastes away into nothingness. Belonging includes togetherness, marriage, family, kinship, church, community, city, state, world, universe. Belonging means relationships. This requires understanding of one's self and of others. What does a person owe to himself and what does he owe to others? Belonging includes laws — ethics — morality. It includes the meaning of democracy and dictatorship. Does the individual owe his whole life to the state without having anything to say about his life and his liberty? Or is the purpose of the state to serve the individual, and does he have the right to participate in his own government? We cannot have laws and morality without understanding the world we live in.

Man's Spiritual Intuition

Since this world is so full of mystery and wonder, the thinking, sensitive man is imbued with a spiritual sense at the greatness of the universe and must therefore come to the conclusion that there must be a Power that rules the world; that controls and directs the universe. Some people have given this mighty force the name of God. Some call it Nature.

Man, looking around this world in which he finds himself begins to question what he sees and what he experiences. Who am I? Where am I? What is Life? What is the purpose of life? What is death? Why must I die? Is death the end of everything or does life go on in a different form — in a different place — for a time — forever? What is the meaning and mystery of it all? Man looks for answers. He is afraid of what he does not understand. He develops guilt. He develops a sense of right and wrong. He develops a conscience.

God is something he can't control — a power — fire — separate gods for separate powers — the sun — darkness — it is frightening. Fear brings a willingness to submit to this great power of the universe. He develops a code — a way of life that will please the gods. Fear brings a certain amount of discipline and direction until outside control becomes internalized and habits and attitudes are formed. He passes this on to his children. Authoritative figures must have ethical and moral values in order to train the child with the wisdom he needs to give him a way of life and a way of death.

The Influence of Religious Observance on the Child

How does belonging to a religious denomination give a child faith, comfort, and security? Every person needs to see meaning and purpose in life. Religion helps provide values that give him goals and direction. Through practice of religious rites, customs, ceremonies, and holidays, the child learns to identify with his group. Families get together and share happy times and important occasions, such as marriage, birth, confirmation. These celebrations are associated with good food, music, songs; but also with religious practices of worship, self examination, and prayer. The unhappy times of belonging and togetherness are during times of sadness, sickness, and death; of funerals that lead to final separations. In these times also, strength comes with belonging.

How does religion help a child when death strikes? Religion is a central theme in attitudes toward death. When a child learns the meaning of life he will know that death is part of life, accept it as such, and live his life with the knowledge that every day, every moment is meaningful. We should not have to wait for the knowledge that we are dying in order to realize the beauty and wonder of life and of the universe.

FAITH AND INTUITION

What is faith? Faith may come from the deep recesses of the "collective unconscious," (Jung) going back to the recurring experiences of life of our remote ancestors, before they had even discovered speech. Faith grows out of that deep intuition, which comes from the unconscious communication between man and his universe, that different individuals have to varying degrees.

People who have little faith believe only in the things they themselves can observe. All other things do not exist for them. They see only the tree, but not the supporting roots that give it life and strength. They are not attuned to the deep rhythms of the universe.

Great leaders who have this spiritual communication may be able to inspire others who will accept the tenets of their teachings and pass their beliefs on to their children. Most great religions that have withstood the test of time are based on high ethical and moral principles; on the belief that man has a conscience that controls his conduct and his relationship to other men and to God.

The person who has faith in God and in his religion finds acceptance and security that give him courage and peace of mind. Faith directs his behavior in constructive channels and helps him accept adversity as the will of God. It is a discipline that guides his conduct with the assurance that there is a divine purpose in all things, although it may be beyond his understanding. Parents who have this faith will unconsciously pass it on to their children by their religious observance in everything they do.

Children gain security through faith in authoritative figures whom they can trust to take care of them and give them discipline and direction, so that they know what they should and should not do. They need faith in parents, in teachers, doctors, government authorities, and faith in God. Whenever we fail them we hurt and confuse them and may be responsible when they lose their way in life.

What can a professional person do to help a patient find comfort and support from his religion at a time of crisis? Every person in the helping professions must respect the other person's religion and try to apply its principles wherever he can to help the patient with his problems.

Never try to force your own religion upon another person. Use his religious beliefs to give him hope, comfort, and reassurance. Give him opportunities to follow his religious practices whenever you can. Call a priest, minister, or Rabbi when he wants to see him. Call a priest when a Catholic is dying. Baptize a dying Catholic child if no one else is there to do it. This will be a great comfort to his parents.

A CHILD'S DEVELOPMENTAL CONCEPT OF GOD

How can we explain God to a little child when he suddenly asks, "What is God like?" A small child who is born into a home where the presence of God abides at all times, where there is faith and prayer, thanksgiving and blessings, observance of religious customs, accepts God as he accepts his mother, as a part of his environment. Any explanation about God to a child who comes from a home where religion is not observed will be foreign to his experience and difficult for him to comprehend.

A child's concept of God and religion follows his cognitive growth and development "which emerge in the course of mental growth" (Elkind, 1970). To an infant, anything that he does not see does not exist. He is not aware that his mother's face exists when it is no longer present. When we play peek-a-boo with him we may help him learn that what disappears can reappear again. He is delighted when he sees his mother's face again after it has disappeared. Only toward the end of his second year is the young child able to understand that objects have a permanence of their own. This capacity to mentally represent objects results in their conservation. "The search for conservation is a life-long quest for permanence amidst a world of change" (Elkind, 1970).

At first the child feels that nothing changes. Everything remains the same. Life is permanent and everlasting. Later, as he grows older, he discovers that change is constantly going on. He may learn that even stars are born, exist, change, then die. He is shocked when he discovers that he and his loved ones must ultimately die. He searches for ways to conserve life.

Whom can he trust? Upon whom can he depend? Parents? No, they, too, may die and leave him. Upon God? Yes! So he is forced to believe in God in order to feel safe and protected, in order that he may never die, in the belief that there is another and even better world beyond the grave, if that is what his religion teaches him. The concept of God is religion's ultimate answer to the conservation of life, and therefore to immortality, for God transcends space, time, and corporality. Every religion contains an organized body of ceremonies based on its history. Through religious worship the young person can relate himself to the deity. The concept of God lies at the very core of personal religion.

How can we help the child gain a wider knowledge of God without misinforming and confusing him? A child's mind is filled with wonder and curiosity. He is always asking "Why?" We can only satisfy his need to know by giving him the kind of information that he will be able to understand at his age and development. But we must always try to be honest with the child if we would develop trust and confidence. We should not teach him anything that we will have to deny later. Some people do not think it is a good idea to teach a child about the myth of Santa Claus who secretly brings him the presents his parents actually provide.

What is a child's idea of God? Concepts of God, religion, Santa Claus, change with age. Religion of childhood differs from religion of adults. A child's religion is not rigid; it is a growing, developing, learning concept.

Children's Questions About God

To gain ideas of some children's concepts of God, pupils from kindergarten through ninth grade were invited to ask any questions they wanted to know about God and religion. The children's questions concerned the existence of God, his power, and what he does.

The kindergarten children were interested in the relationship of God with death. They asked: "Does God die like everyone else? How does God pick up people that are dead?" They wanted to know how God makes himself, how he gets up in the sky, how he sees people, and why we can't see God. They had questions about the activities and power of God. "How does God make the sun, moon, rain, rainbows, lightening, and people? How does God make people happy and why does he make people fight? How does he help the Christ child's mother do all sorts of things, and how does the devil get killed?"

The first grade children wanted to know how God can see if he is invisible.

Most of the third grade's questions were about God himself. "How and when was he born; how old is he; where and how far up in the sky does he live? Is God married; is he Christian or Jewish; and when will God die? How did God create the earth, man, and the first woman?"

The fifth grade children's questions often reflected scepticism about whether there is a God — is he a person or a spirit; is there more than one God, and how did he get his name? Did God make the earth; how was the earth made; and when did God live on earth? Is God always with you wherever you are and is it true that on Rosh Hashanah God writes in the Book of Life?

Children in grade six wanted to know whether there really is a God, "because we can't hear, see, or feel him." They wanted to know whether Moses really heard God or whether the scrolls were just made up stories.

The eighth grade children wanted proof of the existence of God and what does he look like and what is he made of? "Does God ever appear? Is God really real or is he just a blind faith that has been built into religion so that almost everyone believes in God? If we didn't have a God whom would we turn to? Did Abraham and his children really hear God's voice?"

Children in grade nine had many questions about the meaning and existence of God and whether he is a spirit or a physical being. "Does God influence us for good or evil purposes; is he an illusion; is he really something or did someone just make him up? What part does he play in our life and what does he have to do with life on earth? Does God really speak to us and hear our prayers or are we just hearing things? Why is the belief in God so strong? Why is God always referred to as a *he*? Why is God looked upon as being in heaven, instead of on earth or underground? How or why do people draw pictures of a spirit or belief? What is God; what is he like? What is God's meaning to us?" And the skeptical child said, "God does not help me. He never does nothing for me."

The children's questions reflected not only developmental concepts of God but voiced the eternal questions of mankind about the mystery of a creator of life and death and the meaning of the universe.

Answering Children's Questions

How can we answer children's questions about religion? Parents need a clear and definite philosophy of their own religion in order to help their child understand some of its concepts. What is vague in their own mind will certainly be more vague in the child's mind.

When the child asks, "What are we?" Explain the tenets of your own religion. The child needs your faith to lean on. Tell him that all people do not agree about religious ideas and about the meaning of life and death, but all religions teach the need to love and help people of all races, religions, and nationalities. Therefore if everyone would truly follow his own religion there would be peace on earth and good will to men.

There are many things we can teach a child about God that applies to all religions. We can teach him that the spirit of the creator is in everything and unifies the universe. We are all related.

Any harm we do hurts everyone and there is a little less good and beauty and happiness in the world. Any good we do helps everyone. The child should be given the feeling that one person can do a tremendous amount of good or harm. He is a living, acting part of this world, influenced by the past and present and influencing the future.

We need to understand a child's ideas before we can give him positive, helpful information. A four-year-old may make little differentiation between parents, Santa Claus, superman, and God. To him, all four represent power to do anything they want. A five-year-old may believe that God, like a human being, is responsible for anything that happens, good or bad. If a vase is knocked over or the milk is spilled, God may be blamed for it. Many children visualize God as an old man with a beard who is rich and powerful and who may be like a king. Freud says that many people think of God as possessing the same attributes as their own father. The spoiled child who gets almost anything he wants from his parents may think of God as an unkind power if he, too, does not grant all the child's wishes. A child whose parents are overly strict may visualize God as an angry and punishing God whom he must please in order to feel safe.

A child's religious and moral growth can rarely develop much above that of his parents. If his parents have lost interest in their religion the child will know it. Some parents are stimulated to grow in order to meet their child's needs. Parents must be consistent in what they themselves believe, in order not to confuse their children.

Today, we are desperately searching for the true spirit that underlies all religions which lead to better human understanding and human brotherhood. Children need to be given a clear understanding of their own traditions and also respect for the religion of their neighbors.

What idea of God should we give our children? We can only give children the feelings and ideas that we ourselves hold. The child will also get ideas from his friends, school, Sunday school, church, and other sources. In the process of all learning and of growing up, children may get confused and distorted ideas; but under wise guidance, with added knowledge, they attain a clearer view of things. As he grows older, the child needs to participate in discussions with parents and ministers concerning the meaning of religious concepts taught by their own religion.

CONVERSATIONS WITH CHILDREN ABOUT GOD

What are some of the questions about religion that children ask us or which we feel important for them to know? Children want to know about God. The six-year-old will tell you that God is the creator of the universe. He believes in two forces, God and the devil, Heaven and hell, good and bad. This discussion between six-year-old John and his mother gives us some ideas of the child's concepts.

John: Mother, I believe in God. Everyone should believe in God, if not, they'll get punished or won't go to Heaven. If you're nice to God, He will be nice to you. By helping yourself and your father and mother you can help God. If you love God, He will love you. Michael asked me what God looked like.

Mother: What did you tell him, John?

John: I told him that God looks like a man with a mustache. He wears an Egyptian hat and Egyptian clothes. I told him God lives in Heaven. That's in the sky. God rules the whole earth — and other earths, too, in America and even out of America. How old is God, Mommy?

Mother: There is no beginning and no end to God and He never dies.

John: Why doesn't God ever die? He is a fine God and I like Him.

Mother: God isn't like a man. He's different. He is a great Spirit. He is great beyond our understanding. We don't know all the answers. We only know we must have faith in him.

John: They just can't get all the reasons, but God knows. He knows what man is thinking. If people are bad, God will punish them; good ones he loves. He likes a good spirit and a good heart and soul. A soul is your own self. It's inside of you and you can't see it because you can't see through the skin. I would like to know what God does. He watches at night, too. He has to work hard. No one knows what God is doing. Not even you, Mother. But sometimes if people are very good, God will tell them what to do.

When you pray, you tell God that you're kind in your heart. That is why I pray every night. I like to make up my own prayers. God is good and will know what I am trying to say.

As the child grows older he becomes more inquisitive. Seven-year-old Phyllis was seriously interested in understanding about God and religion.

Phyllis: Mother, I just can't understand about God. Can't anybody see him? How do we really know he is there?

Mother: We can never see God directly, but for many reasons we feel sure in our hearts that there is a God and that he is a God of love and goodness. We know that in all history and among all peoples throughout the world there has always been some belief in something or someone greater than man himself. Nobody really knows all about God. It is beyond our understanding. Before people were as civilized as they are today and lived in caves, they already felt that there was some power much greater than themselves who must have made this universe. To some of them, fire seemed very powerful and wonderful, so they worshipped fire. Others worshipped the stars and the moon and the sun. The Indian's belief in God is very much like our own, in many ways. They call him the Great Spirit.

People today do not all agree in their ideas. But the three main religions in America, Protestant, Catholic, and Jewish, all teach the belief in one God. They all teach good things but some of their ways of practicing their religious customs are different. Here, in our wonderful country we have FREEDOM OF RELIGION. This means that everyone has a right to practice his religion the way he believes in his heart. Most people keep the same religion as their parents.

Long ago there were some very great leaders. They were so wise and good that they seemed to be nearer to God and to understand him better. They told their ideas to the people just as our minister explains things to us and the Rabbi explains things to the Jewish people in their temple. Some of the leaders were Abraham, Moses, and Jesus. Many of their thoughts and teachings were written down in a book called the Bible. That book is still the most wonderful book in the world. It tells us how people learned about God long ago and how he helped them. The TEN

COMMANDMENTS found in the Bible are so wonderful that if all people would follow them today, we would have a much happier world. The Bible tells us that God is a God of love and we should love our neighbors as ourselves. That is the beginning of kindness.

Phyllis: Well, Mother, I still can't understand how God takes care of us. There are so many people in this world, and birds and animals, too.

Mother: It is said that not even a sparrow falls without God's knowledge. God also gives everyone responsibilities to do what he can in this world. God has made a world where living things have parents. Children live in families so parents can take care of them and teach them what is right and wrong and how to do things in the best way. He gives us eyes, ears, and minds so we can learn to take care of ourselves. He wants us to learn to think for ourselves and choose right from wrong.

Phyllis: But Mother, it's still very hard to believe in God if you can't see him. How do I know he is everywhere?

Mother: Let us take a little walk in the garden and I will be better able to explain to you what I feel in my own heart. How pleasant it is in this garden with the lovely sun shining and the signs of spring all around us. Look at the beautiful violet growing under this tree. Could it make itself? No. Could you or I or Daddy make a violet? No indeed. The greatest and richest man in the world cannot make a violet, but a tiny seed that comes from violets can grow into a violet if it is in good soil and gets rain and warmth and sunshine. The same thing happens to all growing things. Nobody in the world can make an apple seed. All growing things and all living things, birds, insects, animals, people and everything in the world show a plan in the way they live and grow and act and even in the way they die. All those things couldn't make themselves, so we feel that some great Spirit whom we call God, must have made this great universe. The more people learn about this world the more they can see God's plan and God's laws which all nature follows.

We can always be sure that God's laws will work. We know that night will always follow day, that spring will follow winter and summer will follow spring. All the growing, changing things, the sky, the clouds, the wind and rain, the rivers and oceans and beautiful mountains, the glorious sunsets, all give you a feeling that only someone as great as God could have made such a wonderful beautiful world. We should take care of this world and not polute or destroy it. All the things we learn in science help us to understand God's plans. Scientists help us to see the pattern of the universe and its laws. The more they learn, the more they see how everything is related.

You, my child, are a part of this great world. You enjoy its beauty. You eat the food that grows on the farm and drink the waters that flow in its rivers. You play with children, go to school, take care of your dog, and help you parents. When a bird or pet dies you put it in a box and bury it in the ground, for you know that death, too, is part of God's plan. Even if we don't always understand it we must learn to accept it.

You can help make this world a little better or make it a little worse. If you try to learn, if you are kind and helpful to others, if you do not destroy beautiful things or flowers, you are helping to make this a better world and you are bringing happiness to others. If you give as well as get, then you will be a good and helpful member of this world. The world will then be a little better because you are living in it. So remember, you do not live your life alone; you are an important part of this great universe.

Let me tell you a little story. When I was a Girl Scout our troop went on an all-night hike in the woods one summer. We built a campfire and ate our supper. Then we rolled up in our blankets and tried to go to sleep on the ground around the campfire. I woke up in the middle of the night and it was very, very still. I could really feel the stillness of the night. The heavens were filled with millons of stars. In that quiet peacefulness, in the stillness of the night, I felt closer to God. I felt that I was part of this beautiful world that he created. I couldn't see God but I could feel his presence. People living thousands of years ago, especially shepherds who were out in the hills watching their sheep, must have had the same kind of feelings because in the Bible it says, "The Heavens declare the glory of God, and the firmament showeth His handiwork." (Psalms 19:2). This means that when we see this beautiful world our heart tells us there must be a God who created it.

Phyllis: I like to see the stars and I can find the dipper, too. I am glad that I am part of God's wonderful world. I am going to try to be a good part so I can help make it a better world.

This conversation is an attempt to carry over to the child the relatedness of all things and the thought that God created the universe according to a plan. A better understanding and acceptance of God's plan, of nature's laws, and of the orderliness of the universe will give children faith in God, in themselves, and in the world.

CEREMONIES AND RITES

Customs, rites and ceremonies are an important part of every culture. All religions have rituals and holydays that are meaningful. Children like pageantry and enjoy all religious ceremonies. Such activities are built into feelings of relatedness that give them strength and linger in their memories. It means belonging to the group; doing what others are doing; worshiping and praying together as one group, on happy and serious occasions; belonging to the past as well as to the present; identifying with your people and with the history of your religious affiliation.

Abstractions can be most meaningful when they are tied to a child's experiences. A child may be confused by words whose meanings are limited to his own experiences. Words grow in their meaning just as the child grows. His language is often different from that of adults and there may be no real communication between them. He learns many things with his body as well as with his brain. Dancing, singing, playing, associated with religious activities, leave attitudes built into his body as well as into his mind.

Experiences make things real and concrete. The child who attends a funeral retains a clear and vivid image of what has happened. It remains in his memory and cannot easily be erased. It is very painful and distressful but it must be faced in order to be accepted as a fact, so that the child can go through the experience of grief and mourning; the steps of separation from the dead that are needed in order to turn to a new life without them.

Psychologically, participation with others in religious rites is an emotional experience that is absorbed by the child through imitation and identification, before he has acquired logical reasoning and understanding of their meaning. The child adopts the religion of his fathers without thought and analysis. If the indoctrination "takes" it may last a lifetime. But it may later be rejected by some individuals, especially by the adolescent youth.

When the significant adults in his life really do not live up to the ethical and moral teachings of their religion, the youth may discredit the entire tenets of the church and drop the practice of organized religion as meaningless and hypocritical. Then he may seek other religions with which to identify or he may become disenchanted with life and religion. Adolescents have a great need to find purposes in life with which to identify. This need is especially true at a time of crisis, when misfortune or death strikes.

THE MEANING OF PRAYER TO A CHILD

What does prayer mean to a child? A child's concept of prayer is related to his developmental ideas of God and to his religious training and experience at home and in his practicing religion. Prayer is a time of meditation and is an expression of faith in a Supreme Being. Every religion has formal prayers related to significant events in life. There are also daily prayers of thanks, confessions, and prayers for special occasions.

When we teach a child to pray and encourage him to make up his own prayers, it makes him feel closer to God. It may also reveal to us his thoughts, feelings, and fears. However, older children often like to say their prayers alone, in the privacy of their room. To be meaningful in a child's life, prayer must be a part of his daily living and not used only in times of trouble. There should be prayers before and after meals, at bedtime, and on special occasions, in addition to formal prayers that are a part of every religion. In this way it becomes a natural thing for a child to turn to God at a time of trouble.

Prayer at bedtime gives a child assurance, comfort, and feelings of protection from the fear of separation, of letting go of wakefulness into sleep. Fear of sleep may be associated in the child's mind with fear of death. Therefore his prayers should not include the thought that he might die before he wakes. It should rather include thanks for the daily blessings of food and shelter, for parents and friends, and for other people who help us, such as teachers, doctors, nurses, policemen, so that the child learns to appreciate what other people do for him.

Faith comes with feelings of helplessness as well as wonder, and prayer during times of crisis may be a spiritual experience. When there is illness, prayer should ask for help and strength to face whatever comes and to be able to cope with it. When there is a death, prayer should contain acceptance and faith in the will of God, so that the child will not feel guilty or believe that the death was his fault. There could also be a prayer of thanks for the years the child enjoyed the companionship of the loved one until his death.

Prayer with a child dying of a lingering illness should emphasize the present day with all its joys and beauty. It should help the child feel closer to God and not be afraid of the future. Reading the twenty-third Psalm and other parts of the Bible could help and comfort the child who lives with the fear of death in his heart.

We have to understand children's developmental concepts of prayer. Some children think God is a super-daddy and all they have to do is pray for something and it will be granted.

Bobby: Mommy, I don't think God hears little boys when they pray. I prayed and prayed for a bike and I still didn't get one.

Mother: God doesn't give us everything we ask for. He knows best what we need and should have. Besides, we can't always understand God's plans, but we must have faith in his wisdom and in his love for us. God gives us a chance to work for the things we want. He gives men brains and skillful hands so they can learn to do things.

Bobby: Well, if we don't get what we pray for why should we say prayers?

Mother: When we say prayers we have a quiet time with God and think of his goodness and thank him for what he does for us. Sometimes we are unkind and selfish and forget about others. To pray means to stop and think. When we talk to God we can see the right way better. Then we don't think only of ourselves but we know that we are part of this great world and what we do is important to make it better or worse. God has made a world to run according to laws. He follows those laws himself and does not break them. You can't break God's laws and think that by praying to him he will keep his laws from working in your case.

Bobby: I like to learn God's laws and be happy. But sometimes I really can't understand why God lets us have trouble, like when my puppy got lost.

Mother: Prayer does not mean that we shift our responsibilities onto God. It means rather that we accept our responsibilities and become more willing and able to carry them. Maybe you should have taken better care of your puppy. But when you are in trouble, if you ask God, he will comfort you help you know and do what is right.

Bobby: Mother, does prayer make God forgive us for everything we do that's wrong? Will he forgive me for taking Johnny's new ball, if I pray to him?

Mother: Bobby, you just can't go around doing wrong things and expect God to forgive you for your sins just because you say a prayer asking him to do so. If you are really sorry for your mistakes then you must do something to correct them. First you have to ask Johnny to forgive you. You have to return his ball to him or buy him a new one. You have to promise him that you won't do it again and keep your promise. Then you can pray to God and ask him to forgive you. If you are truly sorry in your heart you won't do it again. When you feel that God has forgiven you, then your heart will feel at ease and happy.

As you grow older you will learn more and more the difference between right and wrong. A still small voice within you, called your conscience, will help you try to do what is right. If you do wrong, you will have a guilty conscience and be unhappy. Sometimes other people make mistakes and are unkind to us. If we forgive others, God will forgive us if we try to correct our mistakes.

Bobby: Mother, I can hear my conscience right now. It is telling me to give Johnny back his ball. But Mother, I lost Johnny's ball. Well I can give him my new ball. He will like that and he will forgive me. Then we can be friends again.

Mother: Now you understand very well. If you will listen to your conscience it will always help you do what is right.

These are suggestions of ways we might use to help a child understand about prayer, faith, forgiveness, and conscience. Spiritual strength grows day by day as the child matures and learns through wise guidance and the examples of adults around him. When trouble comes God is not a stranger to the child and he will more readily be able to turn to him in faith, confidence, and trust.

THE THREE RELIGIONS IN AMERICA

Religion has been a vital force in the history of mankind and people have made many sacrifices in its name. History is filled with the way the power of religion affected people, rulers, and government. Whenever religion has been used as a force to judge, control, or frighten the individual, suffering and sadness, threats and torture were the outcome. Wherever there has been religious freedom it has brought comfort and happiness to its followers. America has been built upon respect for other people's religion and freedom to worship God according to one's conscience. The doctrines of the Catholic, Protestant, and Jewish religions as they influence the child's experiences with death will be discussed here.

The Catholic Way

A child's attitudes toward life and death are acquired in the home and church. The divinely revealed teachings of the Catholic faith are that man's soul will survive its separation from the body and will open up into a new life of eternal fulfillment. Without such belief life would have no meaning. "God sent Christ to fulfill the promise of salvation for those who would believe in him" (Riley, 1967).

The Catholic child finds supernatural security in following the ministrations of the church that promises him victory rather than defeat, when death strikes, according to his religion. In the home, the parents take the place of God, who will punish the child if he transgresses the teachings of the church. The child who believes that life on earth is a preparation for life eternal, will live his life differently from those who have no faith in the teachings of the church. Character and respect for parents is built up in the child who believes in a future life of rewards and punishment.

In the world to come, the union of body and soul will be reestablished and bring happiness and eternal life. The Catholic child is taught from his earliest years to think about death in its relationship to eternal life. At the moment of death, God judges every person. If he truly repents about his sins before he dies, he may hope that God will pardon him. But such repentence will not continue beyond the moment of death. At that time, God will decree eternal happiness or suffering and misery for the soul. This decree is bound up with the mystery of the creation.

For the Catholic, heaven is a promise of perfect happiness that transcends the joys of earthly life, while hell brings eternal misery far worse than the deepest pain and sorrow experienced before bodily death. This represents divine justice. Catholics on earth pray to the saints in heaven for one another and for the souls in Purgatory, asking the saints and those in heaven to intercede with God for the souls in Purgatory, whose sufferings can be alleviated by the suffering of the living.

The presence of the priest at the bedside of the dying Catholic, the services held for the dead before burial, and on the day of burial, are vivid reminders to youth of the need to prepare for eternity (Riley, 1967).

The Protestant Way

The traditional ideas in Protestant thought are the belief in resurrection, restoration of the physical organism of the faithful at some future date, immortality, and continued life of the soul in a place of reward or punishment, heaven or hell, depending upon the behavior of the individual in life. Christ is the savior from sin and death and the personal guarantor of the hopes of the righteous. This life everlasting, immortality, can be achieved without barely tasting death. This illusion of unreality about death has resulted in unwise traumatic deprivation experiences of children (Jackson, 1967).

"Religious education based on the traditional ideas in Protestant thought tend to make religion meaningless for life rather than a source of life's meaning" (Jackson, 1967).

Death used to be a part of homelife and could be faced openly and honestly. The changed social and cultural conditions has resulted in unwise management of acute deprivation experiences, the most traumatic being the loss through death. We now need to reassess our educational processes, theological assumptions, and our religious and social ceremonies to meet current circumstances (Jackson, 1967).

"The church should put a high value on people in life and in death. It should provide the resources to cope significantly with the facts and the emotions that accompany death. When it fails to do this it downgrades life itself" (Jackson, 1967).

Psychological knowledge today provides a sound basis for understanding the relationship of life and death. The child must be told the truth and not things that will later have to be unlearned. The basic concern should be the search for the meaning of life and personal adequacy in meeting its experiences. The resources should be interpersonal relationships strengthened by a firm grip on reality. God would be the "source of ordered processes that can be depended upon," not a scapegoat for man's troubles (Jackson, 1967).

The traditional religious ceremonials surrounding death in which the child should definitely participate give him an opportunity to express his thoughts and feelings. They act as a form of communciation that is more meaningful to a child than words. It gives him a chance to learn that the church values both life and death and the emotions that accompany them (Jackson, 1967).

The Jewish Way

The main tenets of the Jewish religion is the belief in one God who created the universe. "The roots of Jewish tradition, everything we practice, has its origin in the Bible, with our basic moral values reaching out to God," says Rabbi Aaron M. Wise. Judaism is a way of life. It is concerned with loving thy neighbor as thyself and the brotherhood of man. The Jewish child must learn this way of life in order to be a good Jew and be able to fulfill God's commandments. He must have an opportunity to gain spiritual strength in his home, from his parents, if Judaism is to be a meaningful guide to his conduct in everything he does.

Jewish education includes a knowledge of the Hebrew language, the Bible, the Ten Commandments, and all the Jewish customs, rites, and ceremonies that take place at various important occasions of joy and sorrow. For everything there is a prayer – for everything there is a blessing. Through learning and practice the truly religious Jewish child internalizes the Jewish way of life and lives by it. His faith in God will sustain him in times of joy and in times of sorrow. He is taught to face the reality of death as well as the miracle of life.

Judaism prescribes definite rites and ceremonies dealing with every aspect of death. The dying person is not to be left alone as long as he is alive, and is to be treated with great love and tenderness. At his death, the sorrowing family is to be sustained and helped. The ritual of burial and the manner of mourning is clearly prescribed in Jewish law. The child must be encouraged to participate in all the ceremonies of burial, prayers, and mourning.

"The Jewish funeral is a rite of separation. . . The presence of the casket transforms the process of denial to the acceptance of reality" (Grollman, 1967). The child's emotional reactions, his fears and fantasies will be lessened when nothing is hidden from him and he is told the truth about everything that is happening. "No one knows God fully or understands the mystery of death. The door must remain open to doubt, questioning, and differences of opinion. In a family that is open, loving, and truthful with the child, when death is not associated with guilt, superstition, and unchallenging dogma, the child will gain a better understanding of the meaning of death" (Grollman, 1967).

Formal mourning ceremonies reflect the need for the expression of grief in order to realize and learn to accept the reality of separation from the loved one. After the funeral service the *Shivah,* the first seven days of mourning, begins. The bereaved remain at home and receive condolence calls from relatives and friends. The child is able to face the grief with his family. After the seven days of mourning, until thirty days after the death, normal activities are resumed but places of entertainment are avoided. The immediate family, especially the men, continue to recite the *Kaddish prayer* which reinforces both the reality of death and the affirmation of life (Grollman, 1967).

Jewish rituals are community rituals and require a *Minyen,* ten men, who either congregate in the home of the bereaved or in the synagogue or temple. "The observation of the Jewish laws of mourning helps the child face reality, gives honor to the deceased, and guides the bereaved in the reaffirmation of life" (Grollman, 1967).

In Judaism there is no one definite acceptance of the meaning of life after death. There is a wide difference of opinion among different Jewish groups, with no final authoritative conclusion. It says in Genesis, "You are dust and to dust you shall return." In Ecclesiastes it is written, "The dead know nothing." The Talmud says, "For all creatures, death has been prepared from the beginning." Death is considered a logical part of life and is inescapable.

The belief in immortality varies with different Jewish groups and leaders. The Orthodox Jew believes in resurrection, the reunion of body and soul, standing before God, who will judge whether or not they will share in the blessings of the messianic age. The mystical Chassidim believe in the transmigration of the soul, where the soul would enter another body and begin a new life.

The conservative and reform movement retain some concepts about the immortality of the soul. Grollman (1967) quotes O. Lazarus who says, "We cannot believe in the resurrection of the body that perishes with death. We feel however that there is that within us which is immortal, and is not bounded by time and space. It is man's soul . . . which continues to live after death."

And the dust returneth to the earth as it was,
But the spirit returneth unto God who gave it.

Descartes considered the soul a direct gift of God and therefore out of the range of scientific understanding.

Other Jewish leaders varied in their ideas about what happens after the body dies. Some believe immortality is attained through the birth of children and grandchildren, as life goes on from generation to generation. Many people hope they will live on through their contributions to society in their creative ideas and works in medicine, scientific inventions, philosophy, art, music, and literature. Their thoughts and works will live on when they leave a heritage that contributes to a better world. Those who leave money for good causes hope that their name will live on in the social institutions they helped to found.

Death makes life precious. "The Jewish religion offers an abundance of sharing religious resources in the encounter with helplessness, guilt, loneliness, and fear" (Grollman, 1967).

Rabbi Abraham J. Heschel said, "We believe in an afterlife, but we have no information on it. I only know *what life is.* What God wants to do with me after I am in the grave I leave to Him."

A child's religion and death are intimately interwoven. It affects his entire outlook on life from the time he is born until the time he dies.

CONSOLATION VISITS AND NOTES

What can we say to people who have suffered the loss of a loved one through death? How can we help them at the time of their bereavement when they are overwhelmed with grief and sorrow? This is a subject that reveals the emotions we have unfortunately been taught to hide even from ourselves. We have to dare to reach out without fear — or even with fear. But when we have good feelings to share with other people we should not let our feelings fade away and waste in fear of embarrassment. We need a bridge of communication in expressing sympathy as well as in other ways.

First of all, we must overcome our own need to deny death, funerals, and bereaved families. We cannot run away from the reality of death just as we cannot run away from the reality of life, so we must try to face both with wisdom and compassion.

Grief is assuaged by visits and consolation notes to the bereaved, during the mourning period and even later. Letters of condolence, especially if they are personal and express warm feelings and experiences with the deceased, indicate a shared relationship and therefore a shared sense of loss that shows empathy and understanding.

The tendency to avoid the situation may be due to a loss of

what to do and what to say. But it really is not so difficult. A feeling that comes from the heart can be communicated with just the touch of the hand — with just the murmur of a few words, "I'm so sorry." Just by visiting the bereaved you are already showing that you care. If there is a child in the family, speak to him and give him a hug. When you see things to do, get the child to help you and let him know how much he is needed. If everyone seems to be occupied, take him out for a walk and let him talk. He will soon reveal his feelings to you when he senses that you have a listening ear.

Should you feel that a visit to a casual acquaintance or neighbor is an intrusion of their privacy, a card or note might surprise and comfort them. If you meet the bereaved in the market place do not turn away but reach out to them in sympathy and friendship.

If you are unable to visit them at the time of mourning, you can always write. It will show that you cared and took the trouble to say so. What you write depends upon your relationship with the deceased and his family. A personal note is especially meaningful to the recipient. It must be honest and come from the heart. Here is a note about a simple neighbor whom it was easy to respect:

"He was a man of simple dignity and decency, of self-respect and self-dependency. He served his family through love and honest labor. I always found pleasure in chatting with him for a few minutes when I met him on my way to work. I share with you the loss of a truly good man, beloved and honored in all relationships."

When writing to a family, address the letter to include every member of the family by name. A special note to the child, addressed to him in a separate envelope, will make him feel remembered and considered as a person. We should neither worship youth nor belittle small children. The special note will also tend to wipe out any misconceived thoughts that children sometimes have that they were guilty of the death. In writing to children give them comfort and security. Tell them that they are good children, are loved and will be taken care of.

A letter about the death of an older parent or grandparent who was truly worthy of respect, could include the need to honor his name and emulate his teachings. Here is a letter about a wise and unusual woman.

"Dear Cousins, Our hearts were shocked and saddened to hear of the death of your dear mother. She was a great lady of rare intuition and human dignity. Her heart and mind reflected wisdom and understanding, warmth and friendship. Her mind was active and she was very much alive to what was going on in the world, so that it was a privilege to be with her and talk with her. Her wisdom and warmth were contagious and left us a little richer and happier with each contact. We are grateful for the privilege of having known her. We know that it is a great heartache to lose such a mother, but you should find comfort in knowing that at all times you showed her the honor and respect, deep love and loyalty, care and concern that she so well deserved. You were all near to her and dear to her, ever ready to be at her side, while at the same time she had the independence of her own apartment and her own way of life. We shall all miss her, and yet, she will ever remain alive in our hearts, for she was a part of us as we were a part of her. May God comfort us all in this time of sadness and bring us peace. With deepest love and sympathy, Your Cousins."

A personal remembrance, perhaps even unknown to the bereaved, can be very endearing to them. A teacher wrote to the family of a young husband and father:

"We were shocked and saddened to hear of the untimely death of your dear husband and father. Victor was such a precious person. I first knew him when I was a student teacher in the sixth grade at Taft School, and I also knew his mother who loved him dearly. How I enjoyed this serious and interesting boy as he involved himself in his work with effort and enthusiasm. This pattern of his personality continued as he grew up, served in the war with honors, then married and became the father of three sons. Mary, you were a good wife and mother for there was love and understanding in your home. Your family and our family became good friends. When you invited us to dinner we felt that we belonged to your family, too. Memories remain in our hearts and enrich our lives. Children absorb the feelings of their parents for their friends. They carry on the patterns of their parents and pass them on to their own children to make them immortal.

"Although we are greatly saddened by his untimely death, it should be a comfort to all of us to remember that Victor lived the good life, happy with his family, friends and his work. Now we must all continue to carry on in the paths he portrayed for us, with thanks and appreciation for the privilege of having known and loved this precious person. The heart needs time to heal, but our hearts beat in time with yours to give you strength and comfort in your time of sorrow. Your faithful friends."

The son answered, "I would like to thank you for your most kind and sympathetic letter. What is exceptional is the clear encapsulation of dad's life and personality; and reflected in it is your own personal and deep sympathy for all of us who loved him and enjoyed him." The wife wrote, "Thank you for your understanding which gives us strength to continue. We treasure your letter and will keep it always."

Often a brief note can be very meaningful from a friend of the family:

"We feel with you the sense of sorrow that comes with the departure of a wife from this worldly life. We feel the loss with you for it is our loss, too. Old friendships never die, and the memory of your beloved wife will always be in our heart."

In writing to religious people their faith should always be considered. Captain Ferdinand Mendenhall, editor of the *Van Nuys News,* a very socially active and sensitive leader in the community, wrote in his column (Mendenhall, 1970) about a letter he received from a friend when his father died:

"Although you miss him greatly, and grieve in his going, yet you would not want him to return, even if he could do so. He has served his fine mission in life, and now rests with the Father of us all." Mr. Mendenhall states that this letter gave him an entire new outlook on life and death and he has kept the letter as a most valued possession.

To an observant Catholic:

"We know that your faith and trust in God has always been a part of your daily living. His way of life has guided you always and in a crisis like this our faith and trust in him must guide us all. We are thinking of you and praying with you that God may bring you comfort in the assurance that His will is based on wisdom that is often beyond our understanding. Faithfully yours."

To a Jewish family on the death of their father:

"He fell asleep in his armchair. God must have loved him deeply to take him so gently and so quietly on the holy night of Yom Ha Kippur. It is considered a sign of his goodness and righteousness."

It is very important to continue to keep in touch with the bereaved and try to see them or write to them at a later date, especially on holidays:

"But as the New Year approaches, we must look forward to the future with hope and gladness. New relationships must be made as you look ahead for growth and fulfillment. Everyone has a job to do to fill his life with worthwhile work and relationships."

The traumatic effect of the death of a loved one on children will be lessened where there is faith in his religion and observation of its rituals.

SUMMARY

Religion is man's basis for giving his children a moral code of conduct. A child's religion is based on his developmental age and religious training. His religious beliefs influence his attitudes toward death.

Change, separation, and togetherness is a continuous process of living. Every person has a need to belong to a group. The spiritual man senses the unity of the universe and its relatedness to the mystery of life and death. Faith reaches back into the deep recesses of the collective unconscious and grows out of that deep intuition that comes from the unconscious communication between man and his universe. Through his intuition man develops faith in a Creator. Parents who have this faith will pass it on to their children, who gain security and trust in authoritative figures and in God. Religion gives the child goals and direction. As he absorbs faith in God's plan he learns to accept death as part of life. Professional people should use a child's own religion to help him meet adversity and death.

A child's concept of God is a growing thing. The search for conservation is a lifelong quest for permanence amid a world of change. When the child learns about death he is forced to believe in God in order to feel safe and protected, so that he may never die. Children's concepts of God grow with their development and the teachings of their church. The religion of childhood is different from the religion of adults. Conversations with children reveal their concepts about God. Questions children ask about God are concerned with his existence, power, and activities.

A child's concept of prayer is related to his developmental ideas of God and his religious training. Bedtime prayers help him overcome the fear of separation that comes with going to sleep. Prayer during times of crisis may be a spiritually revealing experience. When there is a death, prayer should contain acceptance and faith in the will of God. Prayer with a dying child should help him feel closer to God and not afraid of the future. The child who learns to pray to God will more readily be able to turn to God in times of trouble.

The child needs the parent's faith to lean on. We can teach him that most religions teach the Ten Commandments and the brotherhood of men. Children's concepts of God are absorbed from their environment. A child's religious and moral growth can rarely grow above that of his parents. He should first learn about his own religion and later about other religions, but he should always be taught to respect all religions.

Customs, rites, and ceremonies are expressions of relatedness and belonging to the group. Prayer and participation in rites and ceremonies give the child the security of belonging.

A child's religion and death are intimately interwoven and influence his entire life. The doctrines of the Catholic, Protestant, and Jewish religions affect the child's attitudes toward death.

Consolation visits and letters can be very conforting to bereaved families and people should take the time to visit or write notes to them.

REFERENCES

Allport, G. W.: The Individual and His Religion. New York, Macmillan, 1950.
Elkind, D.: The origin of religion in the child. Rev Relig Res, 6(1):35-42, 1970.
Fitch, F. M.: One God, The Ways We Worship Him. New York, Lothrop, Lee and Shepard, 1944.
Grollman, E. A.: The ritualistic and theological approach of the Jew. In Grollman, E. A. (Ed.): Explaining Death to Children. Boston, Beacon Press, 1967.

Jackson, E. N.: Telling a Child About Death. New York, Channel Press, 1965.

———: The theological, psychological, and philosophical dimensions of death in Protestantism. In Grollman, E. A. (Ed.): Explaining Death to Children. Boston, Beacon Press, 1967.

Mendenhall, F.: You would not want him to return. Van Nuys News and Green Sheet, January 4, 1970. p. 3.

Riley, T. J.: Catholic teachings, the child, and a philosophy for life and death. In Grollman, E. A. (Ed.): Explaining Death to Children. Boston, Beacon Press, 1967.

Zeligs, D. F. Psychoanalysis and the Bible: A study in depth of seven leaders. New York: Bloch Publishing Co., 1974.

———: The Story of Jewish Holidays and Customs. New York, Bloch Publishing Co., 1967.

———: The Story Bible. New York, Behrman House, 1949. vol. 1.

———: The Story Bible. New York, Behrman House, 1951. vol. 2.

Zeligs, R.: Your child and God. Calif Parent-Teacher, 36(5):7-9, 1960.

———: The meaning of prayer. Calif Parent-Teacher, 36(7):16-17, 29, 1960.

AUTHOR INDEX

A

Adelson, L., 21
Adlerstein, A. M., 36, 48, 143, 153
Alcott, L. M., 80, 93
Aldrich, C. K., 123, 124, 126, 138
Alexander, I. E., 36, 48, 143, 153
Allport, G. W., 238
Alschuler, R. H., 10, 21
Alvarez, A., 180, 181, 189
Anthony, S., 26, 32, 45, 49
Aring, C. D., 39, 49
Aronson, G. J., 147, 153
Auster, S. L., 112, 122
Azarnoff, P., 89, 93

B

Bard, B., 134, 138
Becker, D. E., 209
Bender, L., 22, 32
Bergman, A. B., 107
Birk, A., 195, 209
Bogard, H. N., 178, 189
Bowlby, J., 210
Bozeman, M. F., 99, 102, 103, 104, 105, 107, 108
Brauer, P. H., 147, 153
Bryant, P., 164, 189

C

Call, J. D., 131, 133, 138
Carr, A. C., 138
Chadwick, M., 36, 49
Chesser, E., 24, 26, 32, 189
Chodoff, P., 78
Colley, R. S., 143, 153
Cousinet, R., 24
Currie, J. B., 165, 189

Cushing, H., 92, 93

D

Davenport, C. W., 49
Day, S. B., 201, 210
Doctor X., 73, 79
Drake, D. C., 65, 66, 78
Driver, C., 194, 210
Duff, R. S., 66, 78

E

Easson, W. M., 79, 83, 93, 96, 107, 118, 122, 140, 142, 144, 146, 152, 153
Elkind, D., 215, 216, 238
Elmore, J. L., 67, 78
Erickson, F., 125, 138
Evans, A. E., 79, 83, 93, 96, 107

F

Farberow, N. L., 179, 189
Feifel, H., 23, 32, 36, 74, 78
Fitch, F. M., 238
Fletcher, J., 134, 138
Fraiberg, S., 201, 210
Freud, S., 34, 36, 49, 219
Friedman, P., 180, 189
Friedman, S. B., 51, 78
Furst, S. S., 173, 189

G

Gabrielson, I. W., 164, 189
Gellis, S., 51, 78
Glaser, K., 170, 189
Goldberg, I. K., 113, 122
Goldman, A., 163, 189
Green, M., 54, 56, 78, 138

241

SUBJECT INDEX

A

Abandonment
  fear of, 43, 44
Adolescent
  death unnatural experience, 142
  meaning of death, 140
  suicide attempts, 181
  suicide causes, 157
  suicide rates, 169
Amputation
  impact of, 126
Assassination of
  John Kennedy, 45
  Robert Kennedy, 45-47

B

Broken homes, 158, 160
Broken romances, 158, 163

C

Care
  at home, 72
  at hospital, 71
Case reports
  dying child
    in *Little Women,* 80-81
    in *New Year's Eve,* 80
    in Osler's care of, 91-92
  father's death feared, 37-38
  grandmother's funeral, 39-40
  hospital experience
    harmful, 60-62
    helpful, 63-64
  mother's death feared, 40-44
  sibling
    sudden death of, 2-21
  stepfather

    trouble with, 207-208
  suicide attempts, 182-186
  suicide note, 187
Child
  cannot be fooled, 87
  dying at home, 72-73
  senses fatal prognosis, 80, 85
Children
  rural, 27
  urban, 27
  with chronic illness, 59
Cinderella Syndrome, 202
Consolation notes
  visits, 233-238
Conspiracy of silence, 87

D

Death
  and the adolescent, 140-153
  children's fear of, 34-49
  consolation visits, 233-238
  developmental concepts, 22-33
  difficult time of, 110
  earliest concepts, 23-26
  of parent
    remarriage, 206
  of public figures, 44-47
  taboo subject, 22, 88
Denying death by avoiding patient, 74
Doctor
  able to face death, 53
  child's trust in, 52, 55
  communication with, 55
  competent, 54
  friendly to parents, 54
  friendly to patient, 54
  main one needed, 54
  mature emotionally, 54
  patient and, 55